Creation in Crisis

Christian perspectives on sustainability

Edited by

ROBERT S. WHITE

First published in Great Britain in 2009

Society for Promoting Christian Knowledge, 36 Causton Street, London SW1P 4ST

Copyright © The Faraday Institute 2009

The author and publisher have made every effort to ensure that the external website and email addresses included in this book are correct and up to date at the time of going to press. The author and publisher are not responsible for the content, quality or continuing accessibility of the sites.

British Library Cataloguing-in-Publication Data
A catalogue record for this book is available from the British Library

ISBN 978–0–281–06190–7

3 5 7 9 10 8 6 4 2

Typeset by Kenneth Burnley, Wirral, Cheshire
Printed in Great Britain by 4edge Limited, Essex

Produced on paper from sustainable forests

Contents

Contents

Illustrations

Tables

To our children and grandchildren,
who will inherit from us
the responsibility of care for this world*

*including the editor's first grandchild, Caitlin Lucy White,
born as this book went to press

Contributors

Richard Bauckham is Emeritus Professor of New Testament Studies at St Mary's College, University of St Andrews, and Senior Scholar at Ridley Hall, Cambridge. He has published widely in theology, historical theology and the New Testament and has authored, co-authored or edited 23 books. Recent publications include: *Gospel Women: Studies of the Named Women in the Gospels* (T. & T. Clark, UK, and Eerdmans, USA, 2002); *God and the Crisis of Freedom: Biblical and Contemporary Perspectives* (Westminster John Knox Press, 2002); *Bible and Mission: Christian Witness in a Postmodern World* (Paternoster, UK, and Baker, USA, 2003); *Jesus and the Eyewitnesses: The Gospels as Eyewitness Testimony* (Eerdmans, USA, 2006); *The Testimony of the Beloved Disciple* (Baker, USA, 2007); *Jesus and the God of Israel* (Paternoster, UK, and Eerdmans, USA, 2008). He is a Fellow of the British Academy and a Fellow of the Royal Society of Edinburgh. In 2008 he was awarded the British Academy's Burkitt Medal for Biblical Studies.

Richard Carter has worked for 35 years on the natural science, social science and engineering of water development and management, focusing especially on the poorest countries of sub-Saharan Africa. He undertook his undergraduate, Master's and Ph.D. studies respectively at Cambridge, Southampton and Cranfield Universities. After training as a geologist, he took a Master's degree in irrigation and water resources engineering, and later completed a Ph.D. in water policy and management related to semi-arid west Africa. He also completed a postgraduate Diploma in Christian Studies at Regent College, Vancouver. Richard joined Cranfield University at Silsoe in 1981 after several years working for consulting companies in UK and overseas. He was appointed Professor of International Water Development at Cranfield in 2002, and in recent years also ran his own consulting firm. In 2009 he left Cranfield to take up the position of Head of Technical Support Unit at WaterAid, a large UK-based international non-governmental organization.

Flavio Comim is a development economist, currently working for the United Nations as co-ordinator of the 2009 Brazilian Human Development Report. He is an affiliated lecturer of the department of Land

Economy and Visiting Fellow of St Edmund's College, University of Cambridge. He obtained his Ph.D. in economics at Cambridge in 1999. His field of research is poverty, inequality and social capital, with special emphasis on the capability approach. He has worked on history of economic thought and methodology of economics. Dr Comim has written papers on topics ranging from the role of common sense in the Scottish Enlightenment to poverty measurement from a capability perspective. He has published widely in journals such as *History of Political Economy*, *Review of Political Economy* and *Structural Change and Economic Dynamics*. His recent publications include: F. Comim, M. Qizilbash and S. Alkire, eds, *The Capability Approach: Concepts, Measures and Applications* (Cambridge University Press, 2008) and L. Bruni, F. Comim and M. Pugno, *Capabilities and Happiness* (Oxford University Press, 2008).

Calvin B. DeWitt is professor with the Gaylord Nelson Institute at the University of Wisconsin-Madison, on the graduate faculties of Environment and Resources, Water Resources Management, Conservation Biology and Sustainable Development, and Limnology and Marine Science. He is co-founder of the International Evangelical Environmental Network, President of the Academy of Evangelical Scientists and Ethicists, and President Emeritus of Au Sable Institute of Environmental Studies. Recent publications include 'Stewardship: responding dynamically to the consequences of human action in the world' in *Environmental Stewardship*, ed. R. J. Berry (T. & T. Clark International, 2006), 145–58; *Earth-Wise: A Biblical Response to Environmental Issues*, 2nd edn (Faith Alive, 2007); 'The scientist and the shepherd: the emergence of evangelical environmentalism', in *The Oxford Handbook of Religion and Ecology*, ed. R. Gottlieb (Oxford University Press, 2006), 568–87; 'Contemporary missiology and the biosphere', in *The Antioch Agenda*, ed. D. Jeyaraj, R. Pazmio and R. Peterson (ISPCK, 2007), 305–28; 'The place of Creation in today's missionary discourse: evangelical environmentalism in America', in *Missiology and the Environment*, ed. L. Vischer (John Knox Centre, 2007), 174–204; 'To strive to safeguard the integrity of Creation and sustain and renew the life of the earth', in *Mission in the Twenty-First Century: Exploring the Five Marks of Global Mission*, ed. A. Walls and C. Ross (Darton, Longman and Todd, 2008), 84–93.

Ellen F. Davis is Amos Ragan Kearns Professor of Bible and Practical Theology at the Divinity School, Duke University, North Carolina. The author of many books and articles, her research interests focus on how biblical interpretation bears on the life of faith communities and their response to urgent public issues, particularly the environmental crisis and interreligious (mis)understanding. She is a member of the Archbishop of Canterbury's Building Bridges seminar, an international group of Muslim and Christian theologians. Professor Davis held the Hulsean Lectureship at the University of Cambridge in 2005–6. The Lectures have been published in her most recent book, *Scripture, Culture, and Agriculture: An Agrarian Reading of the Bible* (Cambridge University Press, 2009); the book uses biblical interpretation as the basis for a critique of industrial agriculture and food production. She is now working with the Episcopal Church of Sudan to advance theological education in Southern Sudan.

John Guillebaud is Emeritus Professor of Family Planning and Reproductive Health, University College London. He was born in Buye, Burundi, brought up in Rwanda, Uganda and Kenya and trained at St John's College, Cambridge, and St Bartholomew's Hospital, London. He has made regular training and support visits to Africa for healthcare professions. He was formerly Medical Director of the Margaret Pyke Centre for Family Planning and is currently vasectomy surgeon at the Churchill Hospital, Oxford, as well as consulting for the World Health Organization and other international and national bodies. Professor Guillebaud has been invited to lecture in 42 countries, spread throughout all the continents, on contraceptive technology and related issues. He has authored eight books and 260 original articles, editorials and book chapters, covering the topics of birth control, reproductive health, population and environmental sustainability. Recent publications include E. McVeigh, R. Homburg and J. Guillebaud, eds, *Handbook of Reproductive Medicine and Family Planning* (Oxford University Press, 2008) and *Contraception – Your Questions Answered*, 5th edn (Churchill-Livingstone/Elsevier, 2009). He is the originator of the Environment Time Capsule Project at <www.ecotimecapsule.com>, a Trustee of TASKwh (Towards African Solutions through Knowledge for Women's Health), Co-Chair of <www.populationandsustainability.org> and Chair of Planet 21 (<www.peopleandplanet.net>).

Donald Hay is now retired. He stepped down in 2005 after five years as Dean of Social Sciences at Oxford University, and served as Acting Pro Vice Chancellor (Planning and Resources) in 2006–7. He had previously held posts in the Department of Economics and Jesus College from 1970. His main areas of research and teaching were industrial organization and economics in the UK, Brazil and People's Republic of China, and the reform of competition policy in the UK. Among his publications was a major text, co-authored with Derek Morris, *Industrial Economics and Organisation*, 2nd edn (Oxford University Press, 1991). He has had a long-standing interest in the relationship between economic analysis and a Christian understanding of society. He authored *Economics Today: A Christian Critique* (Apollos, UK, and Eerdmans, USA, 1989): more recently in this field he has worked on climate change, and on the economics of marriage and divorce.

Contributors

Sir Brian Heap was Master of St Edmund's College, Cambridge, and is now an Honorary Fellow both at St Edmund's College, Cambridge, and Green College, Oxford, Senior Member of King's College, Cambridge, and Special Professor at the University of Nottingham. He has doctorates from the Universities of Nottingham and Cambridge, and has published widely on endocrine physiology, biotechnology, sustainable consumption and science policy. He was formerly Director of the Institute of Animal Physiology and Genetics Research (Cambridge and Edinburgh) and Director of Research at the UK's Biotechnology and Biological Sciences Research Council, as well as President of the Institute of Biology, UK Representative on the European Science Foundation, Strasbourg, and UK Representative on the NATO Science Committee, Brussels. Professor Heap was elected a Fellow of the Royal Society in 1989, member of Council in 1994, and Foreign Secretary and Vice-President from 1996 to 2001. He served as a member of the UK's Nuffield Council on Bioethics, the Department of Health's Expert Group on Cloning, and an expert on the Advisory Group on Biotechnology for the President of the European Commission. He was engaged in issues including population growth, the environment and biotechnology in developing countries, particularly in China with the World Health Organization. His recent publications include: 'Embryonic stem cells, a challenge to universal values', in *Science, Technology and Human Values,* ed. L. G. Christophorou and C. Drakatos (The Academy of Athens, 2007), 277–88; and 'Higher education, scientific research and social change', in *Higher Education and National Development: Universities and Societies in Transition,* ed. D. Bridges, P. Juceviciene, R. Jucevicius, T. McLaughlin and J. Stankeviciute (Routledge, 2007), 265–78.

Sir John Houghton is currently Honorary Scientist of the Hadley Centre for Climate Prediction and Research at the Meteorological Office; a Trustee of the Shell Foundation; and President of the John Ray Initiative. Previously Sir John was a Member of the UK Government Panel on Sustainable Development (1994–2000); Chairman, Royal Commission on Environmental Pollution (1992–8); Chairman or Co-Chairman, Scientific Assessment Working Group, Intergovernmental Panel on Climate Change (1988–2002); Director General (later Chief Executive), UK Meteorological Office (1983–91); Director Appleton, Science and Engineering Research Council (also Deputy Director, Rutherford Appleton Laboratory) (1979–83); and Professor of Atmospheric Physics, Oxford University (1976–83). During the 1970s Sir John was also Principal Investigator for Space Experiments on NASA Spacecraft. Sir John has received numerous honours and awards, most recently the prestigious Japan Prize (2006), and among others, the Glazebrook Medal (Institute of Physics, 1990), the Bakerian Prize Lecture of the Royal Society (1991), and the Royal Astronomical Society Gold Medal (1995); he has received Honorary Doctorates of Science from 12 universities including those of Wales (1991) and Oxford (2006). Recent publications include: *The Search For God: Can Science Help?* (JRI, UK, and Regent College Bookstore, Vancouver, 1995); and *Global Warming: The Complete Briefing*, 4th edn (Cambridge University Press, 2009).

Hilary Marlow has a particular interest in religious motivations for environmental concern and is part of a joint research project between the Faraday Institute and the Kirby Laing Institute for Christian Ethics. Her research involves exploring biblical portrayals of the purpose of human beings and their relation to the world in the context of current environmental concerns. She is an affiliated lecturer in the University of Cambridge where she teaches biblical Hebrew to theology students in the Faculty of Divinity. She also gives occasional lectures on the biblical prophets in the Cambridge Theological Federation. She holds BA honours degrees in Social Administration (University of Manchester) and in Biblical Studies (King's College London). Her Ph.D. from the University of Cambridge on the Old Testament and the environment has recently been published as *Biblical Prophets and Contemporary Environmental Ethics: Re-reading Amos, Hosea and First Isaiah* (Oxford University Press, 2009). For the past ten years Dr Marlow has been involved in the Christian environmental charity, A Rocha, and she is also a board member of the John Ray Initiative and a member of the Ely Diocese Environment Committee. Other recent publications include: 'The other prophet! The voice of earth in the book of Amos', in *Exploring Ecological Hermeneutics*, ed. N. Habel and P. Trudinger (Society of Biblical Literature, 2008), 75–83; *The Earth is the Lord's: A Biblical Response to Environmental Issues* (Grove Books, 2008) and 'Justice for whom? Social and environmental ethics and the Hebrew prophets' in *Ethical and Unethical Behaviour in the Old Testament: God and Humans in Dialogue* (T. & T. Clark, 2009).

James J. McCarthy is Alexander Agassiz Professor of Biological Oceanography, and from 1982 to 2002 he was the Director of Harvard University's Museum of Comparative Zoology. He is also the Master of Harvard's Pforzheimer House. Jim McCarthy received his undergraduate degree in biology from Gonzaga University, and his Ph.D. from Scripps Institution of Oceanography. His research interests relate to the regulation of plankton productivity in the sea, and in recent years have focused on regions that are strongly affected by seasonal and inter-annual variation in climate. He has authored many scientific papers and currently teaches courses on biological oceanography and biogeochemical cycles, marine ecosystems, and global change and human health. He has served and serves on many national and international planning committees, advisory panels and commissions relating to oceanography, polar science and the study of climate and global change. From 1986 to 1993 he chaired the international committee that establishes research priorities and oversees implementation of the International Geosphere–Biosphere Program, he was the founding editor for the American Geophysical Union's *Global Biogeochemical Cycles*, and was involved in two of the recent international assessments on climate impacts. He served as Co-chair of the Intergovernmental Panel on Climate Change, Working Group II, which had responsibilities for assessing impacts of and vulnerabilities to global climate change for the Third International Panel on Climate Change Assessment (2001). He is one of the lead authors on the recently completed *Arctic Climate Impact Assessment* (Cambridge University Press, 2008). He is President of the American Association for the Advancement of Science, a Fellow of the American Academy of Arts and Sciences, and a Foreign Member of the Royal Swedish Academy of Sciences.

Douglas Moo is Blanchard Professor of New Testament at Wheaton College, Illinois. He is Chair of the Committee on Bible Translation, the group of scholars charged with oversight of the New International Version (NIV) and Today's New International Version (TNIV) Bibles. He formerly taught for 20 years at Trinity Evangelical Divinity School, Illinois. Professor Moo's research interest is in New Testament exegesis and theology, particularly the letters of the apostle Paul. He is currently working on a commentary on Galatians and a Pauline Theology. He has a particular interest in the way the created world is presented in the New Testament, with implications for current environmental issues. His recent publications include: *The Epistle of James*, Pillar Commentary (Eerdmans, 2000); *Romans: NIV Application Commentary* (Zondervan, 2000); D. Moo and D. A. Carson, *Introduction to the New Testament* (Zondervan, 2005); and D. Moo, *The Epistles to the Colossians and to Philemon*, Pillar Commentary (Eerdmans, 2008).

Jonathan Moo has recently completed a Ph.D. at the University of Cambridge (with a dissertation entitled 'Creation, nature and hope in fourth Ezra') and works as a research associate at the Faraday Institute for Science and Religion, St Edmund's College, Cambridge. He is presently working on a project sponsored jointly by the Faraday Institute and the Kirby Laing Institute for Christian Ethics on 'Hope for creation: a biblical vision for contemporary environmental policy'. In addition to his research in biblical theology, exegesis and environmental ethics, Jonathan also does some lecturing in New Testament for the Divinity Faculty in the University of Cambridge and gives occasional lectures and seminars elsewhere. He holds degrees in Biology and English (BA, Lake Forest College, Illinois), Wildlife Ecology (MS, Utah State University), and Theology (Cert. Biblical Studies, Trinity Evangelical Divinity School, Illinois; MA Old Testament, MA New

Testament, Gordon-Conwell Theological Seminary, Massachusetts). In 2010 he will take up a teaching post in the Department of Theology and Philosophy at Whitworth University, Spokane, Washington. Recent publications include: 'The sea that is no more: Rev 21.1 and the function of sea imagery in the Apocalypse of John', *Novum Testamentum* (forthcoming); 'Romans 8.19–22 and Isaiah's Cosmic Covenant', *New Testament Studies* (2008) **54**: 74–89; 'Review of environmental stewardship: critical perspectives – past and present', in *Science and Christian Belief* (2008) **20**: 216–18; and 'A Messiah whom "the Many do not Know"? Rereading 4 Ezra 5:6–7', *Journal of Theological Studies* NS (2007) **58**: 525–36.

Peter Moore is freelance science communicator based near Bristol, UK, a visiting lecturer in ethics at Trinity College Bristol, and a Course Tutor on the Science Communication MSc course at the University of the West of England, Bristol. He is a Fellow of the Royal Society of Arts and has worked as a rapporteur at private meetings in the House of Lords, and at St George's House, Windsor Castle. He is also director of The Wonder Project, a company building white-board resources for British schools. Over the past 15 years, Dr Moore has contributed to national and international publications, including *Nature* and the *Journal of Biology*, and has written more than a dozen books that reflect on the way that science and technology has had an impact on humanity, including *Being Me – What it Means to be Human* (Wiley, 2003) and *Enhancing Me – The Hope and Hype of Human Enhancement* (Wiley, 2008). He was Chairman of the Medical Journalists Association from 2002 to 2005. He has appeared on British radio and television and has won six national awards for his work.

Michael Northcott was educated at the Universities of Durham and Sunderland. He taught at the Seminari Theologi Malaysia in Kuala Lumpur before moving to the University of Edinburgh in 1989. Former graduate students teach at universities and colleges in Australia, North America, Africa, Asia and the Far East. He is an ordained Anglican priest, a trustee of the Fair Trade organization Traidcraft, and Honorary Canon Theologian of Liverpool Cathedral. He has been visiting professor at the Claremont School of Theology, Duke University, Flinders University, and the University of Malaya. He is best known for his work in environmental theology and ethics, and his book *The Environment and Christian Ethics* (Cambridge University Press, 1996) is in its fourth printing. More recently published books include *Life After Debt: Christianity and Global Justice* (SPCK, 1999) and *A Moral Climate: The Ethics of Global Warming* (Darton, Longman and Todd, and Orbis Press, 2007). Forthcoming co-edited volumes include M. Northcott and K. Vanhoutan, *Diversity and Dominion: Dialogues in Ecology, Ethics, and Theology* (Cascade Press, 2009) and

M. Northcott and R. J. Berry, *Theology After Darwin* (Paternoster Press, 2009). Professor Northcott has written more than 60 scholarly articles and is presently pursuing a number of research projects including an interdisciplinary collaborative work on the theological and ethical implications of the present extinction crisis, and a longstanding project on the theology and ethics of work and its technological reshaping.

C. René Padilla is passionate about social justice and the part that the Church plays in bringing this about. He was a member of the staff of the International Fellowship of Evangelical Students for Latin America (1959–82) and General Secretary of the Latin American Theological Fellowship (1983–92). He is a founding member and Emeritus President of the Kairos Community of Buenos Aires, Argentina, which encourages Christians to meet the physical, social, psychological and spiritual needs of poor communities. Dr Padilla grew up in Ecuador and Colombia, studied in England, and has lived in Buenos Aires since 1967. He is the President of the Micah Network, a worldwide group of campaigning organizations aimed at mobilizing Christians against poverty. He has spent his life practising what he preaches. The local church of which he is a member works among slum dwellers and drug addicts and has become a model for 'integral mission', fusing evangelism and social action. At the pivotal International Congress on World Evangelization (held in Lausanne, 1974) and at various consultations organized by the Lausanne Movement, he was instrumental in advocating a more active role among evangelicals in addressing social issues. He has edited or co-authored several books and has written many articles. His main work, *Mission Between the Times: Essays on the Kingdom of God* (Eerdmans, 1985) has been published in English, Spanish, Portuguese, German, Swedish and Korean.

Robert S. White graduated in geology from Emmanuel College, University of Cambridge, in 1974 and was awarded a Ph.D. in marine geophysics in 1977. After spells as a postdoctoral researcher at Woods Hole Oceanographic Institution, Massachusetts, and in Cambridge, he was appointed to the academic staff at Cambridge University in 1981 and to the Chair of Geophysics in 1989. He was elected a Fellow of the Royal Society in 1994. He runs a research group in the Department of Earth Sciences investigating the dynamic earth, in particular using seismology to study the structure of the earth's crust and the relationship between continental break-up and the production of massive outbursts of volcanism. He has led 13 research cruises at sea in the Atlantic and the Indian Oceans, and recently has organized fieldwork on volcanic systems in Iceland, New Zealand and the Faroe Islands. His research is published in more than 200 academic papers. In 2006 he founded with Denis Alexander the Faraday Institute for Science and Religion at St Edmund's College, Cambridge. Recent publications include: D. Alexander and R. White, *Beyond Belief: Science, Faith and Ethical Challenges* (Lion, 2004), and N. Spencer and R. White, *Christianity, Climate Change and Sustainable Living* (SPCK, 2007).

George Wilkes read History at Gonville & Caius College, University of Cambridge, before completing a Ph.D. at Cambridge on the debate over European integration in Britain at the turn of the 1960s. An Affiliated Lecturer at the Faculty of Divinity and Cambridge Theological Federation, he has lectured on Israeli–Palestinian and Jewish–Christian relations, on Jewish thought, and on contemporary European political history, in the universities of Cambridge and Birmingham and at the Centre for the Study of Jewish-Christian Relations in Cambridge. His latest research, the subject of a research programme at the Von Hügel Institute, St Edmund's College, University of Cambridge, focuses on just-war theories and respect for international law in wartime, with a particular focus on the politics of human rights and humanitarian protection within the UN human rights institutions. He has also published work on religion and politics in Israeli–Palestinian relations, on the history of Jewish–Christian relations in the twentieth century, and on contemporary European history. His recent publications include: 'Christianity, Islam and religious indifference – the prospects for coexistence in the European Union', in *The Borders of European Integration*, ed. J. Leszek (Tischner European University, 2006), 41–70; and 'Reforming the Commission on Human Rights', in *For the Sake of Humanity: Essays in Honour of Clemens Nathan*, ed. R. Walden (Brill, 2006), 367–79.

Acknowledgements

We are indebted to Sandi Irvine, our Managing Editor, who brought our chapters into a coherent whole, cajoled us into sticking to deadlines and gave much sage advice. We thank Polly Stanton, Barbara Dyson and Zoë Binns for their efficiency in organizing the conference and writers' workshop, and Sharon Capon for her drafting. We are grateful to Alison Barr and the editorial and production teams of SPCK, and also to Kenneth Burnley for their part in bringing the book to publication so rapidly. The project was made possible by funding from the John Templeton Foundation, the John Ray Initiative and the Hinchley Trust.

Foreword

It was in the Millennium year, as I met with and listened to thousands of young people, that I realized there was a generational gap on attitudes to the environment. It forced me to go back to the Bible and to the teachings of Jesus to see if there were any Gospel foundations for young people's aspirations to inherit from their parents an earth that had a future. I wish that I had had this book to hand! It is an exposition of the earthing of heaven. After reading this book, I had the same reaction that I had to realizing that, at the heart of the Lord's Prayer, there's an unequivocal petition for God to do his will on earth as it is done in heaven. How could I have overlooked for so long that the earthing of heaven is central to the mission of God?

In these pages, Robert White has assembled a remarkable cast. Indeed, if you were to lay on an international conference of specialists with expertise from different disciplines to reflect on the present state and the future hope of the earth, from a Christian perspective, you could hardly get a finer line-up! Here are theologians, scientists, economists and development experts writing with authority and clarity about the crisis that is breaking upon the earth.

Crisis is the Greek for judgement. This word tends to get journalists into a lather! Judgement in the Bible is not the vindictive flailings of a peeved deity. Judgement is the moment of truth when what is sown is revealed by what is reaped in a divinely ordered world. It is not only people of faith who are recognizing that we are reaching such a moment of truth in the history of the planet. What you will find on these pages are the deliberations of specialists with expert knowledge of the earth's condition from within their own field of expertise. Their gift to the reader is that they are able to write so that those of us who are not experts might understand.

This book is written with Christians in mind. And it is urgently needed by us, to persuade us (as Professor Ellen Davis does) that we should not overspiritualize the beatitude which holds before us the promise of inheriting the earth. Christians should be grounded and earthed, treading the planet with humility and praying, as Jesus taught us, for the earthing of heaven.

Shortly after my own conversion to this biblical understanding of the kingdom of God (see Richard Bauckham's chapter) a friend of mine asked me, very gently, whether I had gone off the boil spiritually! He said that others were beginning to wonder! The truth is that these discoveries of the earthy dimensions of God's kingdom have enlarged my vision of Jesus. They have helped me to see that he 'without whom not one thing came into being' (John 1:3) and 'through whom and for whom all things have been created' (Colossians 1:16) is indeed the one who 'sustains all things by his powerful word' (Hebrews 1:3). Such revelation from the primary chapters of the New Testament has brought me to my knees in adoration, and filled me with hope.

Although this book is about the ecological crisis, it is also full of hope. So much environmental prophecy is laden with doom. The prophets blame humanity for its anthropocentric view of the world and for the anthropogenic causes of climate chaos. The conundrum of this prophetic analysis is that the solutions proposed are also anthropocentric and anthropogenic! The distinctive feature of this book is that all the writers proceed from a theocentric and christocentric view of the cosmos. It is Christ's environment, for it is he who stands at the centre of creation. To desecrate creation is not just a crime against humanity; it is a blasphemy, for it is to undo God's creative work in, through and for Christ.

I am honoured to be invited to introduce these experts to you. They will not disappoint. They will disturb you with hope.

I pray this book will change people's attitudes. What I know is that the climate of opinion on this issue needs to change more rapidly than the climate itself if we are to avoid some of the disasters imagined in these chapters.

The earth is the Lord's and all that is in it, the world, and all those who live in it.

The Rt Revd James Jones
Bishop of Liverpool

Abbreviations

AIDS	*see* HIV/AIDS
CCS	carbon capture and storage
CFCs	chlorofluorocarbons (ozone-damaging chemicals previously used for example as propellants in aerosols and still used as coolants)
CO_2	carbon dioxide
CO_2e	carbon dioxide equivalents
ESV	English Standard Version
EU	European Union
FAO	Food and Agriculture Organization (run by the UN)
G8	the world's leading industrialized nations (Canada, France, Germany, Italy, Japan, Russia, UK, USA)
GDP	Gross Domestic Product (the total market value of all final goods and services produced within the country in a given period of time)
GFN	Global Footprinting Network
gha	global hectares; *see* ha
GHGs	greenhouse gases
GM	genetically modified
ha	hectare, metric unit equivalent to approximately 2.5 acres
HIV/AIDS	human immunodeficiency virus/acquired immune deficiency syndrome
IAASTD	International Assessment of Agricultural Knowledge, Science and Technology for Development
IEA	International Energy Agency
IPCC	Intergovernmental Panel on Climate Change
MDGs	Millennium Development Goals
metre	metric unit equivalent to approximately 1.1 yards or 3.3 feet
NAB	New American Bible
NASB	New American Standard Bible
NET	New English Translation
NIV	New International Version

Abbreviations

NLT	New Living Translation
NRSV	New Revised Standard Version
OECD	Organization for Economic Co-operation and Development
p.p.m.	parts per million
RSV	Revised Standard Version
TFR	total fertility rate
TNIV	Today's New International Version
tonne	metric unit equivalent to approximately 1.1 tons
UN	United Nations
UNICEF	UN Children's Fund
WHO	World Health Organization

I

Introduction

ROBERT S. WHITE

There is a sufficiency in the world for man's need but not for man's greed.

(Mohandas K. Gandhi (1869–1948))

If everyone lived in the same way as we do in the West we would need three whole planets like earth to fuel our habits. You don't have to be a genius to work out that our lifestyle is not sustainable. But it is seductively easy to ignore. Or at least it is if you have an abundance of food in your refrigerator and live in a heated or air-conditioned house full of plentiful clean water, electricity, gas, umpteen gadgets and an enormous amount of stuff to cushion your life. It is rather more difficult to ignore if you are unsure where your next meal will come from, if changing weather patterns mean your crops have failed or been washed away for the third year running, or if you do not have transport to get to the weekly clinic in the village 20 kilometres away along a dirt track. Some of us (mostly the sixth of the global population who live in the high-income countries of Europe and North America) are taking more than our fair share of the cake: so much that we are wolfing down most of the cake and actually making ourselves ill in the process. And not just metaphorically. There are now over 1,000 million overweight people in the world, with consequently diminished lifestyles, increased health problems and shortened lives. Yet, shockingly, there are also over 850 million undernourished people living on this same small planet and famine is a major factor in the annual deaths of 6 million children under five years of age.

Our overconsumption is not only unsustainable but is also an ethical issue because, if there are only finite resources available and some of us take more than our fair share, then inevitably others will have less. Those who lose out are the poor and disempowered. Sometimes they are on our own doorsteps, because as nations get richer so the inequalities between the richest and the poorest citizens tend to increase rather than decrease. But often those who suffer are out of sight and mostly out of mind on the other side of the world. Or indeed they are not yet born. The consequences of what we have already done, in polluting and degrading the world in which we live, by causing the destruction of habitats and the loss (extinction) of entire species and by burning huge quantities of fossil fuels are that our world is permanently damaged.[1] Our actions to date will continue affecting the climate and sea level for generations to come and the damage and losses we have caused are in many cases irreparable. In a real sense we are cheating our children and grandchildren if they inherit a severely degraded world.

The purpose of this book is to explore the root causes of environmental unsustainability: why do we continue in activities that are manifestly harmful to ourselves and to others? Part of the answer is undoubtedly ignorance about what we are actually doing. But part is also that we do not want to face up to the fact that the material comforts we enjoy are bought at a cost to other people and to the natural world. We can only begin to formulate an appropriate response if we first identify what we are doing wrong, and then have an ethical basis on which to build. In this book we adopt the approach that the material world is part of God's creation and then explore humankind's place in it.

In summer 2008 we gathered a group in Cambridge, England, at the Faraday Institute for Science and Religion, for a workshop to address these issues. We included experts in both science and theology because a lasting response to the problems that the world faces needs input from both. For three days we challenged and enriched each other's viewpoints, bringing theology as it were down to earth and seeking to give wings to science and technology. This cross-fertilization continued as we critiqued and revised each other's written chapters.

The resulting synthesis portrays both the seriousness of environmental degradation and climate change, and the contribution of Christian thinking in seeking possible solutions and ways forward. Our goal is to promote the transformation of society towards sustainability and a more equitable distribution of the world's riches. If this book helps to educate people who may be sceptical about issues of environmental and social justice and encourages them to take them seriously, we will have succeeded. Our motivation is the Christian imperative of loving both God and our neighbours.

The first half of the book is concerned largely with setting out the evidence for how we, humankind, are affecting the world. It starts, appropriately enough, with global climate change and the way we use energy (Chapter 2). Climate change is a truly worldwide problem where what we do in our own backyards quite literally affects people everywhere else in the world. Over the past century Europe and North America have been the major contributors to so-called 'greenhouse gases' present in the atmosphere. Almost half of the greenhouse gases introduced into the atmosphere by humans were emitted from Europe and North America by the burning of fossil fuels.

Since our standard of living in the West is built on the back of greenhouse gas emissions, then it is not unreasonable to suggest that we have a moral responsibility to help others affected by those same greenhouse gases. That is not a message we necessarily like to hear if it is going to affect, as it must, our own lifestyles. One of the fascinating, and many would say depressing, responses to the increasing evidence of climate change has been a denial by some that it is caused by human beings. There is clear evidence that there has been a targeted process of denial and misinformation, backed by millions of dollars and instigated by industries with vested interests (Chapter 3). The techniques are reminiscent of the campaigns by the tobacco industry in the 1980s to discredit the links between smoking and lung cancer, and even used some of the same organizers and lobbyists: first draw attention to the inevitable uncertainties in the science and then suggest that we 'wait and see'. But we don't have the luxury of waiting. Or at least, if we do delay addressing the problems of climate change, not only will hundreds of thousands or even millions of people suffer unnecessarily, but it will probably cost us much more to address in the future than if we take action now (Chapter 4).

The problem of unsustainability is of course a much wider issue than just the effects of climate change, but like greenhouse gases it is largely a global problem. In late 2008 the rapid spread of economic downturn and then recession across the globe, initiated by problems with subprime mortgages in the USA, demonstrated vividly just how interconnected is the world economic system. Although numerous international summit meetings have sought to address some of the issues that arise from overconsumption, resource depletion and the inequitable distribution of goods and services, none of them has had much traction in changing things. Chapter 5 argues that this is largely because international negotiations are based primarily on self-interest or purely economic factors and, since only 25 per cent of the world's population control 86 per cent of the wealth, such negotiations are always one-sided. We suggest that the formulation of co-operative policies and mechanisms have to pay far more attention to value systems that go beyond mere economic self-interest, and Chapter 5 gives some examples of how biblical principles and values might map onto an approach that takes sustainability seriously.

A problem that is often tiptoed around when talk is of resource usage and how it can be made sustainable, is the unprecedented increase of global population over the past century (Chapter 6). The world population increased by two-thirds in the nineteenth century, which in itself is quite a large increase, but it has quadrupled since the beginning of the twentieth century. More mouths to feed and bodies to house means that more resources are needed; habitats for other species are altered or destroyed; and more pollutants, be they greenhouse gases or other wastes, are produced. It is not a complicated concept. But rather than taking population growth as a 'given', something for which we must forever attempt to provide, Chapter 6 argues that we should accept and even promote a benign intervention that reproductive science now offers: namely voluntary contraception. An important proviso is that contraception should always be available for use voluntarily, wisely and democratically, and ought to be part of a sweep of measures that includes better education, improved health provision and empowerment of women.

Alongside issues related to population size is the natural justice that demands that the poorest people in the world should have a proper standard of living and should be able to live with dignity. That means addressing the scandal that almost half the world – 3 billion people – live below the poverty line on less than $US2.50 per day and that the richest 20 per cent of the world account for 75 per cent of world income. People may rightly argue about the optimum number of people on this earth, but they cannot easily argue against the gross inequities where the rich get richer, usually at the expense of the poor.

One of the consequences of massive population increase is an increased vulnerability to disasters such as earthquakes, floods and famines, simply because more people are packed together into mega-cities of 5 million people or more (Chapter 7). So if an earthquake strikes a megacity, it can potentially kill more people than ever before. It is likely that, despite our increasing technological ability and scientific understanding of the natural world, there will be an earthquake in the coming decades that kills more than a million people. But the main killer in the world is floods. By the middle of this century it is estimated that half the world's population will be at risk from floods. The culprit is often unsustainable agricultural practices, which strip away restraining trees and vegetation, coupled again with global climate change, which brings increased intensities of storms and changed rainfall patterns. Though we often talk of 'natural' disasters, in reality the vast majority of deaths and suffering can be traced to the behaviour of humans. This gives pause for thought as we consider the relationship between a creator God, his creation and the people he made.

There are several chapters devoted to agriculture and ecology because food is the most basic of human requirements and eating is one of the must fundamental cultural activities. We grow food on an industrial scale, in the process using vast quantities of fossil fuels for fertilizers, agricultural vehicles, food processing and transport. Modern industrial agriculture is manifestly unsustainable, which is why hunger is again on the rise worldwide. Industrialized agriculture is also harmful to native habitats and species, and is destructive of the very soil upon which it depends. Until recently, we took sustainability of the biosphere and its ecosystems for granted. We can do so no longer. Humankind has become a major biological and geological force, and, whether recognized or not, is now challenging the very sustainability of the biosphere upon which our and every other living creature's lives depend.

Chapter 8 draws out the lessons from a biblical perspective on agriculture. The Bible consistently represents the care of arable land as a primary religious obligation. In the high-income countries we do not now live in agrarian societies, and the loss of the link between the food on our plates and the earth from which it comes, and on which all of us ultimately depend, has not only impoverished our lives but leaves us dangerously out of touch with creation. There is a call here for a grounded life that can be realized through reinstituting practices of decentralized agriculture, horticulture and marketing.

Chapter 9 addresses not only issues surrounding land use for agriculture, but also illustrates the point that institutional structures strongly affect the way things are done by both individuals and communities. Crises of changing global climate, worldwide loss of biodiversity and degradation of land and soils require us to understand better both the biosphere that sustains all life and the human institutions that guide and shape the thoughts and actions of human individuals and societies. Only then can we understand and be effective in implementing corrective actions. The task that faces humanity is to transform all degrading and destructive human domination into responsible stewardship of the biosphere in its entirety. That will need transformation not just of individuals, but of the institutions we have developed.

If food is essential to life, so too is water (Chapter 10). The biblical writers lived in an arid land and so were perhaps much more conscious than ourselves of the life-giving power of water. Yet today water problems affect half of humanity. Some 1.1 billion people in developing countries have inadequate access to water, and 2.6 billion lack basic sanitation. It is not merely an inconvenience to have to spend several hours a day collecting water, as do millions of women. Some 1.8 million child deaths occur each year as a result of diarrhoea caused by waterborne infections, and nearly half of all people in low-income countries suffer at any given time from a health problem caused by water deficits or poor sanitation.

Drawing back to a wider perspective, Chapter 11 links the root causes of two of the greatest problems affecting humankind today – ecological collapse and poverty – to an economic system rooted in an obsession for economic growth and unbridled consumerism. Many of the low-income countries of the world are actually rich in natural resources – minerals, agricultural products, timber, land, water, oil, medicinal herbs, and so on. Nevertheless many people in these countries are poor or even destitute. If the earth belongs to God, as the Bible states (Leviticus 25:23), then human beings are not owners but only tenants of the land. It is appropriate therefore to seek both a lifestyle that reflects an appreciation of 'enough' and ways to promote the responsible stewardship of natural resources. From a biblical perspective the basic cause of poverty is the oppression of the weak by the powerful, and this ultimately is a relational problem. Because God loves justice, he is against every kind of oppression and he expects justice to be done to the poor. The cause of justice, therefore, is not optional for Christians.

6

The inter-relationship between social injustice and the well-being of both society and the natural environment is explored further in Chapter 12, using prophetic passages from the Old Testament. The relationships between human beings, God and the natural world each affect and interact with one another. The Bible has a theocentric orientation, with neither human interests nor those of the environment being of paramount importance. But the prophets proclaim that it is neglect of justice and righteousness for the poor that results in the desolation of the land. This is the opposite of today's thinking – that it is neglect of the earth by overuse, exploitation and climate change that results in injustice for the world's poor. Maybe these are just two ways of saying the same thing: that the world is an interconnected whole and we ignore this at our peril. The call for social justice by the prophets is just as relevant today as it was two and a half millennia ago, and challenges us to consider the impact our own actions have, not just on other human beings, but on the rest of the natural world.

The New Testament Gospels also proclaim the same message of the interconnectedness between human beings and the created order of which humankind is a part. The main message of the Gospels is to explain the mission of Jesus the Messiah in inaugurating the kingdom of God. That kingdom involves the renewal of all creation, putting to rights the broken relationships between human beings and the creator God and between human beings and the rest of the creation. God's plan of salvation does not mean removing humans from nature to some purely spiritual heavenly future as so many have assumed, but rather healing the relationship between humanity and the rest of creation and bringing God's purposes to fulfilment in the new creation. The goal is the renewal of all things (Matthew 19:28), not of humankind alone (Chapter 13). This is a crucial perspective in the current environmental crisis.

If we are to live sustainably, we need to wean ourselves from the ideology that assumes we should liberate ourselves from the bounds of nature and live in a world of our own devising where we have supremacy over all things. In practical terms this means living within the limits given to us by the created order to which we belong. Western society and current economics is built largely on an obsession not just to maintain our standards of living but constantly to demand more growth. That attitude is at the root of the ecological crisis. Jesus' teaching, by contrast, highlights the insidious seductiveness of acquiring material wealth and possessions, which distracts attention from restoring a proper relationship first with God the creator and then with other people and the rest of creation. The teaching of Jesus on the kingdom of God, which has already broken into this present world, as the final chapters discuss, has the practical aspect of bringing us down to earth to live as an integral part of God's creation.

As discussed in Chapter 14, much of the present environmental crisis, which has arisen from unsustainable consumption, is driven by a form of idolatry. Such idolatry arises from the lie that possessing more material 'stuff' brings greater happiness, that continued economic growth is essential to well-being. Yet the truth, as the world's great religious traditions have always proclaimed, is that the true sources of human well-being arise from loving God and one's neighbour, the pursuit of justice and mercy, and the quest for beauty, goodness and truth. The power and danger of images as idols have long been apparent to the religious traditions of Judaism, Christianity and Islam. In our modern age, advertising often generates those idols and fosters an environment where humans love created things above the creator, where they worship cars and clothes and computers. Yet ultimately these things can kill us – quite literally in the case of cars, which, globally, cause 1.3 million deaths annually in accidents, injure a further 10 million and cause ill-health from pollution to hundreds of millions more. If a move to a more sustainable society is to have real bite, it will come about only by a combination of enlightened self-interest and by counter-cultural movements recognizing that pursuing the gods of mammon may be satisfying in the short term but ultimately prevents us from realizing the true 'good life'. Though the religious among us ought to hear this message earlier and more clearly than those who reject such faith, eventually the harm being done to humanity and to the earth will become clear to everyone.

We finish this book, appropriately enough, with a discussion of eschatology – of what will happen eventually to the world when it ends (Chapters 15 and 16). This is an arena where secular views can offer little encouragement. Ultimately, astrophysicists suggest that the universe will die not with a bang but with a cold, silent whimper. In the more immediate future, influential writers such as James Lovelock suggest that we are close to, or have already passed, the tipping point where climate change will run away out of control. In 2006 he wrote that billions of people would be likely to die as a result,[2] with only a handful of those now alive surviving.[3] The President of the Royal Society, Lord Rees of Ludlow, who certainly knows a lot about science, and astrophysics in particular, has written that he thinks there is only a 50/50 chance that our present civilization on earth will survive to the end of the twenty-first century without a serious setback.[4] He said in 2006 that 'Even in a cosmic or a geological time-perspective, there's something unique about our century: for the first time in its history, our entire planet's fate depends on human actions and human choices.'[5]

In contrast, the Christian perspective is of the certain hope of a new creation. This is the cornerstone of the Christian gospel. It is alluded to by numerous authors in this book, and rightly so because it is the thread that runs right through Scripture. The Bible narrative is bracketed by creation at the beginning and re-creation at the end. The New Testament is directed almost entirely towards this future, and the ramifications it carries for how we should live in its light in bearing witness to the reality of the kingdom of God, which is already breaking into this world. This hope does not derive from humankind's cleverness in human projects or from the Enlightenment idea that continual progress is what we should expect. Instead it is based on the death and resurrection of Christ, which demonstrated for all time that the natural processes of death and decay have been overturned by the creator God and in the fullness of time will be mirrored in the whole cosmos. There are elements of both continuity and discontinuity in the way the new creation is described, giving us good reason to work at stewarding this creation well, because that effort will bear fruit in the future.

When Jesus was asked by a sceptical lawyer how it was possible to enter into the eternal life that is part of the new creation, he answered with the pithy summary, 'Love the Lord your God with all your heart and with all your soul and with all your strength and with all your mind' and 'Love your neighbour as yourself' (Luke 10:27). To love God must include valuing and caring for the things he loves and being good stewards of them. Judging by God's pronouncement in the very first book of the Bible, that everything he had made was 'very good' (Genesis 1:31), this means caring properly for all of creation. And if we are to put all our energy into it, all of our heart, soul, strength and mind, we are, among other things, to use all of our scientific, technological, social and political skills, as well as curbing the worse excesses of our selfish desires.

Though non-Christians may not sign up to the concept of loving God, there must be few in the world who would argue with the second part of Jesus' answer, that we should love our neighbours in the same way as we take care of our own interests. The world would certainly be very different if everyone took that command seriously. Our neighbours are people all over the globe, especially now that we live in a world of instant global communications and inter-relatedness. And we cannot love those other people without caring for the environments in which they live and which we affect through our actions – by our greenhouse gas emissions, our purchasing and consumer decisions, our economic structures.

The ecological crisis has arisen because of human actions – it is in our power now to move towards sustainable ways of living. Whether or not we do so will affect not only our own well-being but also that of billions of other people both now and for generations to come.

2

Sustainable climate and the future of energy

JOHN HOUGHTON

Mostly we know what to do, but lack the will to do it.
(C. Tickell, *The Doomsday Letters*, BBC Radio 4 (1996))

Climate varies a great deal both over space and in time. There are natural variations due to interactions within the climate system itself (for example, between the ocean and the atmosphere), or the influence of natural events such as volcanoes, or changes in the input of solar radiation or its distribution over the earth. Ice ages occurring over the past million years, for instance, were triggered by regular changes in the geometry of the earth's orbit around the sun, known as Milankovitch cycles (see Chapter 3).

The term 'sustainable climate' refers to the relationship between human beings and the climate. Humans have had an impact on their local climate over a long time, for example through deforestation. The history of Easter Island in the seventeenth century is one case where such action had great adverse consequences. However, it is only during the past century that increases in human population and the development of large-scale industry have begun to have widespread and severe effects on our climate. So much so that climate change due to human activity is often stated as the biggest challenge facing the world in the twenty-first century. The change we are experiencing and which is rapidly growing is described as unsustainable because its impacts are largely adverse and will negatively affect our children and subsequent generations, many human communities (especially the poor and disadvantaged) and many ecosystems, which will experience great losses of species and biodiversity.

In this chapter I describe our latest understanding regarding the science and the impacts and then address the action that needs to be taken, especially as it affects the energy sector and its sustainability.

The science of climate change

By absorbing infra-red or 'heat' radiation from the earth's surface, so-called 'greenhouse gases' (or GHGs) present in the atmosphere act as a blanket over the earth's surface, keeping it warmer than it would otherwise be. Examples of these GHGs are water vapour, methane and carbon dioxide (CO_2). The existence of this natural 'greenhouse effect' has been known for nearly 200 years; it is essential to the provision of our current climate to which ecosystems and we human beings have adapted.

Since the beginning of the Western industrial revolution, around 1750, CO_2 has increased by nearly 40 per cent and is now at a higher

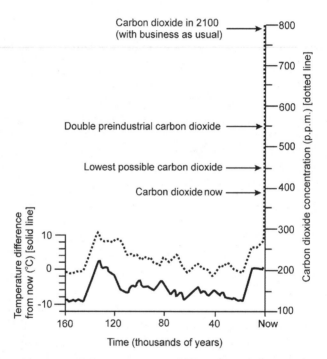

Figure 2.1 Changes of atmospheric temperature and CO₂ concentration in the atmosphere during the last ice age. As shown from the Vostok ice core drilled from Antarctica. This reveals information from the 160,000 years during which the ice in the core has been laid down. Temperature changes can be deduced from variations in the ratio of oxygen isotopes incorporated into the ice, and CO₂ concentrations from inspection of bubbles of air trapped in the ice. The main triggers for ice ages have been small, regular variations in the geometry of the earth's orbit about the sun. The next ice age is predicted to occur in about 50,000 years' time. (Adapted from D. Raynaud, J. Jouzel, J. M. Barnola *et al.*, 'The ice core record of greenhouse gases', *Science* (1993) **259**: 926–34.)

concentration in the atmosphere than it has been probably for millions of years (Figure 2.1). Chemical analysis demonstrates that this increase is due largely to GHG emissions into the atmosphere, including each year about 25 billion tonnes of CO_2 itself, as a direct result of the burning of coal, oil and gas. If no action is taken to curb these emissions, the CO_2 concentration will rise during the twenty-first century to two or three times its pre-industrial (1750) level.

The climate record over the past 1,000 years shows a lot of natural variability – including the medieval warm period (950–1100) and the European little ice age (approximately 1450–1850). The rise in global average temperature (and its rate of rise) during the twentieth century is well outside the range of known natural variability (Figure 2.2).[6] The warmest year in the instrumental record was 1998. A more striking statistic is that each of the first eight months of 1998 was the warmest on record for those individual months. There is very strong evidence that most of the warming over the past 50 years is due to the increase in GHGs, especially CO_2. Confirmation of this is also provided by observations of the warming of the oceans. The period of cooling noted from about 1950 to 1970 is most likely due to an increase in atmospheric particles (especially sulphates) from industrial sources. These particles reflect sunlight (global dimming), hence tending to cool the earth's surface and mask some of the warming effect of GHGs.

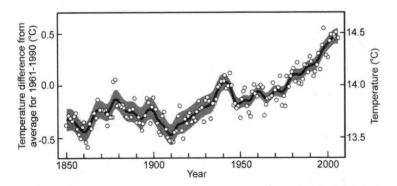

Figure 2.2 Observed changes in global average surface temperature relative to average for the period 1961–90. Broadened curves represent decadal averaged values while circles show yearly values. Shaded area indicates the statistical degree of uncertainty in each measurement. (From 'Summary for policymakers', in *Climate Change 2007, The Physical Science Basis, Working Group I Contribution to the Fourth Assessment Report of the IPCC Intergovernmental Panel on Climate Change*, ed. S. Solomon, D. Qin, D. Manning *et al.* (Cambridge: Cambridge University Press, 2007), 1–18.)

Over the twenty-first century the global average surface temperature is projected to rise by between 2° and 6° Celsius (°C) from its pre-industrial level; the range represents different assumptions about emissions of GHGs and the sensitivity of the climate model used in making the estimate (Figure 2.3). For global average temperature, a rise of this amount is large. The temperature difference between the middle of an ice age and the warm periods in between is only about 5° or 6°C. So, associated with probable warming in the twenty-first century will be a rate of change of climate equivalent to, say, half an ice age in less than 100 years – a larger rate of change than for at least 10,000 years. Adapting to this will be difficult for both human beings and many ecosystems.

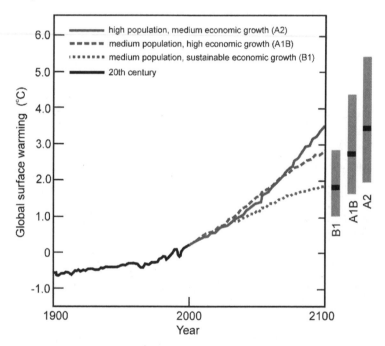

Figure 2.3 Global average surface warming relative to 1980–99, for the twentieth century from observations, for the twenty-first century, for three representative scenarios of GHG increases as projected from multi-model estimates with climate models. The grey bars on the right indicate the best estimate and range of statistical uncertainty for 2100 for the three scenarios. (Adapted from *Climate Change 2007, The Physical Science Basis, Working Group I Contribution to the Fourth Assessment Report of the IPCC Intergovernmental Panel on Climate Change*, ed. S. Solomon, D. Qin, D. Manning et al. (Cambridge: Cambridge University Press, 2007).)

Climate change impacts

Talking in terms of changes in global average surface temperature, however, tells us little about the actual impacts of global warming on human communities. Some of the most obvious effects will be due to a rise in sea level caused mainly by ocean water expanding as it is heated. The projected rise due to ocean warming, together with that due to melting glaciers, is of the order of half a metre per century and will continue for many centuries. Warming of the deep oceans as well as the surface waters takes a long time. Acceleration in the melting of the Greenland and the West Antarctic ice sheets is beginning to make a further contribution; the best estimates of total average sea level rise by 2100 now approach 1 metre.[7] Such a rise will cause very great problems for human communities living in low-lying regions: areas such as Bangladesh (where about 10 million live within the 1 metre contour; Figure 2.4), southern China and other major river deltas, and also islands in the Indian and Pacific Oceans, will be impossible to protect and many millions of people will be displaced.

Figure 2.4 Land that will be affected in Bangladesh by various amounts of sea-level rise. (Adapted from J. D. Millman, 'Environmental and economic implications of rising sea level and subsiding deltas: the Nile and Bangladeshi examples', *Ambio* (1989) 18: 340–5.)

There will also be impacts from extreme events. The extremely unusual high temperatures in central Europe during the summer of 2003 led to the deaths of over 20,000 people – an event that caused myself and others to describe climate change as a weapon of mass destruction. Careful analysis has led to the projection that such summers are likely to be the norm by the middle of the twenty-first century and cool compared to those expected in 2100.[8]

Water is becoming an increasingly important resource (see Chapter 10). A warmer world will lead to more evaporation of water from the surface, more water vapour in the atmosphere and, on average, more precipitation. Of greater importance is the fact that increased condensation of water vapour in clouds leads to the release of heat (the latent heat of condensation). Since this release of latent heat is the largest source of energy driving the atmosphere's circulation, the earth's hydrological cycle (water cycle) will become more intense. This means there will be a tendency to more intense rainfall events but also less overall rainfall in some semi-arid areas.

On average, floods and droughts are the most damaging of the world's disasters. Between 1975 and 2002, as a result of flooding due to rainfall, over 200,000 lives were lost and 2.2 billion affected; as a result of drought, over half a million lives were lost and 1.3 billion affected.[9] The greater frequency and intensity of these events is bad news for most human communities and especially for regions such as Southeast Asia and sub-Saharan Africa, where they already occur only too frequently. For floods, a typical increase in risk of a factor of five can be expected by 2050.[10] Currently, extreme droughts affect about 2 per cent of the world's useable land area at any one time, a figure that has doubled in the past 20 years (defined according to the Palmer drought index that distinguishes between moderate, severe and extreme droughts). Recent estimates suggest that by 2050 over 10 per cent of the world's land area will be so affected,[11] and, if no action is taken to stabilize climate change, by 2100 it could be about 30 per cent. Further, extreme droughts will tend to be longer and measured in years rather than months, again leading to many millions of displaced people.

Sea-level rise, changes in water availability and extreme events will lead to increasing pressure, on less affected areas, from environmental refugees. A cautious estimate has suggested that, due to climate change, there could be more than 150 million extra refugees by 2050.[12] The severity of impacts will affect not only human communities. Many ecosystems will be unable to adapt to the changes or to the rate of change and many millions of species will be lost; indeed, the rate of species loss is already beginning to accelerate.

In addition we will experience longer-term changes, about which there is less certainty, but which, if they were to occur, would be highly damaging and possibly irreversible. For instance, large changes are being observed in polar regions. With rising temperatures over Greenland, it is estimated that meltdown of the ice cap could begin during the next few decades. Complete meltdown is likely to take many centuries but eventually would increase sea level by 7 metres.

A further concern is what may happen to the Thermo-Haline Circulation, which involves all the oceans in which the Atlantic Gulf Stream plays a key part. Increased fresh water from rainfall and melting ice in north polar regions could weaken this circulation or even cut it off, leading to large regional changes in temperature in the North Atlantic. Paleoclimate history (that is, climate change evidence in the geological record) indicates occurrence of such changes in the past. It is such an event that is behind the highly speculative happenings in the film *The Day After Tomorrow*.

There are also some positive impacts from global warming. For instance, in Siberia and other areas at high northern latitudes, winters will be less cold and growing seasons will be longer. Also, increased concentrations of CO_2 act as fertilizer on some plants, and, provided there are adequate supplies of water and other nutrients, will lead to increased crop yields in some places, probably most notably in northern mid latitudes. However, careful studies have demonstrated that adverse impacts will far outweigh positive effects, the more so as temperatures rise more than 1° or 2°C above pre-industrial levels.[13]

A recent review of the economics of climate change by Sir Nicholas Stern provides estimates of the likely economic cost of climate change impacts:[14] up to 3 per cent of global world output for a warming of 2°–3°C and up to 10 per cent (over 10 per cent in some low-income countries) if warming rises more than 5°C, as is likely to occur next century if there is no action to reduce GHGs (see also Chapters 4 and 5). These economic estimates do not take into account the human cost in terms of, for example, deaths, dislocation, misery and lack of security that would accompany large-scale climate changes.

Many people ask how sure we are about the scientific story I have just presented (see also Chapter 3). Let me explain that it is based very largely on the extremely thorough work of the Intergovernmental Panel on Climate Change (IPCC) and its last major report published in 2007. I had the privilege of being chair or co-chair of the Panel's scientific assessment from 1988 to 2002. Hundreds of scientists, drawn from many countries, contributed to and reviewed these assessments. Our task was honestly and objectively to distinguish between those areas that are reasonably well known and understood from those with large uncertainty. The IPCC has produced four assessments (1990, 1995, 2001 and 2007) covering science, impacts and analyses of policy options. The IPCC 2007 report is in three volumes, each of about 1,000 pages and containing many thousands of references to the scientific literature.[15] Because the IPCC is an intergovernmental body, at the meeting to agree the 'Summaries for Policymakers' that were included in the reports, the scientists were joined by government delegates (also mostly scientists) from about 100 countries – including all the world's major industrialized countries. At these meetings, scientific accuracy and clarity governed the decisions; no influence from political or other agendas was allowed. No assessment on any other scientific topic has been so thoroughly researched and reviewed. In June 2005, just before the G8 Summit in Scotland, the Academies of Sciences of the world's 11 most important countries (the G8 plus, India, China and Brazil) issued a statement endorsing the conclusions of the IPCC and urging world governments to take urgent action to address climate change.[16] The world's top scientists could not have spoken more strongly.

Unfortunately, there are vested interests that have spent tens of millions of dollars on spreading misinformation about the climate change issue (see Chapters 3 and 12). First they tried to deny the existence of any scientific evidence for rapid climate change due to human activities. More recently they have largely accepted the fact of anthropogenic, or human-initiated, climate change but argue that its impacts will not be great, that we can 'wait and see' and in any case we can always 'fix' the problem if it turns out to be substantial. The scientific evidence cannot support such arguments.

Adapting to climate change

To combat climate change it is necessary not only to mitigate the changes by reducing GHG emissions but also to adapt to the changes that are unavoidable and are already becoming apparent. Adaptation will be required in most sectors of human activity. For instance, since a high proportion of the world's population lives in coastal areas, sea-level rise will demand substantial and expensive work on sea defences. Because of large changes in water availability in many areas, water conservation, water resources and water management must be urgently addressed (see Chapters 7 and 11). New flood control measures are already being considered in many areas. Extensive adjustments will also be required in the agricultural sector, for instance in the development of new crop strains appropriate to higher temperatures or possessing drought resistance. Improved land management will also be essential, for instance in erosion control or crop relocation. As adaptation studies develop, it is becoming increasingly clear that preparation for large adjustments and changes in the future must begin immediately.

International action on climate change

Because of the work of the IPCC and its first report in 1990, the Earth Summit at Rio de Janeiro in 1992 was able to address the climate change issue and the action that needed to be taken (see also Chapter 5). The Framework Convention on Climate Change – agreed by over 180 countries – stated that Parties to the Convention should take 'precautionary measures to anticipate, prevent or minimize the causes of climate change and mitigate its adverse effects. Where there are threats of irreversible damage, lack of full scientific certainty should not be used as a reason for postponing such measures.'

More particularly the Objective of Article 2 of the Framework is 'to stabilize GHG concentrations in the atmosphere at a level that does not cause dangerous interference with the climate system … that allows ecosystems to adapt naturally to climate change, that ensures food production is not threatened and that enables economic development to proceed in a sustainable manner'.[17] Such stabilization would also eventually stop further climate change. However, because of the length of time that CO_2 remains in the atmosphere, the lag in the response of the surface temperature to changes in GHGs (largely because of the time taken for the ocean to warm) and the time taken for appropriate human action to be agreed, this stabilization will take the best part of a century.

Stabilization cannot, of course, remove all the adverse consequences of climate change for human communities or for ecosystems.

According to the definition given at the start of this chapter, therefore, some unsustainability is bound to remain. But by minimizing unsustainability, the Objective of the Climate Convention can be seen as providing a working definition of a sustainable climate.

Global emissions of CO_2 to the atmosphere from fossil fuel burning are currently approaching 25 billion tonnes per annum and rising rapidly. Unless strong measures are taken they will reach two or three times their present level during the twenty-first century and stabilization of climate will be nowhere in sight. To stabilize CO_2 concentrations, emissions during this century must reduce to a fraction of their present level before the century's end.

What stabilization targets need to be set? One that has often been talked about limits the concentration of equivalent CO_2 (CO_2e, see Box 2.1) in the atmosphere to double its pre-industrial value, that is about 550 p.p.m. CO_2e, which would cause a rise in global average temperature of about 3°C over its pre-industrial (1750) value. Although climate change would eventually largely be halted – but not for well over 100 years – the climate change impacts at such a level would be very large, of the kind and magnitude I described earlier.

It is now widely recognized that a limit lower than 3°C must be the aim if such unacceptable damage is to be ameliorated. A limit of a 2°C rise in global average surface temperature (that implies a CO_2e concentration limit of about 450 p.p.m.) was first put forward by the European Union Council in 1996. That 2°C limit has now become widely accepted and intense discussions are taking place to see how it can be achieved. It would require global emissions of CO_2 to peak within the next ten years and by 2050 to be reduced by over 50 per cent from 1990 levels (see Figure 2.8, below). Some prominent climate scientists led by James Hansen of Columbia University, USA, are arguing that the 450 p.p.m. limit for CO_2e is insufficient to prevent a serious risk of widespread, unacceptable changes and that a target of 380 p.p.m. should be the aim. Since 380 p.p.m. is below the present level of atmospheric CO_2, such a target could not be reached this century. However, Hansen and others are beginning to look into how large amounts of CO_2 can be removed ('drawn down') from the atmosphere and captured in trees, soils or other reservoirs (know as carbon sinks). It is important that preparations of this kind are begun as it may well turn out that we need more drastic action than is currently planned.

Box 2.1 Carbon dioxide equivalents (CO_2e)

GHGs other than CO_2 that are increasing because of human activities, for instance methane and nitrous oxide, also contribute to global warming. It is often helpful to convert the effect of these other gases into equivalent amounts of CO_2 (written as CO_2e). If we consider these other gases on their own, their combined effect at the moment is approximately the same as if we added 75 p.p.m. to the 'normal' CO_2 concentration (about 385 p.p.m.), which gives a total CO_2e value of 460 p.p.m. However, in addition to GHGs, small atmospheric particles called aerosols also contribute to global warming or cooling by absorbing solar radiation or by reflecting it back into space. Their effect also can be given a CO_2e value. Most aerosols tend to cool the atmosphere so, at the moment, their net cooling effect is about the same as the warming effect of GHGs other than CO_2. This means the effect of non-CO_2 gases and that of aerosol particles balances each other out and the value of CO_2e is approximately the same as the concentration of CO_2 alone (385 p.p.m.).

An important question is whether aerosols will continue to provide cooling at the same level as today. Because of the lifetime of particles in the lower atmosphere, typically only a few days, the answer to the question depends on whether, for example, sulphur dioxide (the source of sulphate aerosol particles) will continue to be released into the atmosphere from power stations that burn coal or oil. Future scenarios continue to include aerosol contributions for the next few decades, but with substantial reductions after 2040 or 2050. When these reductions become imminent it will be necessary to find ways of reducing CO_2 itself even further to compensate. It would be prudent to begin now to explore technologies through which these additional reductions could be achieved.

The reductions in emissions must be made globally; all nations must take part. However, there are very large differences between GHG emissions in different countries. Expressed in tonnes of CO_2 per capita (per person) per annum, they vary from about 25 for the USA, 10 for Europe, 5 for China and 2.5 for India (Figure 2.5). Ways need to be found to achieve reductions that are both realistic and equitable – for instance a mechanism called Contraction and Convergence, suggested by the Global Commons Institute, proposes that, within a few decades, countries' emissions should converge to the same per capita allowance of CO_2 and that there should be trading of emissions equivalents to this end.[18]

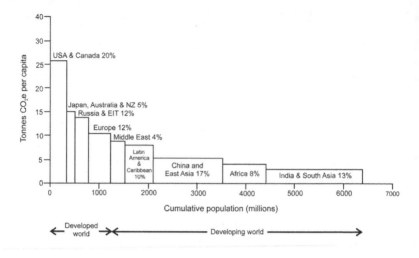

Figure 2.5 Distribution of regional GHG emissions per person (that is, all gases included in the Kyoto Protocol including land-use change) expressed as tonnes of CO₂e emissions in 2004 from different countries or groups of countries, plotted against population numbers. The percentages in the bars indicate each region's share in global GHG emissions. EIT is economies in transition; to convert tonnes CO_2 to tonnes of carbon, divide by 3.66. (Adapted from 'Summary for policymakers', in *Climate Change 2007, Mitigation of Climate Change, Working Group III contribution to the Fourth Assessment Report of the IPCC Intergovernmental Panel on Climate Change*, ed. B. Metz, O. Davidson, P. Bosch, R. Dave and L. Meyer (Cambridge: Cambridge University Press, 2007), 1–24.)

In order to allow some growth in emissions by developing countries as they grow economically, it is necessary for larger reductions than the global average to be made by developed countries. For instance, the UK government has taken a lead on this issue and, in the Climate Change Bill that became law in December 2008, sets a mandatory target of a reduction of 80 per cent in GHG emissions from 1990 levels by 2050.

Required actions and technologies

Three kinds of action are required to achieve these reductions. First, there is energy efficiency. Very approximately one-third of any country's energy consumption goes in buildings (domestic and commercial), one-third in transport and one-third in industry. Large energy savings can be made in all three sectors, many with significant economic savings. But to achieve these will require encouragement and incentives from central and local government and a great deal of determination from all of us.

Take buildings, for example. Standards of insulation and energy efficiency in buildings need to be brought closer to those of Scandinavia in many countries including the USA and the UK. Why in the UK, for instance, is combined heat and power (i.e. from a power station providing electric power, using the 'waste' heat for domestic heating) not the norm for new housing estates? Recent projects demonstrate that 'zero emissions' buildings are a practical possibility – initial costs are a little larger than for conventional buildings but running costs are a lot less. For example, in south London the BedZED development (ZED is zero emissions development) – the largest carbon-emissions-neutral housing project in the UK – is a complex of 82 homes obtaining its heat and power from the use of forestry residue. Bringing older housing stock up to a much higher standard is also essential. In the transport sector, large efficiency savings are also possible. For cars, a progression of technologies between now and 2050 is anticipated, beginning with petrol/electric hybrids, then moving on to fuel cells and hydrogen fuel from non-fossil fuel sources.

Within the industrial sector some serious drives for energy savings are already happening. A number of the world's largest companies have already achieved savings in energy that have translated into savings of billions of dollars.[19]

Second, there are possibilities for capture of carbon underground, for instance in spent oil and gas fields or in suitable rock formations.[20] Because of the large number of coal-fired power plants being built, especially in China and India (China is building new electricity-generating capacity of about 2 gigawatts per week), rapid development, demonstration and implementation of carbon capture and storage (CCS) in all new plants is a very high priority (Figure 2.6). The European Union is working with China on a demonstration CCS project but many more such projects are urgently needed.

Third, a wide variety of non-fossil-fuel sources of energy is available for development and exploitation, for instance biomass (including waste), solar power, hydro, wind, wave, tidal, geothermal energy and nuclear power. The potential of solar power, both photovoltaic and concentrated solar power (where solar energy is harnessed to drive heat engines), is especially large, particularly in developing countries and

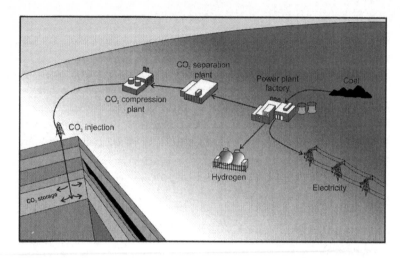

Figure 2.6 Schematic of carbon capture and storage from coal-fired power stations. (Adapted from IAE, *World Energy Outlook* (Paris: IAE, 2007).)

near desert areas with high levels of sunshine. Large solar projects are envisaged that couple electricity and hydrogen generation with desalination in desert regions where water is a scarce resource.

Within industry, the opportunities for innovation, development and investment in all these above-mentioned areas are numerous. A simple presentation of the type of reductions required has been created by Robert Socolow and Stephen Pacala of Princeton University, New Jersey, USA.[21] To counter the likely growth in global CO_2 emissions from now until 2050, seven 'wedges' of reduction are proposed, each wedge amounting to 1 gigatonne of carbon (equivalent to 3.66 gigatonnes CO_2) per year in 2050. To provide the reductions that are required to meet the 2°C rise limit mentioned above, 13 such wedges would be needed. Some of the possible wedges that Socolow and Pacala propose are as follows. They illustrate the scale of what is necessary.

- Buildings efficiency – reduce carbon emissions by 25 per cent.
- Vehicle fuel use – from 30 to 60 miles per gallon (about 10–20 kilometres per litre) in 2 billion vehicles.
- Carbon capture and storage at 800 gigawatts of coal-fired power plants.
- Wind power from 1 million windmills each working at 2 megawatts peak power output.

- Solar photovoltaic power derived from an area 150 kilometres by 150 kilometres.
- Nuclear power –700 gigawatts, twice current capacity.
- Stop tropical deforestation and establish 300 million hectares of new tree plantations.
- Biofuel production from biomass on 250 million hectares of land.

In June 2008 the International Energy Agency (IEA) published its *Energy Technology Perspectives,* which describes in detail the technologies and investment required by the world's energy industries to reduce global fossil fuel emissions sufficiently to have some chance of meeting the 2°C target by 2050.[22, 23] Figure 2.7 details the reductions required in different sectors. In addition, global deforestation, especially in the tropics, which today accounts for about 20 per cent of CO_2 emissions, would need to be halted almost immediately.

The costs of stabilization at 450 p.p.m. CO_2e have been estimated by the IPCC and the *Stern Review*[24] as equivalent to the loss of a small percentage of world GDP by 2050, that is one or two years' economic growth over a 40-year period. The IEA has also estimated the cost in terms of the additional financial investment in global energy required to meet the BLUE Map scenario (see Figure 2.7).[25] They begin with an estimate of the total cumulative energy investment needs for 'business as usual' (their reference scenario) from 2005 to 2050 of about $US250 trillion (million million), or about 6 per cent of world GDP. By far the largest part of this relates to investments that consumers make in energy-consuming capital equipment: from vehicles to light bulbs to steel plants. In fact transport vehicles alone account for 84 per cent of the total investment. To follow the BLUE Map scenario over this period, additional investment needs are estimated at $US45 trillion, an increase of 18 per cent over the reference scenario and equivalent to just over 1 per cent of world GDP over the period – a figure similar to that quoted by the IPCC for the likely mitigation cost of stabilizing CO_2e at 450 p.p.m. The IEA also point out that, compared with the reference scenario, the BLUE Map plan will result in significant fuel savings amounting to about $US50 trillion, approximately wiping out the additional investment cost.[26]

In addition to climate-change mitigation, there are many beneficial moves towards other aspects of sustainability associated with this revolution in energy generation and use that I have outlined. The net cost,

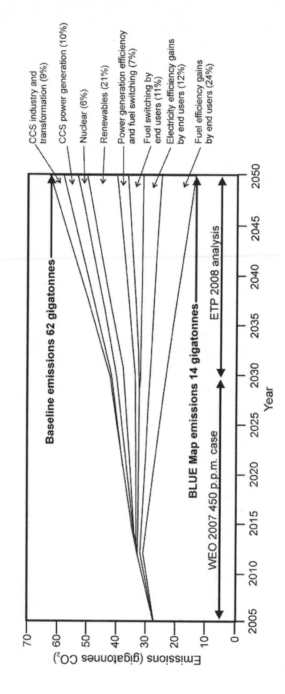

Figure 2.7 Reductions required in CO$_2$ emissions below the 'business-as-usual' reference scenario, over the period 2005–50, to meet the requirements of the International Energy Agency (IEA) BLUE Map emissions scenario, showing contributions from different energy sources. WEO, IAE Report *World Energy Outlook*; ETP, IEA Report *Energy Technology Perspectives*. (Adapted from IEA, *Energy Technology Perspectives* (Paris: IEA, 2008).)

often quoted as a main concern, would appear to be small, even possibly negligible, and certainly far less than the cost of taking no action.

At the end of this section on action, we are bound to ask, 'Can it be done?' Figure 2.8 summarizes for global emissions elements of the 'road map' that will have to be followed to 2050 for a 50 per cent chance of success in achieving the 2°C target. Note that emissions peak around 2015 reduce from 1990 levels by at least 50 per cent by 2050. Beyond 2050 our discussion of the last section implies that the emissions reductions required will need to aim at a 'zero-carbon future' as quickly

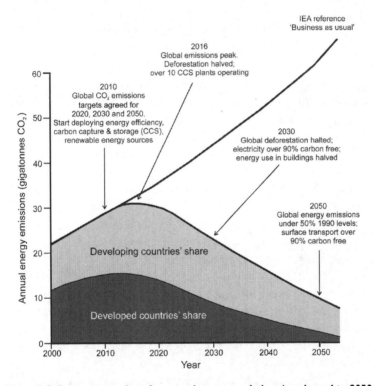

Figure 2.8 Some waymarkers for annual energy emissions 'road map' to 2050 showing IEA Reference scenario and a profile aimed at targets of less than 2°C temperature rise from pre-industrial levels and 450 p.p.m. CO_2e stabilization. The division between developed and developing countries from today until 2050 is a construction based on the developed countries' share, compared with that of developing countries, peaking earlier and reducing further, for example by at least 80 per cent by 2050. CCS is carbon capture and storage. (Adapted from J.T. Houghton, *Global Warming: The Complete Briefing*, 4th edn (Cambridge: Cambridge University Press, 2009).)

and expeditiously as possible. The energy future before us represents an extremely ambitious timetable that can only be fulfilled if the programme of energy transformation is raised to a very much higher level of urgency – more like that prevailing in time of war. In 1941, under the Presidency of Franklin Roosevelt and his remarkable programme of Lend-Lease, the US industrial machine turned itself over, within a few months, to providing military equipment – tanks, aircraft, etc. – on a very large scale. I believe that the threat of climate change is such that concerted action of a similar kind is now needed.

A strategy for future energy

It is relatively easy to present written solutions of the kind I have just listed, but harder to see how they can be implemented. 'What are the best options?' is typical of the questions that arise. But there is no one best solution and no best technology. Different solutions will be appropriate in different countries or regions. Simplistic answers I have heard many times have been, 'Leave it to the market' and 'The three solutions are Technology, Technology and Technology'. The market and technology are essential tools but poor masters. Solutions need to be much more carefully crafted than these tools can provide on their own. So how can the process start?

A long-term perspective is required. I like to think of it in terms of a voyage. For the boat we are taking, technology can be thought of as the engine and market forces as the propeller driven by the engine. But where is the boat heading? Without a rudder and someone steering, the course will be arbitrary; it could even be disastrous. Every voyage needs a destination, a detailed map and a strategy to reach it. Energy requires a strategy for the long term. In the following paragraphs I list briefly some important components of the strategy that should direct any solutions.

First, the economy and environment must be addressed together. It has been said that 'the economy is a wholly owned subsidiary of the environment'.[27] In a speech in 2005, Gordon Brown, then UK Chancellor of the Exchequer, expanded on this idea when he said:[28]

Environmental issues – including climate change – have traditionally been placed in a category separate from the economy and from economic policy. But this is no longer tenable. Across

a range of environmental issues – from soil erosion to the depletion of marine stocks, from water scarcity to air pollution – it is
clear now not just that economic activity is their cause, but that
these problems in themselves threaten future economic activity
and growth.

Take the market. It responds overwhelmingly to commodity price and
the short term. But in its raw form it takes no account of environmental or other external factors. Although there is general agreement
among economists that such factors should be internalized in the
market, for instance through carbon taxes or 'cap and trade' arrangements, most governments remain slow to introduce such measures (see
Chapter 4). An example where it is working comes from Norway where
the levy of a carbon tax makes it economic to pump CO_2 back into the
strata from where natural gas is extracted. Aviation presents a contrary
example where the absence of any economic measures is allowing
global aviation to expand at a highly unsustainable rate. Governments
need urgently to set a stable financial framework so that industries can
do their part to work for effective solutions.

Second, not all potential technologies are at the same stage of development. For good choices to be made, promising technologies must
be brought to the starting gate so that they can compete fairly. This
implies joint programmes between government and industry, the
provision of adequate resources for research and development, the
creation of demonstration projects and sufficient support to see technologies through to maturity. (That government energy research and
development in the UK is now less than 5 per cent of what it was 20
years ago shows the lack of commitment or urgency on the government's part.) The market will provide little of this on its own. A prime
example of where this is vital is in the CCS technology already mentioned. Another is the exploitation of tides and tidal streams where
the UK, with some of the largest tides in the world, has a particular
opportunity.

A third part of the strategy is to address the social and 'quality of life'
implications arising from the way energy is provided to a community.
For instance, energy coming from large central installations may be
appropriate for cities. But large-scale migration to cities that is now
occurring tends to reduce the quality of life for many in poorer countries. The introduction of local energy schemes on a farm or village

scale to the billions of people currently without access to commercial energy is essential if rural communities in the developing world are going to survive and grow economically.

In rural communities, biomass is a valuable renewable energy resource. The CO_2 that is emitted when biomass is burned, digested or turned into biofuel is 'fixed' by the next crop as it is grown. When fossil fuels are burned, no such replacement occurs. Waste is a component of biomass, increasingly recognized as an important energy source. The potential energy value in agricultural and forestry wastes and residues could, if realized, meet at least 10 per cent of the world's total energy requirement. Suitable crops can also be used for the production of liquid biofuels. In Brazil, sugar cane has been successfully grown to produce ethanol for many years. A strong focus of recent work is commercial-scale production of biofuels from lignocellulose from grasses, woody material or from the residue from cereal or other crops; the IEA scenarios I have presented assume that these second-generation biofuels, as they are called, can be successfully developed on the scale required.[29]

However, decisions about the large-scale production of biofuels, or indeed any biomass, must be guided by thorough and comprehensive assessments that address their overall efficiency and contribution to the reduction of GHG emissions.[30] Also requiring careful assessment is the degree to which their use of land is competing with food crops (for example, the use of maize) or adding to deforestation of tropical forests (as for instance with some palm oil plantations) that itself contributes substantially to GHG emissions (see Chapter 11). Examples have recently come to light of adverse consequences, for instance on world food prices, arising from a lack of adequate assessment.

In addition to biomass (including food and plant waste), biogas or biofuels, solar energy (photovoltaic or thermal) can provide another important local source of energy. For instance, in a reasonably sunny area, an array of solar cells of about 1 square metre in area coupled with a small car battery to provide for energy storage can provide for basic lighting, a small refrigerator and some television – such an arrangement is called a Solar Home System. In Bangladesh, there is a plan for 1 million biogas systems and 1 million solar home systems to be provided by 2015, financed in ways similar to microfinance provided through the Grameen banks (no-collateral banks owned in large part by the borrowers and providing for the very poor).[31]

Fourth, energy security must be part of the strategy and is increasingly being addressed by governments in many countries. How safe are gas pipelines crossing whole continents? How safe are nuclear power stations from terrorist attack or nuclear material from proliferation to terrorist groups? It is such considerations that put into question any large expansion of the contribution from nuclear energy.

Diversity of source is clearly important. But thinking about security could be more integrated and holistic. Admiral Sir Julian Oswald, UK First Sea Lord (1989–1993) suggested more than ten years ago that defence policy and spending could be broadened to consider potential causes of conflict such as the large-scale damage and insecurity that will arise increasingly from climate change.[32] For instance, funding on the scale of the many billions of pounds and dollars spent on the Iraq war, if directed at combating climate change, would accelerate enormously the realization of GHG reductions on the scale required.

Fifth, as is both stated and implied in the 1992 Framework Convention on Climate Change, partnerships of many kinds are required. All nations (developed and developing) need to work closely together with national, international and multinational industries and corporations to craft solutions that are both sustainable and equitable. Technology transfer from developed to developing countries is vital if energy growth in developing countries is going to proceed in a sustainable way.

There are those who argue that we can 'wait and see' before action is necessary. That is not a responsible position. The need for action is urgent for three reasons. The first is scientific (see also Chapter 3). Because the oceans take time to warm, a lag exists in the response of climate to increasing GHGs. A commitment to substantial change already exists, much of which will not be realized for 30 to 50 years. Further emissions just add to that commitment. The second reason is economic (see also Chapter 4). Energy infrastructure, for instance in power stations, lasts typically for 30 to 50 years. It is much more cost-effective to begin now to phase in required infrastructure changes rather than having to make them much more rapidly later. The third reason is political (see also Chapter 5). Countries like China and India are industrializing very rapidly. I heard a senior energy adviser to the Chinese government speak recently. He said that China by itself would not be taking the lead in reducing GHG emissions.[33] When the big emitters in the developed nations take action, China will take action.

Moral and spiritual issues

People often say to me that I am wasting my time talking about global warming. 'The world', they say, 'will never agree to take the necessary action.' I reply that I am optimistic for three reasons. First, I have experienced the commitment of the world scientific community (including scientists from many different nations, backgrounds and cultures) in painstakingly and honestly working together to understand the problems and assessing what needs to be done. Second, I believe the necessary technology is available for achieving satisfactory solutions. My third reason is that I believe we have a God-given task of being good stewards of creation (see also Chapters 8 and 9).

How can we take on this task of sustainable stewardship? To begin with, it is helpful to expose the root causes of unsustainability, some of which are listed below:

- Ignorance – we didn't know.
- Denial – we didn't want to know.
- Procrastination – we said, 'Not now'.
- Lack of will – we knew but didn't do.

The first 'root cause' – ignorance – is well illustrated when it is recognized that in developed countries we have already benefited over many generations from abundant fossil fuel energy that has been the main source of our wealth. We had not realized the damage this is causing or that it falls disproportionately on the world's poorer countries. The demands on our stewardship take on a special poignancy as we recognize the strong moral imperative for those of us in the rich world to limit the damage by reducing our emissions of GHGs as quickly as possible and also by sharing our wealth and skills with the developing world assisting them to develop sustainably.

The last of my 'root causes' points up the problem of resolve. Many recognize this lack of will to act as a spiritual problem. Our obsession with the material and the immediate means that we fail to act according to values and ideals that transcend the limited horizons controlled by our selfishness and greed. Because of this, it has been proposed that at the basis of stewardship should be a principle extending what has traditionally been considered wrong – or in religious parlance as sin – to include lack of care for the environment or for those severely disadvantaged by the pollution we have introduced.[34] Those with religious belief often emphasize the importance of coupling together the relationship of human beings to the environment to the relationship of human beings to God (see Chapters 12 and 13). For Christians, God's commitment to the earth and its future could not have been demonstrated more strongly than by the sending of Jesus, God's son, into the world to redeem it. For me as a Christian, the implication of this is that our stewardship of the earth need not be pursued on our own but in partnership with God, who not only provides us with strong motivation for action but who has promised to work alongside us as we care for the earth he has created (John 15:5, 15). I can personally bear testimony to the value and excitement of that partnership. That religious belief can provide an important driving force for action is often also recognized by those who look elsewhere than religion for a solution.

For our fulfilment as human beings we need not just economic but moral and spiritual goals. Near the top of the list could be long-term care for our planet and its resources. Reaching out for such a goal could lead to nations and peoples working together more effectively and closely than is possible with many of the other goals on offer.

Finally, I would like to indicate the sorts of action that individuals can take. There are some things that all of us can do. For instance, when purchasing vehicles or appliances we can choose ones that are fuel efficient; we can buy 'green' electricity and ensure our homes are as energy efficient as possible; we can think before we travel and use public transportation or car-share more frequently and we can support leaders in government or industry who are advocating or organizing the necessary solutions (see also Chapter 14). Both the challenge and the opportunity for all of us are unmistakeable. And we all can contribute. To quote from Edmund Burke, a British parliamentarian of 200 years ago, 'No one made a greater mistake than he who did nothing because he could do so little.'[35]

3

Climate science and its distortion and denial by the misinformation industry

JAMES J. McCARTHY

Science is a self correcting process. To be accepted, new ideas must survive the most rigorous standards of evidence and scrutiny.

(C. Sagan, *Cosmos*, television series:
Episode 4: 'Heaven and Hell', 1980)

It is important to realize that science progresses when scientists question every aspect of scientific understanding. Sometimes new findings, seemingly credible, or perspectives that prevailed for decades are subsequently proved to be wrong. The process of science is one of always questioning and challenging both new and well-established findings; hence all knowledge of physical, biological and chemical aspects of planet earth should be open to re-examination. Does evidence adequately support the prevailing view of how a particular process works? Is there a contradictory body of evidence? Is there an alternative explanation that is also, or perhaps even more, consistent with the highest quality evidence?

All good scientists ask these questions about everything they have either been taught or discovered themselves. We train our students to go beyond what we can teach them – to use newer methods for gathering evidence, to subject their data to ever more sophisticated analyses, always to keep their minds open to other views in order to advance, in the most genuine sense of the word, the science. The very best students may discover errors and inadequacies in what their mentors thought, in their time, to be the best understanding of the natural world.

It is not surprising therefore that many scientists are upset by the regularity with which the press confers the title 'sceptic' on any individual, regardless of credentials, who challenges the prevailing understanding of climate science. The implication is that scientists who are leaders in the climate science community are not as 'sceptical' as they should be. Those who criticize the current understanding of climate science on the basis of opinion unsupported by science are more appropriately described as 'climate science contrarians' or 'climate science deniers'.

There are many examples of when prevailing views in science shift dramatically with the introduction of a new piece of evidence. Examples include the discovery of plate tectonics (1960s), the linking of an asteroid impact to animal extinctions 65.5 million years ago at the Cretaceous–Tertiary boundary (early 1980s), and the role of chlorofluorocarbons in ozone depletion in the Antarctic stratosphere (late 1980s). In these and many other instances, although a consensus among experts emerged within a few years, it is noteworthy that a small number of experts, some very senior and distinguished, remained unconvinced for the rest of their lives that the new mainstream view was correct.

John P. Holdren, Director of the Woods Hole Research Center in Massachusetts, USA, has written in the *International Herald Tribune* about the untenable position of the climate science contrarians. While they reject the science that links changes in so-called greenhouse gases to changes in the earth's surface temperature, they are unable to advance a credible alternative hypothesis for either the documented increase in that temperature or the changes in frequency, intensity and persistence in extreme weather events that have been observed across all regions of the planet over the past few decades.[36]

A brief history of contemporary climate science

In the early 1800s, the French mathematician and physicist Joseph Fourier pondered the regulation of earth's surface temperature. What kept our planet from warming inexorably? He is widely acknowledged as the first scientist to posit that the combined effects of the earth's emission of infra-red radiation and the presence of atmospheric constituents that absorb that radiation could keep the earth's surface temperature bounded within a fairly narrow range. Fourier used the analogy of a glass box that allows sunlight to enter the box while trapping the re-emitted energy as heat. Today we call Fourier's absorbing atmospheric constituents 'greenhouse gases' or GHGs. The role of carbon dioxide (CO_2) as one of these constituents was identified in 1859, when the British physicist Sir John Tyndall discovered that this gas absorbs infra-red irradiation.[37]

By an interesting coincidence, it was also in 1859 that Edwin L. Drake opened the first commercial oil well in Titusville, Pennsylvania, USA. Daily crude oil production from this 20-metre-deep well at that time was 25 barrels per day.[38] The combustion of coal, oil and natural gas worldwide fuelled the industrial era, and today global use of these fossil fuels provides about 80 per cent of the energy that we consume to heat our buildings, power our industries and vehicles, and generate our electricity. We now know that physical and biological systems in the ocean and on land that remove CO_2 from the atmosphere are unable to absorb or assimilate additional CO_2 at the rate at which it is being produced by the combustion of fossil fuels. About half of the fossil-fuel carbon released by human activities today will remain in the atmosphere for up to a century.

In the 1890s the Swedish chemist Svante Arrhenius became interested in the possible consequence of the CO_2 released from fossil-fuel combustion on earth's surface temperature. In 1896 he calculated that, if releases of fossil-fuel emissions were to double the content of CO_2 in the atmosphere, it would cause a globally averaged temperature rise of 5°–6°C. For comparison, this is about twice the temperature rise estimated by the Intergovernmental Panel on Climate Change (IPCC) for a doubling of CO_2 by year 2100 (see Chapters 2 and 5).

In the 1930s, Guy Callendar, a British meteorologist, pursued a more rigorous analysis of the CO_2–surface temperature relationship. He was confident that the warming that had been observed from the late 1800s to the 1930s was attributable to an atmospheric accumulation of fossil-fuel emissions, and he predicted an even warmer future if this trend continued.[39] Arrhenius and Callendar were both aware that many natural processes have influenced earth's climate on longer timescales. The theory of cyclic glacial episodes was advanced by Louis Agassiz in the 1840s, and there was a great deal of speculation as to whether a period of intense volcanic activity could, by means of dust clouds, initiate a cool period and give rise to an expansion of glaciers. Another mechanism that could drive the pacing of glacial cycles – variations in the sun–earth orbital properties – was promoted by James Croll and others.[40]

Callendar lived until 1964, and he probably puzzled about the apparent levelling off or downwards trend in the earth's average surface temperature during the 1940s and 1950s. It would be decades later before it could be shown that other anthropogenic or human-instigated effects on the atmosphere, in addition to natural processes, were responsible for this period of slight cooling while the CO_2 content of the atmosphere was continuing to increase.[41]

Callendar would probably, however, have known of the refinement of the orbital theory by Milutin Milankovitch for the origin of ice ages, advanced early in the 1900s.[42] Oceanographer John Imbrie showed in 1992 that the fossil data in the marine sedimentary record fits Milankovitch's theory.[43]

In 1957 the oceanographer Roger Revelle, expressing concern about the consequences of CO_2 release from fossil-fuel combustion, wrote: 'our society is performing a great geophysical experiment'.[44] The problem, which any experimental scientist would recognize immediately, is that there is nothing against which to measure this experiment – we have only one planet earth. Revelle knew that it was essential to establish precise measurements of the CO_2 content of the atmosphere, and so he recruited a bright young chemist, Charles David Keeling. A graph of the continuous record of measurements for CO_2 from 1958 to present has come to be called the 'Keeling curve' (Figure 3.1). It shows the rhythm of seasonal cycles in terrestrial photosynthesis and respiration, and an annual average rate of CO_2 increase that is constant around the globe, regardless of latitude.

Over the past three decades the extraction of ancient air bubbles from glacial ice cores in Antarctica, Greenland and even tropical mountains has allowed the analysis of past atmospheric CO_2 content and temperature. These data clearly show a rise in atmospheric CO_2 from the mid-1700s, when land use practices, such as forest clearing and agriculture, resulted in increased release of carbon into the atmosphere from vegetation and soils. This rise then steepened with widespread industrialization. Importantly, the atmospheric CO_2 content recovered from ice core data and from the direct measurements begun by Keeling in 1958 now join seamlessly.[45]

The modern era in climate science

Because of the complex dynamics of climate, understanding past climate change and ascertaining whether recent and current change is

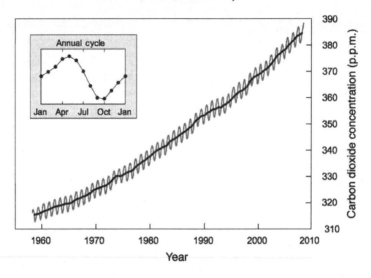

Figure 3.1 The increase in atmospheric CO_2 since direct measurements began in 1958. Seasonal oscillations result from higher values during winter when respiration exceeds photosynthesis, and lower values during the summer when the converse is true (see inset graph). The black line represents an averaged annual trend, showing a 20% increase over the period of these measurements. (The original figure was created by Dr Robert A. Rhode (UC Berkeley) from published data (NOAA ESRL); modified from <www.globalwarmingart.com/wiki/Image:Mauna_Loa_Carbon_Dioxide_png>.)

within the boundaries of natural variation took time to sort out. Has earth warmed in unusual ways since the mid-1800s? Could the amount of GHGs produced by human beings be large enough to cause a change in temperature averaged globally? If accumulating GHGs can explain the rise in earth's average surface temperature early in the 1900s (as Callendar believed they could) and the rise in temperature since 1970, how could the slight cooling of the 1950s and 1960s be explained? These and many other sensible questions were common motivators of scientific studies over the past three decades. In the mid-1990s, key aspects of the relationship between increases in concentrations of GHGs and climate became clear.

For example, even though atmospheric CO_2 (and the sum total of anthropogenic GHGs) increased relatively smoothly over the twentieth century, globally averaged surface temperatures show a slight downwards trend from 1940 to the mid-1970s (Figure 3.2). This apparent dichotomy, over decades, between trends in GHGs and temperature is sometimes held up by climate contrarians as a major inconsistency in climate science. However, if we take into account the effects of natural forces (such as solar variability or volcanic eruptions) and those of anthropogenic aerosols (such as sulphur and organic carbon emissions from fossil fuel and wood combustion; see Chapter 2), there are no significant unexplained portions of the observed temperature record of the twentieth century (Figure 3.3).[46]

We now know with a high degree of certainty that, as a consequence of the heat-absorbing property of CO_2 discovered by Tyndall, the accumulating inventory of this gas and other GHGs in earth's lower atmosphere has the potential to alter our planet's climate for decades and centuries to come. The fact that our species is now changing the conditions that define suitable habitats for most species led Paul Crutzen, a Nobel Laureate in chemistry, and oceanologist Eugene Stoermer to suggest that we have entered the Anthropocene epoch of earth history (see also Chapter 14).[47]

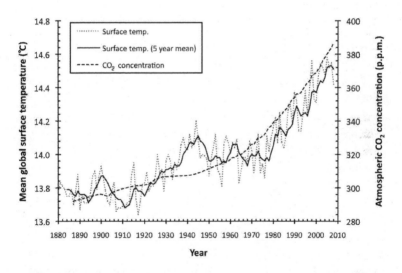

Figure 3.2 Atmospheric CO_2 concentrations from direct measurements (see Figure 3.1) plus 'proxy' measurements from ice cores, and globally averaged temperature over the past century. Graphs such as this have been used by climate science contrarians to cast doubt on any direct relationship between temperature and CO_2 concentration. (Data from A. Neftel, H. Friedli, E. Moor *et al.*, 'Historical CO_2 record from the Siple Station ice core', in *Trends: A Compendium of Data on Global Change* (Carbon Dioxide Information Analysis Center, Oak Ridge National Laboratory, US Department of Energy, Oak Ridge, TN, 1994).)

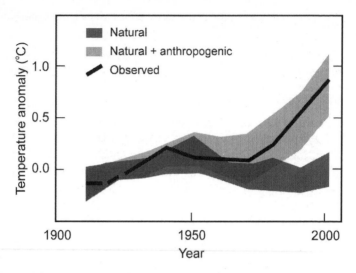

Figure 3.3 A comparison of a smoothed trend for temperature observations over the past century and the results of model studies designed to simulate climate during this period. Clearly, without the human effect on climate, we would expect there to have been very little change in earth's temperature over the past century. (Redrawn from IPCC, *Climate Change 2007: Synthesis Report* (Fourth Assessment Report of Intergovernmental Panel on Climate Change, 2007); see <www.ipcc.ch>.)

Change in climate is now evident at regional scales in precipitation patterns, in storms, in diminished land and ocean ice, and in rising sea level. Furthermore, during the past decade scientific studies have shown that these changes in climate are now affecting the distributions of plants and animals and the timing of their reproductive cycles on all continents.

Extrapolations from recent trends in the anthropogenic releases of GHGs can be used to project plausible future conditions in earth's climate. Within a few human generations the effect of these climate changes could put the survival of many species at risk. The natural processes that have determined where and when on this planet individual species thrive can now be swamped by the actions of a single species, *Homo sapiens*. For more than a million years the roughly 100,000-year cycle of glacial advance and retreat has altered the geographical ranges of terrestrial and marine species. When glaciers advance, populations move equatorwards; then when glaciers retreat, population ranges expand polewards. We are now at a point of historical maxima in range expansion. With the exception of certain 'ice age mammals', there is little evidence of widespread extinctions either on land or in the sea over the course of the most recent glacial–interglacial cycle. The history of extant species as read in their genes reflects a capacity to survive prior compressions and expansions of habitats. A very different prospect is now unfolding with current warming trends. Rather than repeating history, which with natural processes would have the planet heading again to a 100,000-year period of cooling, earth is projected to become warmer than at any time in the past million years. Moreover, it is warming at a rate that is 100 times more rapid than the warming that followed the last glacial maximum in 16,000 BC. As the Arctic warms to conditions perhaps not experienced for tens of millions of years, critical habitat space for many species will evaporate.

If we are unsuccessful in reducing substantially our dependence on sources of energy that release CO_2, it is also abundantly evident that some of the likely projected changes in climate will, on average, also be bad for humanity. We know from examples over the past decade that many of the world's nearly 7 billion people will be adversely affected by the projected impacts of a significantly warmer earth. Studies show that tropical storm intensity has increased, heatwaves of unusual intensity are becoming more frequent and sea level is rising faster than thought likely only ten years ago.[48]

Over recent decades the occurrence of tropical storms of record intensity across Asia and the Americas has taken many thousands of lives and has left countless people homeless, even displaced permanently from their communities. Heatwaves like those that occurred in India and across Europe during the summer of 2003 disproportionately affect people who most lack the means to attain relief from unbearable heat day and night. Worldwide water shortages and crop failures from intense hot, wet or dry spells are also taking their tolls in human life and well-being (see Chapters 7 and 10). Climate science tells us that we have the opportunity to avoid the most dire of these adverse impacts, but delays in taking action diminish our prospects for success in doing so.

Communicating climate science findings

Paradoxically, as the science that underpins this understanding has become increasingly robust, both the communication of the science to the public and its use in the formulation of wise policy at all levels of governance have lagged behind. Although it can be said that difficulty in deploying strategies that would effectively address the growing climate problem has contributed to the slow policy response to date, the communication problem has been in large part due to relatively small but powerful efforts to convince the public that they should doubt the robust findings of climate science.

Over the past 25 years, many national academies of science have reviewed climate science and have spoken with increasing confidence regarding the observed changes in earth's climate and the evidence that human activities are the primary source of heat-trapping emissions responsible for global warming. Several international conferences have reviewed scientific understanding of climate change, the most comprehensive of which is the above-mentioned IPCC (see also Chapter 2).[49] Its overall aim is 'to assess on a comprehensive, objective, open and transparent basis the scientific, technical and socio-economic information relevant to understanding the scientific basis of risk of human-induced climate change, its potential impacts and options for adaptation and mitigation'. IPCC reports do not prescribe policy, but they do undertake reviews of scientific, technical and socio-economic factors germane to the application of particular policies. As with a premier peer-reviewed scientific journal, independent editors ensure that authors fully address concerns raised by reviewers.

The IPCC is unique in many regards. No other body of scientific knowledge is regularly assessed in such a comprehensive multinational manner for the express purpose of advising governments on the relevance of knowledge in the formulation of national and international policies. A small number of paid staff administer the assessment process, but the bulk of effort, the scientific leadership and the work of the authors, is accomplished without any monetary compensation. The full range of perspectives on climate science contained within the published peer-reviewed scientific literature is represented by the authors who contribute to the IPCC reports. Importantly, the finalization of the reports by the authors and the review and approval of the summary reports by national delegations of the Panel are consensus processes. There are no majority and minority reports. There are no votes. Discussion continues until all parties are satisfied that the report is consistent with their understanding of the science. A little-appreciated fact is that this leads to a conservative report. That is to say, that views not supported by the weight of multiple lines of evidence have little chance of tilting the main message of the report.

The four IPCC assessments (1990, 1995, 2001, 2007) have provided progressively more specific messages regarding climate change and its causes. The 1990 report concluded that earth's average surface temperature was increasing at an unusual rate.[50] Largely in response to these conclusions the United Nations Framework Convention on Climate Change was presented for consideration at the Rio Earth Summit in June 1992 (see Chapter 5). This treaty, now ratified by 192 nations, states that parties will seek to stabilize 'greenhouse gas concentrations in the atmosphere at a level that would prevent dangerous anthropogenic interference with the climate system'. To make progress towards this objective, parties to the convention pledged to return 'individually or jointly to their 1990 levels [of] anthropogenic emissions of carbon dioxide and other GHGs'.[51]

By 1995 earth had warmed even more, and science had progressed to allow the IPCC assessment to state that human activities were a discernible component of the observed warming. Nothing conclusive could at that stage be said about unusual behaviour or extreme events, and widespread climate impacts were still largely hypothetical.[52]

In the 2001 IPCC assessment it could by then be said that 'most of the warming observed over the last 50 years is attributable to human activities'. Moreover, it had also become clear that the frequency, intensity and persistence of extreme events had changed in recent decades, and for the first time the impacts of climate change could be documented on all continents.[53]

This message was further amplified by an unprecedented joint statement in 2005 of the academies of science in each of the G8 nations plus India, China and Brazil, the three largest developing countries. They declared:[54]

there is now strong evidence that significant global warming is occurring . . . It is likely that most of the warming in recent decades can be attributed to human activities . . . This warming has already led to changes in Earth's climate . . . The scientific understanding of climate change is now sufficiently clear to justify nations taking prompt action. It is vital that all nations identify cost-effective steps that they can take now, to contribute to substantial and long-term reduction in net global greenhouse gas emissions.

Pre-eminent scientific societies and professional organizations across the globe have all made similar statements about recent climate change.

In 2007, the fourth IPCC assessment concluded that earth is unequivocally warming, and with 90 per cent confidence stated that the warming we are seeing is due primarily to the combustion of fossil fuels. The 17 warmest years since 1850 have occurred in the past 20 years.[55] Despite this strong scientific evidence and serious efforts by the IPCC, national academies of science and other distinguished science organizations to convey a consistent message to the public and elected officials, media coverage and political debate on global warming science often give undue credence to the views of little-known organizations and statements by individuals purporting to be experts on climate science. A medical analogy comes to mind. Official position statements of most academies and institutes of medicine, as well as heart disease and cancer charities, state that medical evidence strongly links cigarette smoking to lung and heart disease. What would motivate people who are not experts in this field of medical science to challenge the views of these august bodies?

It is sometimes claimed by climate science contrarians that organizations such as the IPCC, the professional societies of climate scientists and the various national academies of science are exaggerating the consensus within the climate science community. Naomi Oreskes, a historian of science, examined the widely respected climate science journals to determine to what degree the publications in leading journals were consistent with the message of the IPCC and similar assessing bodies.[56] Her sample, using articles from 1993 to 2003, revealed that 928 of them used the phrase 'global climate change' in their abstracts. She found that *none* of the 928 disagreed with the consensus position that climate is changing in unusual ways and that human activities are a major contributing factor. How is it then that non-scientific organizations and a few individuals, some with scientific credentials, are able to convince many people in politics, the news media and the public at large that scientists disagree widely as to whether climate is changing and why?

Unfortunately, people who are unfamiliar with the methods of science do not always appreciate that science is an evolving body of knowledge that is always open to challenge and new ideas. Most non-scientists are not fully aware of the process by which new evidence and new interpretations become part of the body of scientific knowledge.

New information and new ideas in science gain credibility and legitimacy when they are published in peer-reviewed scientific journals. This entails subjecting research methods and results, in all their details, to the scrutiny of peers (typically anonymous) under the supervision of an editor. The editors' reputations as scientists with sound judgement and the stature of the journals rely upon the integrity of this process.

Unfortunately, reports issued by organizations with impressive, scientific-sounding names, and 'op-ed' pieces in newspapers, authored by persons with the title doctor or professor, can at times sound very convincing. Unless, however, this information is based upon published, peer-reviewed scientific work (and it may be difficult for a non-scientist reader to determine this) the report or op-ed column may contain misinformation, or worse, disinformation.

Several aspects of climate science are often presented by climate science contrarians in either incorrect or incomplete form in order to fabricate an apparent contradiction. For example, it is often suggested incorrectly that recent warming is as natural as the medieval warm period (AD ninth to fourteenth centuries) or the little ice age (sixteenth to nineteenth centuries). It is also still said incorrectly that the surface temperature data used by the IPCC are contradicted by satellite temperature data. Similarly uninformed statements asserting that the warming of the last half-century can be explained by solar variability cannot be supported by any published studies.[57]

One particularly repetitious assertion of amateur climate contrarians is that 'scientists thought that earth was cooling during the 1970s, and now they think it is warming. Why should someone conclude that they have it right this time?' A recent thorough review of climate science publications from 1965 to 1979 definitively answers this.[58] Selective reading of scientific publications and misrepresentations of these works in the media by those wishing to cast doubt on the credibility of climate science propagated the myth of a 1970s consensus that 'earth is cooling rather than warming'. In fact, in the 1970s, climate scientists widely embraced the view that for the foreseeable future any known cooling trend would be overwhelmed by GHG warming.

Individuals who wish to dismiss the gravity of the scientific assessments and projections will at times mischaracterize the IPCC. In May 2001 hearings of a United States Senate Committee, Senator Chuck Hagel (Republican, Nebraska) said, 'The summaries of [IPCC] reports

are written not by the scientists, but by UN environmental activists
. . . The summaries are political documents, drafted by government
representatives after intense negotiating sessions . . . [they] take very
alarmist view points.'[59] No one truly knowledgeable of the IPCC
process could make such ludicrous assertions. Scientists draft all of the
assessment reports. Changes in wording are proposed by representatives of governmental delegations, but they are accepted only if they
add both clarity to the message and remain completely consistent with
the underlying science.

A more widely known distortion of the IPCC process and of climate
science in general can be found in a British Channel 4 television show
produced by Martin Durkin and entitled *The Great Global Warming
Swindle*. Among its multiple errors is a fabrication about one person's
experience with IPCC authorship. In July 2008 the British Office of
Communications (OfCom) ruled that Channel 4 had violated its
broadcasting fairness principles, and required a public admission of
this transgression. Most of the people interviewed in this film are not
practising climate scientists. They may have opinions about climate
but they do not publish evidence in support of these opinions in the
widely respected climate journals. One of the few, and the most distinguished, of the true climate scientists interviewed by Durkin was
Professor Carl Wunsch from the Massachusetts Institute of Technology,
USA. In the film his words were taken out of context and used in
support of views that are at odds with his own. A description of his
experience and what it took to get his interview removed from future
television repeats of this show is available on his website.[60]

Books, some by well-known and highly regarded people, have
attempted to cast doubt on the validity of climate science. A recent
example is *An Appeal to Reason: A Cool Look at Global Warming* by
Nigel Lawson, Baron Lawson of Blaby, former Chancellor of the UK
Exchequer (1983–9).[61] In my opinion it is a prejudiced and superficial
examination of the findings of climate science. As Sir John Houghton
pointed out in his review 'Full of hot air', Lawson's selective use of data
for trends in earth's temperature, and his apparent unfamiliarity with
the impact studies of IPCC Working Group II, allow him to conclude
that serious future climate impacts are unlikely.[62]

Lord Lawson and some economists also argue that climate mitigation efforts designed to stabilize atmospheric CO_2 concentrations at
1.5–2 times pre-industrial (that is, before 1750) levels are unaffordable.

Some recent economic analyses, such as those of McKinsey and Company have, however, concurred with IPCC reports that initial efforts to reduce CO_2 emissions more than pay for themselves. The recent study by Sir Nicholas Stern on the economics of climate change demonstrates that the costs of aggressive climate mitigation could be a very small percentage of Gross Domestic Product (see also Chapters 4 and 5).[63]

Manufacturing doubt

If one wanted to minimize the likelihood that the public would take the scientific message about climate change seriously, might doubt be manufactured explicitly for this purpose? Clearly this has been considered. Frank Luntz, a political consultant to the US Republican Party, wrote in 2002: 'Should the public come to believe that the scientific views are settled, their views about global warming will change accordingly. Therefore, you need to continue to make the lack of scientific certainty a primary issue in the debate.'[64]

But why do people go to such measures to cast doubt on climate science? Do they believe that climate scientists have not been objective in the interpretation of their findings? Are they concerned that their lifestyle or their nation's economy would be selectively disadvantaged by collective action to address the causes of rapid climate change? Motives are difficult to discern. Why did American President George W. Bush disavow his 2002 campaign pledge to regulate CO_2 emissions only a few months after taking office? Could it be related to his administration's ties to the fossil-fuel industry? Is it a simple coincidence that within the US Congress two outspoken climate science contrarian positions, Representative Joseph Barton (Republican, Texas) and Senator James Inhofe (Republican, Oklahoma), have both received generous financial support from the fossil-fuel industry? If instead they had advocated government policies informed by authoritative climate science, would the funds have flowed so readily from the energy industry?

The ExxonMobil case study

In January 2007, the Union of Concerned Scientists (UCS) released a study entitled *Smoke, Mirrors and Hot Air*.[65] The report documents how

ExxonMobil, the world's largest energy company, had for years under-written a sophisticated disinformation campaign the aim of which was to deceive the public and policy-makers about the reality of global warming. The campaign bore striking similarities to the tobacco indus-try's effort to mislead the public about the scientific evidence linking smoking to lung cancer and heart disease. In fact, some of the same organizations and individuals involved in the tobacco industry effort were also part of ExxonMobil's disinformation campaign.

Like the tobacco industry in previous decades, ExxonMobil:

- raised doubts about even the most indisputable scientific evidence;
- funded an array of front organizations to create the appearance of a broad platform for a tight-knit group of vocal climate-change contrarians who misrepresent peer-reviewed scientific findings;
- attempted to portray its opposition to action as a positive quest for 'sound science' rather than business self-interest;
- used its access to the Bush administration to block federal policies and shape government communications on global warming.

Between 1998 and 2005, ExxonMobil funnelled close to $US16 million to a network of 43 ideological and advocacy groups that sought to manufacture uncertainty about the strong scientific consensus on global warming. These groups promoted spokespersons who misrep-resented peer-reviewed scientific findings or cherry-picked facts in an attempt to mislead the media and public into thinking there was vig-orous debate in the mainstream scientific community about climate change. Almost all of the 43 organizations publicized the work of a nearly identical small group of people who worked to misrepresent climate science and confuse the public's understanding of global warming. Most of these organizations also included these same individuals as board members or scientific advisers.

In addition to providing this information, though, the report also details links in strategy and personnel between ExxonMobil's efforts and those of the tobacco industry. It includes the text, for instance, of a seminal 1998 memo that ExxonMobil helped to draft as part of a small group called the Global Climate Science Team that set much of the company's strategy in motion. As the report shows, this internal memo not only mimicked the tobacco industry's strategy, it even drew upon key personnel who had implemented it. From internal documents made public by court order, it is now known that the tobacco firm Philip Morris actually hired a public relations firm to create a group – called the Advancement of Sound Science Coalition – in 1993 to mislead the public about the dangers of second-hand smoke. Thus, in an effort reminiscent of the tobacco industry, ExxonMobil has helped to create an echo chamber that serves to amplify the views of a carefully selected group of spokespeople whose work has been largely discredited by the scientific community.

The Union of Concerned Scientists' report shows, however, that ExxonMobil's influence over government policy may have surpassed that of the tobacco industry. During the 2000–6 election cycles, Exxon-Mobil's Public Accounts Committee and individuals affiliated with the company gave more than $US4 million to federal candidates and parties. Shortly after President George W. Bush took office, Exxon-Mobil began to wield its influence. In 2001, ExxonMobil participated in Vice President Richard Cheney's 'Energy Task Force', which recommended a continued reliance on fossil fuels.

ExxonMobil also successfully urged the Bush administration to back away from the US Commitment to the Kyoto Protocol. Notes from a 2001 talk by state department official Paula Dobriansky confirm the role ExxonMobil played in persuading the administration to abandon the international agreement. Another 2001 memo from ExxonMobil urged the administration to hire Harlan Watson, a vocal opponent of climate action, as the lead negotiator for the US on international climate policy. Since then Harlan Watson has steadfastly opposed any American engagement in the Kyoto process.[66] Other documents reveal that, in February 2001, following the release of the IPCC *Third Assessment*, ExxonMobil successfully lobbied the White House to withdraw its support for the renomination of Robert Watson to a second term as chairman of the IPCC.

In London in September 2006, the Royal Society sent a letter to ExxonMobil urging the company to stop funding the dozens of groups spreading disinformation on global warming and also strongly criticized the company's 'inaccurate and misleading' public statements on global warming. On 27 October 2006, US Senators Olympia Snowe (Republican, Maine) and John D. Rockefeller (Democrat, West Virginia) sent a letter to ExxonMobil urging the company to stop funding climate contrarian groups.

In response to public pressure, ExxonMobil launched a public relations campaign aimed at softening its image as a climate science contrarian. Although the company has recently acknowledged the global warming threat, and has announced that it has cut off funding for some of the groups involved in the disinformation campaign, including the Competitive Enterprise Institute, it has not yet pledged a complete halt to its bankrolling of the scores of groups that disseminate misleading information on global warming. In a letter responding to Senators Snowe and Rockfeller, ExxonMobil claimed to have no control over the activities of the groups it supports.

During spring 2008, Rockefeller family members holding shares in ExxonMobil attempted to change the governance structure of the corporation and encourage corporate policies and practices that acknowledge the findings of climate science. If future business success in the energy market includes a greater reliance on wind and solar energy sources, then ExxonMobil is lagging behind other oil companies in directing its resources to develop these markets. This effort and a similar one in 2007 fell short of success with only about 40 per cent investor support.[67]

Much of the mischief that ExxonMobil funded in the past will continue to have influence, and, to the degree it does, governments will take longer to enact the needed policies to reduce GHG emissions.

So where does this leave us?

Some who in the past questioned the validity of conclusions drawn by the IPCC and other climate assessment groups now argue not with the science but rather that the economic cost of reducing GHG emissions sufficiently to stabilize world climate is too great.[68] This is Holdren's third stage of climate science denial: 'Finally, they acknowledge that climate change matters but it's too late to do anything about it.'[69] Bjørn Lomborg further asserts that funds necessary to address climate change could be put to better use in reducing human misery and mortality by investing in poverty reduction and in medical and public health measures to combat diseases such as malaria and malnutrition.[70]

There are multiple flaws in this logic. A comprehensive economic analysis, such as the *Stern Review*, referred to above, projects a contrasting view of the costs to stabilize climate compared with the costs of projected climate impacts of greater warming. Because of the long residence time of CO_2 now being added to the atmosphere by fossil fuel combustion and land-use changes, along with inertia inherent in the climate system, little can be done today to affect climate over the next three or four decades. In other words, there is no known strategy whereby emissions can be reduced fast enough to prevent an anthropogenic warming of less than 2°C, globally averaged, above pre-industrial temperatures. Stabilization scenarios point to 2050 as the soonest that this can be attained. Importantly, however, the climate of the second half of this century will depend greatly on actions taken in the very near term, over the next few years, to place global GHG emissions on a declining trajectory.

Another flaw relates to non-linearities and the likelihood of 'surprises' in the climate system. In 2001 the IPCC could not identify any body of science that pointed to a likelihood of a large reduction in Greenland ice during the present century.[71] Since then, major outlet glaciers for the Greenland icecap have shown changed behaviour. The termini of many are retreating and thinning at unusual rates, and increasing frequency of 'ice-quake' seismic events spatially coincident with exit glaciers signal that an acceleration of ice loss is now under way.[72]

The 2007 IPCC projects 0.28–0.59 metres of sea-level rise by 2100.[73] Importantly, these estimates do not preclude higher rates of rise due to increased rates of ice loss on Greenland and Antarctica, which may cause a threefold increase in sea-level rise estimates, to 0.8–2.0 metres by 2100.[74]

Think for a moment about the impact of a 1–2 metre rise in sea level on lives, livelihoods and property in coastal regions across the globe. Major cities, large portions of nations, indeed entire island nations will become uninhabitable. Add additional tropical storm intensity (an IPCC projection[75]) and damage from any rise in sea level becomes intensified (see Chapter 7). Recently the presidents of the island nations of Kiribati and the Maldives have stated that their people must prepare to evacuate. President Anote Tong of Kiribati has promoted training programmes that will make his citizens welcome as immigrants to other nations. For example, with the assistance of Cuban medical professionals, a programme that trains nurses has been very successful in preparing Kiribati citizens for employment abroad where there are shortages of nurses.

An important finding of the 2001 IPCC was that those who have the least resources have the least capacity to adapt and are thus the most vulnerable to climate change. Needless to say, as more areas experience water shortages, as food security declines and as geographical ranges of tropical insects expand (all IPCC projections for a warmer world), the consequences of poverty and disease in tropical and subtropical regions will be exacerbated.[76]

The concerted efforts of climate science contrarians and their financial patrons to deny the validity of climate science have contributed to delays in formulating and implementing meaningful policies to address climate change in developed and developing nations. The recent suggestion that we need to choose between investing in combating poverty and disease or in climate change, and that the former is a better investment in human well-being than addressing climate change, is a false choice, with cruel implications for our children and grandchildren.

4

Responding to climate change: how much should we discount the future?

DONALD A. HAY

'Why should we do anything for future generations? They will never do anything for us.' Discuss.
(Oxford University Economics Final Examination, 1970s)

Environmental unsustainability develops over time: we harvest biological resources such as forests and fisheries to destruction or extinction, and we accumulate carbon dioxide (CO_2) and other so-called greenhouse gases (GHGs) in the atmosphere (see Chapter 2). The consequences will be felt principally by our grandchildren and subsequent generations, not by us. There are many dimensions to this process,[77] including our apparently insatiable desire to consume more and more goods (see Chapter 14) and our failure to account fully for these consequences in our pursuit of economic growth (see Chapters 5 and 11). But the limited focus of this chapter is specifically on the time dimension and the practice in economic analysis of discounting future costs and benefits, a practice not widely understood by non-economists. Discounting raises the issue of being fair towards future generations: so it is no surprise that a proper analysis goes well beyond the usual territory of economic analysis, as we shall see later in this chapter. But first we need to check our understanding of what discounting is about, taking the specific example of climate change policy.

Discounting the future and climate change policy

The old adage that if three economists are asked for advice on some public policy issue they are likely to provide (at least) four conflicting solutions is not entirely without foundation when it comes to the literature on responding to global climate change. The publication of the *Stern Review* in 2007 provided a good example.[78] Stern proposed immediate global action to curb the emission of GHGs, to stabilize their concentration in the atmosphere in the range 450–550 parts per million (p.p.m.) carbon dioxide equivalents (CO_2e). This proposal attracted some very critical commentary from other economists, notably from William Nordhaus, who argued for a gradualist policy, starting with a limited programme of GHG abatement, and ramping up the policy over the rest of the century.[79]

Such disagreement often comes as a surprise to non-economists who imagine that there should be a 'technical' solution. Before coming to the core of the disagreement, we note that the protagonists are generally agreed that there is a problem to be addressed, even if they differ in their evaluations of the scientific findings: they also agree on the framework of economic analysis to be applied to the problem. So they would probably sign up to the following. First, GHGs are a classic example of an 'externality': an economic action that has consequences for others who are not linked to the initiating actor through a market. Second, emissions have global effects: the damage is independent of where the emissions take place. Third, the effects are cumulative over time, and persistent. Fourth, the predicted effects represent a step change in the environment, and have the potential for catastrophic outcomes. Fifth, the whole analysis is permeated by uncertainty – about the degree of climate change, its effects on the environment, and the consequences for economic activity across the globe. Sixth, there is agreement that in assessing the costs and benefits of global warming it would be right to include health, education and the environment itself. Seventh, economists agree that in assessing costs and benefits it is right to take into account whether the persons to whom they accrue are rich or poor. The scientific analysis indicates that the costs will fall disproportionately on poor people.

What then is the main area of disagreement? It is the rate at which future costs and benefits should be discounted. The basic concept is that costs or benefits that occur at a date in the future should not be given the same weight as costs and benefits in the current period. The commonsense explanation for discounting is that it is implicit in our experience of investing funds now with the expectation of accruing interest over time. A sum invested now in a deposit account will be worth more in a year's time (£100 invested at 5 per cent will be worth £105 after one year). Hence a sum to be received in a year's time is worth less in current values (the present value) than the same cash sum received now (£100 received in a year's time is worth approximately £95.25 now, since investing the latter at 5 per cent would generate £100 in a year's time). The degree to which the sum is worth less, that is the degree to which it is 'discounted', depends on the interest rate assumed (in our example, 5 per cent). Evidently the higher the interest rate the greater the discount in arriving at present values. Over a single period, the differences may not be particularly large, but when the values are discounted over many years, the discount is compounded year on year (just as compound interest accrues to an investment held over a number of years). Then apparently quite small differences in interest rates can generate very large differences in present values. This is illustrated in Table 4.1 and Figure 4.1, which show the present value of £100 accruing at dates in the future, with interest rates varying between 0.0 per cent and 6.0 per cent.

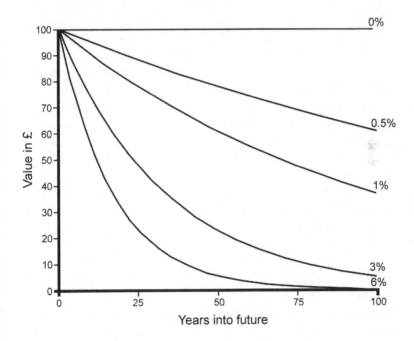

Figure 4.1 Interest rates and the present values of £100 accruing at dates in the future. (See also Table 4.1.)

Table 4.1 Interest rates and the present values of £100 accruing at dates in the future. (See also Figure 4.1.)

Interest rate	25 years hence	50 years hence	100 years hence
0.0	100	100	100
0.5	88	78	61
1.0	78	61	37
3.0	48	23	5
6.0	23	5	0.3

Turning to climate change, the choice of interest rates is clearly critical where we are looking to assess costs that may not be incurred until 50 or even 100 years hence. If, for example, we are considering a cost of £1 million that will appear in 50 years' time, then the present value is £780,000 if we use a 0.5 per cent interest rate for discounting, but only £230,000 if 3.0 per cent, and £50,000 if 6.0 per cent. Why is this so important for policy? Because investment now of say £250,000 to eliminate that cost will be worthwhile if the interest rate is 0.5 per cent or 1.0 per cent, but not if it is 3.0 per cent or 6.0 per cent. The *Stern Review* apparently works with rates of 2.1 per cent for the current century, 1.9 per cent for the next century, and 1.4 per cent thereafter.[80] Economists such as Nordhaus, who believe that a rate of about 6.0 per cent is appropriate, argue that it is too early to begin to invest in mitigation of or adaptation to climate change, since there are other opportunities with a higher return. In particular, they point to the returns on investment in human capital in poor countries, and propose that we should address those first, so that people in those countries will be better placed in terms of wealth and capabilities to tackle climate change problems as they arise. The argument is not that we should not act on climate change, but that, *contra* Stern, we should not take precipitate action.

The choice of interest rate enters another debate about climate change policy – the social costs of carbon emissions. If we could estimate the expected costs of carbon emissions going forward, then in principle we could resolve the externality problem by imposing an equivalent tax on emissions now. The costs have to be estimated in an integrated assessment model, which begins with the trajectory of carbon emissions over time, and then assesses the climatic and hence economic impacts. This is not the place to go into the details of such modelling, but we note the role of the assumed interest rate in evaluating the current costs of emissions. A higher rate, implying greater discounting of future costs, will generate a lower current cost of emissions (and hence a lower implied tax rate), than a lower interest rate. That is one of the reasons (but not the only reason) why Richard Tol reported such a wide range in his comprehensive review of published studies.[81]

Non-economists may well be perplexed that economists hold such divergent views about a key economic parameter. In the rest of this chapter, we explore the reasons for this divergence: the discussion takes us beyond economic analysis into questions about the provision we should make for future generations in terms of delivering to them an environment that is compatible with human flourishing and not despoiled. We will then explore the extent to which Christian ethics may contribute to the resolution of those questions. I begin in the next section with the normative analysis of inter-temporal allocation which underpins analyses of climate change policies, including the *Stern Review*. Nordhaus and Partha Dasgupta[82] accept the framework, but challenge the implications as presented by Stern. In the third section we consider an alternative economic framework that characterizes the issue as one of insurance against uncertain future outcomes. In the fourth section, we outline an approach developed by political philosophers that considers the 'rights' of future generations. We conclude with Christian commentary on the issues raised.

Economic analysis: what should we provide for future generations?

This generation makes provision for future generations by saving and investment; that is, we don't consume everything available in the present period. We save and invest in various ways. In the case of renewable resources, such as fish, animals, plants and trees, we are conscious that overuse can deplete stocks over time to a point of extinction. So we preserve ('save' and 'invest') some of the stock to allow it to be renewed by organic growth. Whether we preserve enough is an important question, though not one pursued in this chapter.[83] We also refrain from using all the productive potential of the economy to provide current consumption goods and services, and produce capital goods to provide consumption goods in future. Savings arise from the decisions of households to provide for the future (retirement, bequests to descendants). Savings are collected by financial institutions, and loaned on to firms investing in plant or research and development, to enable products and services to be supplied at a later time.

The question is whether this decentralized system of saving and investment makes appropriate provision for future generations, or more specifically whether the interest rate in financial markets is the 'right' rate. This was explored in a classic analysis, by Frank Ramsey,[84] that provided the framework for work on the economics of climate change.[85] It is assumed that human well-being in each generation derives from its level of consumption. The analysis identifies two reasons why we might wish to discount the consumption of future generations, and thus apply a discount rate.

The first reason is the concept of a pure rate of time preference (delta, δ, in the technical literature): a non-zero value implies that, everything else being equal, the consumption of future generations is given a lower weight than the consumption of the current generation. Two arguments have been advanced for this. One is that people display 'impatience', or preference, 'for jam today rather than jam tomorrow'. While that may or may not be the case, it is not evident that what individuals prefer for themselves as individuals should necessarily determine the allocation of resources across generations. A more substantial argument is that there is a non-zero probability that the human race and/or the earth as we know it will be destroyed, for example by the impact of an asteroid, an epidemic, a nuclear war, or global warming. A hazard rate of 0.1 per cent, implying a 99.9 per cent probability that we will survive to the next year, generates a probability of 95 per cent that we will still be here in 50 years' time, and of 91 per cent in 100 years' time. A higher hazard rate of 1 per cent generates a probability of survival of only 61 per cent over 50 years and 37 per cent over 100 years. So might it be appropriate to discount the future, as future generations may not exist?

The second reason is that we expect future generations to be wealthier than us. In principle, an additional unit of consumption assigned to someone who is poor is worth more in social terms than the same unit given to someone who is rich, and this is captured by a parameter (eta, η, in the technical literature).[86] A higher value implies a more egalitarian stance. If income per capita (per person) is expected to grow, then we would wish to give less weight to an additional unit of consumption assigned to a member of a future generation. In the Ramsey framework, this is included in the derivation of the discount rate, by multiplying η by the expected growth rate of consumption. If the growth rate is expected to be negative (contracting), this component of the discount rate will also be negative. Note therefore that the discount rate will vary depending on the expected growth rate of consumption. The discount rate to be applied is given by the sum of these two components: the pure rate, δ, and the expected consumption growth rate multiplied by η.

As noted above, the *Stern Review* assumes values of δ equal to 0.1, of η equal to 1.0, and the growth of consumption at 2.1 per cent per annum in the current century, giving a discount rate of 2.2 per cent. This compares, according to Nordhaus,[87] to a 'trio of twos' assumed by other economists, giving a discount rate of 6.0 per cent. The *Stern Review* assumptions have been subject to an elegant critique by Dasgupta.[88] His principal objection is that it is wrong to have a low value of η, implying a not very egalitarian stance on income redistribution between generations, since it requires the current generation to make additional sacrifices of consumption in favour of future generations, who will be much wealthier than we are.[89]

Nordhaus makes further trenchant criticisms of the *Stern Review*. He describes the stance of the *Review* as 'Government House utilitarianism', where the policy-maker determines the rate on the basis of his or her own presuppositions. He proposes instead a rate based on observed returns in the market, which reveals the actual preferences of consumers.[90] But why should only the preferences of the current generation be considered? Future generations do not have a voice in current financial markets but have to rely on the current generation to make provision for them. The political authorities have a good reason to intervene if they believe that greater provision should be made for future generations: their responsibilities are not limited to the current generation.

Insuring against climate change extremes

One feature of the 2007 Report by the International Panel on Climate Change (IPCC)[91] is the range and distribution of climate outcomes generated in global models, and this is picked up in the *Stern Review*. While the mean outcomes fall within bounds of what can reasonably be achieved in mitigation of and adaptation to climate change, some of the more extreme outcomes are much more worrying, even though their probability is quite low. Thus the *Review* predicts a mean rise of 2.8°C by the end of the twenty-first century, but notes that there is a 15 per cent probability of a rise in excess of 4.5°C, and a 3 per cent probability of a rise in excess of 6°C. The higher temperature rises are likely to bring with them disproportionate environmental and economic damage (see Chapter 2). Martin Weitzman[92] has suggested that our response should involve investments that are essentially insurance against low probability but extreme outcomes. An analogy may help to elucidate this idea. We are all accustomed to insuring our homes against such risks as fire, flood and destructive storms. But how would we react if no insurance market existed to enable us to take out the relevant insurance policies? The probability that our home will be totally destroyed by fire is not high, but the consequences would be dire. So our response might include more fire prevention in the home: the fitting of alarms, the installation of sprinklers, and the choice of non-inflammable materials for construction and furnishings. The analogy is that we cannot 'insure' the planet against the outcomes of climate change. The economic risks from climate change affect everybody: in insurance terms, all climate-related risks are correlated, so everyone will be making a claim. However, all is not lost, since we can take steps to reduce the probability of extreme outcomes. Investment in mitigation shifts the distribution of temperature changes, decreasing not only the mean, but also the probability of extreme temperatures.

How does this approach fit into the standard economic analysis of climate change? The claim of the *Stern Review* is that the 'precautionary principle' is implicit in its analysis of the probability distributions of future global incomes (across rich and poor countries) arising from the range of outcomes predicted by the climate scientists. In formal terms, the *Review* applies expected utility analysis, where the outcomes in human well-being are weighted by their probabilities. If extreme negative outcomes are possible, then they will be weighted more heavily (the weight depending on the value of η applied to convert income into utility), and thus feature more prominently in the calculation despite low probabilities. This does not, however, capture the argument of the previous paragraphs, since in evaluating investment in mitigation the approach will also give weight to outcomes that are relatively benign, which will dilute the (negative) contribution of the extremes, making it less likely that investment will generate sufficient returns to justify proceeding. The insurance approach focuses solely on avoiding extremely unfavourable outcomes.

What elements of the future should be discounted?

Discounting the future has attracted the attention of philosophers and political theorists in recent years, frequently in discussions about the ethics of environmental change. John Broome[93] noted that in practice economists discount because discounting is an implicit characteristic of commodity and financial markets, whereas moral philosophers are dealing with human well-being and tend to argue that it should not be discounted. Economists often agree: Ramsey in his seminal article described discounting as ethically indefensible, the result of 'weakness of imagination'.[94] However, in practice economists have to restrict their cost–benefit analysis to commodities either with market prices, or with prices that can be inferred. This is a short cut to evaluating projects where the impacts on human well-being cannot be quantified or aggregated.[95] Broome complains that economists stray into discounting things that should not be so treated. For example, if current pollution is going to cause birth defects in future, it is ethically indefensible to discount the human and other costs that will accrue to future generations.

An alternative approach focuses on human rights, and in particular the right not to suffer from potentially harmful climate change.[96] The key arguments have been summarized succinctly by Simon Caney.[97] The starting point is the principle enunciated in the 1972 Stockholm Declaration of the United Nations Conference on the Human Environment: 'Man has the fundamental right to freedom, equality and adequate conditions of life, in an environment of a quality that permits a life of dignity and well being, and he bears a solemn responsibility to protect and improve the environment for present and future generations.' Caney summarizes the gist in the proposition: 'Persons have a right not to suffer from dangerous climate change.' The definition of a right is from Joseph Raz, who argues that 'to say that X has a right is to say that X has interests which are sufficiently weighty to impose obligations on others'.[98] The successive reports of the IPCC have shown that climate change jeopardizes the interests of some people: in poor countries, climate change may threaten food supplies; rising sea levels and extreme weather events may undermine the ability of some people to support themselves; and in some countries public health will be adversely affected. These interests are surely 'sufficiently weighty' to require us to identify a right to a climate that has not been changed dramatically. However, the argument also needs to establish that we should consider the interests of future generations. One counter-argument is that because they do not exist, they cannot have rights. But when they are born they will have as much moral status as us, and a set of rights that should be respected.

If our descendants have rights to climate, then it is hard to imagine why their interests should be discounted solely because they will exist in the future. The rights of persons in the twenty-second century have the same moral standing as the rights of a person in the twenty-first century. The appropriate pure rate of discount for rights should be zero, even if the discount rate in markets for commodities is positive. None of the reasons advanced by economists for discounting the future apply. Their first reason is the discounting implicit in market behaviour, which the political authorities should take into account when making decisions. But discount rates in markets do not tell us anything about how people might evaluate the human rights of their descendants. However, the authorities should make their ethical presuppositions clear, and in a democracy persuade the voters that these are a reasonable basis for policy. Their second reason is that without it we are committed to making disproportionate consumption sacrifices to benefit future generations. But what we are talking about is not the pattern of consumption over time, but human rights. The former probably should be discounted, but the latter should not. In any case, if the *Stern Review* calculations are accepted, the consumption sacrifice required to address the problem of climate change is actually quite limited – perhaps 2 per cent of world Gross Domestic Product (see Chapter 5). Their third reason is the argument that future generations will be much better off than we are: that argument does not have any validity when what is under consideration is a human right. We could imagine an immensely wealthy future generation that lived in an utterly degraded environment. Their wealth could not compensate for a lost environment: the two cannot be traded off. In any case, future generations may not be better off: people displaced by rising sea waters may be very much worse off.

Bringing Christian ethics into the picture

Much has been written about a Christian understanding of the relationship between the human race and the natural order. David Bookless contrasts the theocentric and anthropocentric approaches.[99] The theocentric approach claims that the world, in both its human and non-human aspects, derives its value from being created and sustained by God. Its key elements, many of which are developed in Chapters 8, 12,13, 15 and 16, are as follows:[100]

- The natural order, including the human race, is the result of God's act of creation, is sustained by him, and is affirmed to be God's possession. It has intrinsic value to God, regardless of human valuations.
- Humanity is distinguished from the rest of the creation by being created in 'the image of God', implying a delegation of responsibility to the human race, rather than conferral of privilege. 'Dominion' describes the exercise of delegated authority, which permits us to use the natural order to provide for material needs, but does not legitimize exploitation.
- The human race is charged with the tending of creation. 'Covenantal stewardship'[101] implies both responsibility and accountability. The instructions in Genesis 2:15 to 'till' and 'keep' creation imply sustainability.
- The fallen nature of human beings predisposes us to take possession of the natural order, and use it for its own ends: that is the root of the environmental crisis.

By contrast, the anthropocentric approach sets the human race above, and separate from, the natural order. The world is here for human use and enjoyment, to satisfy our needs and aspirations. Sustainability is no more than a responsibility to provide for other human beings, and for future generations. Environmental problems can be solved by appropriate human solutions.

The analyses of the previous sections fall squarely within the anthropocentric approach. In the second and third sections the focus of the economic analysis is the well-being of human beings over time. In the fourth section the focus is on the rights of future human beings to an acceptable climate. What is entirely missing from these approaches is the Christian perspective that the natural order belongs to God, that our authority over it is delegated by him, and that our responsibility is to care for it within a framework of stewardship. How does that omission affect our assessment of those analyses? The specifically utilitarian framework within which the standard economic analysis of the second section is conducted is not a framework that a Christian can adopt uncritically.[102] Its vision of human flourishing is far too narrow, with its focus on the individual as producer/consumer, with little consideration of our relationships with God, other human beings and the creation.

However, if constrained to work within the utilitarian framework, our sympathies will surely be with Stern and not with Nordhaus. The appropriate discount rate should be low. First, consider the rate of pure time preference, δ. There are no good *a priori* moral reasons to discount the future, as a positive δ would imply. We have no right to discount the well-being of future generations of human beings, each of whom will be loved by God as we are. And speculations about the survival probability of the planet seem beside the point, given the Christian understanding of the role of the creator in sustaining the natural order: the discussion in Chapter 16 effectively counters the argument that the natural order will be destroyed on 'the day of the Lord', so that we should not care about its future. On the value of η, the weight assigned to a unit of consumption by poor people compared to rich, our understanding of God's concern for the poor[103] will lead us to prefer a higher value. However, this only enters the discount rate in combination with the growth rate in consumption, and future generations may not be wealthier than us if climate change takes hold. Moreover, Christians would be right to reject the argument that we should regard market rates as definitive in determining our evaluations of the future. Those rates, as we have seen, arise from the behaviour of economic actors in markets: the idea that they should be prescriptive for analysis of climate change represents a capitulation to the devices and desires of the current generation of fallen human hearts.

Within the utilitarian framework, Christians would also wish appropriate weights to be given to non-consumption goods, such as health, education and the natural environment. The danger is that because they cannot be as easily quantified as consumption, they are not given the weight they should be. The valuations should not be merely instrumental to production (education and health to supply more productive workers, natural environment to develop the tourist industry). They contribute to other human values regardless of economic activity. For example, education contributes to our functioning in the 'image of God', ill health was a particular concern of Jesus in his earthly ministry with healing as a sign of God's kingdom, and the natural order is valued by God for the delight that it gives him as creator.

The discussion of climate change investments as collective insurance in the third section is consistent with our role as stewards of the natural order. We have a responsibility not to destroy or degrade God's possession. That responsibility must surely include being alert to the possibility that our actions may cause irreversible damage to the environment, and taking steps to reduce the probability of disastrous outcomes. It is not just that the consequences might be serious for the human race in terms of consumption and the physical environment in which our descendants will live, but also that the natural order might be destroyed.

The analysis of rights should also attract Christian support. Indeed, the argument can be greatly strengthened. The rights of succeeding generations to an undamaged environment come from the responsibility that God has delegated to the human race to care for, and to benefit from, his creation. That delegated authority is the same whether we happen to be living in the twenty-first or twenty-second century or beyond. Discounting the rights of future generations has no moral basis. Moreover, a Christian framework resolves the concerns about whether future generations can have rights. Their existence is presumably known to God, and he has assigned the same responsibilities to them, whoever they may be, as he has to us. Our task is to ensure that they have scope for exercising covenantal stewardship, and not to deprive them either of that responsibility or of the opportunities for human flourishing that we enjoy.

Finally, we need to address the consequences of fallen human nature for the environment. The economic model displays a degree of realism about the true nature of human beings, in its assumption that economic behaviour is motivated by the selfish satisfaction of material wants. The question is how that behaviour can be regulated so as to minimize the harm it could do to the natural world. Nordhaus argues that the authorities should not gainsay what the current generation is revealing as its wishes via decisions in financial markets. The Christian understanding is that the political authorities, acting under authority delegated from God, should seek to prevent evils and to promote the good. This suggests that the political authorities should act on climate change, and that their decisions should be informed by the well-being not just of their current citizens but also by that of citizens of other countries and of future generations. They need the wholehearted support and encouragement of Christians as they embark on policies that are likely to prove unpopular.

This chapter started with what might appear to be a rather narrow technical issue in economics – the choice of interest rate to discount future consumption. The question is why this is such an important issue in the framing of public policy on climate change; the puzzle is why it should be so contentious. As the chapter has proceeded, it has become clear that the issues cannot be resolved within economic analysis alone. The debate over the *Stern Review* has clarified the issues in the framework employed by economists to analyse the use of resources over time. Weitzman has helpfully added the concept of investment as insurance against extreme outcomes. A parallel debate has been generated in political philosophy over the putative rights of future generations to a natural environment that has not been too drastically modified or damaged by the current generation. We have identified a strand of Christian moral thinking that has enabled us to strengthen some of the previous arguments, and to decide on which side to come down in the debates. In summary, this chapter argues that Stern was right to argue for a low discount rate in assessing the costs of climate change and in framing policy, though not perhaps entirely for the reasons the *Review* advanced. Certainly the concept of investment in climate insurance and the identification of the rights of future generations can be made more secure within a Christian framework. The implication is that Stern was right to call for immediate action on climate change, and that his critics are wrong to argue that we should wait and see.

5

International governance and root causes of unsustainability

BRIAN HEAP, FLAVIO COMIM
AND GEORGE WILKES

Government and co-operation are in all things laws of life;
anarchy and competition are the laws of death.
(J. Ruskin, *Unto This Last* (1862), Essay 3, 102)

Since the Report of the Brundtland Commission on Environment and Development in 1987,[104] brave intentions have been voiced at numerous international summit meetings to address the problem of unsustainability. Here, we examine why discontinuing unsustainable practices at the international level has proved intractable. Negotiations are usually based on the limited application of the co-operative efforts of self-interested agents, such as multinational companies. We argue here that summits should pay more attention to value systems that look beyond these limited co-operative efforts and ask what could happen if policies and processes were formulated that served wider claims rather than merely the economic self-interest of the participants.

Unsustainability is commonly seen as a result of overconsumption, resource depletion, inequitable distribution of goods and services, and the inadequacy of remedies for intergenerational justice. Jared Diamond reviewed the historical reasons why this has occurred in some societies but not in others.[105] He attributed societal collapse to one or more of the following elements: climate change, galloping long-term human reproductive growth rates, human environmental impacts and resource depletion, unstable trading relationships, and socio-religious factors. For example, in the Pacific the Easter Island social system collapsed due to the overexploitation of local resources; in the Yucatán Peninsula the Maya succumbed to population growth and socio-political failure; and in Greenland a medieval Viking colony was unable to develop stable trading partnerships with Native Americans. Societies that have survived differ widely. Traditional caste groups in India traded with each other and married within caste. The ten poorer states of Eastern Europe were received into the European Union (EU) of richer states, which pledged support to enable the less well-off members to catch up, a powerful reply to those who believe the relationship between rich and poor states is all about the pursuit of power and wealth to the detriment of the poor. Diamond's assessment is that survival can be linked to how individual rights are subjugated to group interests, even if such rights were fought for dearly in earlier generations.

So, is this lesson learned from Diamond's analysis one that could help us to tackle the root causes of unsustainability? Or are international summits directed towards unsustainability so wedded to pragmatism that only the 'law of the jungle' applies, masquerading as negotiated international agreements?[106] Is it possible that growing liberal interdependence will strengthen regional structures and non-state-grounded actors (such as multinational corporations and religious and humanitarian organizations) leading perhaps to a United Nations (UN), for example, that functions more effectively as one body in public policy, binding agreements and world governance? We examine, below, three examples of international summit meetings concerned with climate change, population growth and food security and ask how their impacts might have been enhanced.

Rio de Janeiro 1992 and Kyoto 1997

The first serious attempt to engage international co-operation on climate change came from an agreement at the UN Conference on Environment and Development held in Rio de Janeiro, Brazil, in 1992. The Intergovernmental Panel on Climate Change (IPCC) had been set up in 1988 to provide an objective source of scientific information about the dangers of so-called greenhouse gas (GHG) emissions (see Chapter 2). It was recognized that GHG emissions had risen significantly in the atmosphere by over 50 per cent equivalents of carbon dioxide (CO_2e) between 1850 and 2005. The Kyoto Protocol of 1997 followed: here political leaders aimed to cut by 5.2 per cent the average CO_2 emissions of 1990 by 2010 and achieve 'stabilization of greenhouse gas concentrations at a level that would prevent dangerous anthropogenic [human-instigated] interference with the climate system'.[107] In November 2007 the Protocol was ratified, and by May 2008 182 parties had signed up, representing 63 per cent of countries overall, with many governments persuaded that action is urgently needed (see also Chapter 3). Countries responsible for GHG emissions are predominantly those that experienced an industrial revolution in the eighteenth and nineteenth centuries; the greatest emitter is the USA, though China and India with their very rapid industrial expansion are also becoming major contributors. International scientific assessments indicated that if the GHG concentration doubled, the average global temperature would increase by about 3°C. The EU and the UN have adopted a stabilization target change of 2°C in order to avoid danger-ous climatic consequences (see also Chapters 2 and 3).

An early embarrassment was the inability to secure a politically acceptable international agreement on how the Protocol would operate. As a result the Kyoto agreement proved to be largely symbolic as a governance measure because various loopholes were left and the overall outcome is expected to result in cumulative carbon emissions *increases* of 4,480 million tonnes instead of a reduction of 770 million tonnes.[108] A technological approach to the problem has been advocated but so far there is no international agreement about which 'technolog-ical fixes' are best. Reports have been published about how 15 specific applications could help to significantly diminish the damaging effects of GHGs, the so-called 'Princeton wedges', which could potentially each save 1 gigatonne (1,000 million tonnes) of carbon emissions per year by 2054 (see also Chapter 2).[109] While many technologies already exist, some are currently too expensive for immediate application and mit-igation of carbon emissions therefore is a matter of economics rather than lack of ideas. Other schemes have been promoted on the basis of financial inducements: the Clean Development Mechanism aims to help industrialized countries to contribute to sustainable development in less-developed economies by the purchase of carbon credits.[110] Dubbed a 'medieval indulgence' by the journalist George Monbiot because it lets people off the hook, voluntary payment of a carbon-offset tax helps to calm the consciences of the many millions of us who use air transport.[111] The European Emissions Trading Scheme is another possible way forward. It is a 'cap and trade' policy whereby each EU Member State government has an allocated emissions allowance for a given period. Currently, the scheme is the biggest in the world and means that the polluter pays, a principle that gives priority to policies that improve the life of those who are at the bottom of environmental sustainability league tables, among whom are the most impoverished in terms of their ability to adapt to change, and lack of access to relief mechanisms or migration routes.

Today's estimates for preserving the earth and cutting emissions starting immediately suggest costs of about 1 per cent (now 2 per cent) of Gross Domestic Product (GDP) compared with likely future costs of climate change of 5–20 per cent of GDP (GDP is defined as the total market value of all final goods and services produced within the country in a given period of time; see also Chapter 4).[112] The *Stern Review* on the economics of climate change[113] makes the case for governments in more developed countries stepping in now to promote adaptation (for example, National Adaptation Programmes) rather than relying on the market (which is sluggish) to solve all our problems; it points out that any delay will only increase vulnerability and lead to higher costs later. However, if international policies continue to fail to meet the stabilization target of a 2°C rise in global temperature, as seems likely, adaptation to higher temperatures rather than mitigation of climate change could become a dominant feature of the policy-makers' agenda.[114] Adaptation involves action by national governments and citizens, with policies and actions ranging from building flood defences, through more efficient vehicles on the roads, to energy-efficient light bulbs in homes. As more secure scientific data have become available, there has been a diminution in controversies about whether global warming is a reality but the challenges to technical and fiscal solutions persist.[115] There are demands for a cost–benefit analysis to see whether it would be better to switch some of the estimated funding for the elaborate and expensive climate change interventions now being considered into environmental solutions, HIV/AIDs and malaria research and development, and other ways to reduce global poverty.[116] Clearly, we would wish to do all these things but the outcomes of Rio and Kyoto were aimed at binding and collective action and coalitions between nation states to reduce emissions overall as well as inequalities in emissions: these aims have met with mixed success.[117]

Cairo 1994 and Millennium Development Goals 2000

Another example of international intervention concerns the growth of world population, which was 200–400 million in the first century AD, when Jesus lived. It is now over 6,000 million, illustrating that humankind has had great success in filling the earth according to the dictat of Genesis 1:28: 'be fruitful and increase in number, fill the earth and subdue it'. While the annual global population growth rate has actually declined from about 2 per cent in 1970 to about 1.2 per cent today, doubling in about 61 years, this rate is now applied to the much larger population base of about 6,500 million (and rising) so that the added yearly increments are larger. Even if couples began having an average of two children now, the world population would still grow to more than 8,000 million because of the demographers' so-called 'population momentum' (see Chapter 6).

In 1994 the International Conference on Population and Development in Cairo signalled the seriousness of the global population growth rate. At that meeting the cost of a broad agenda of contraception was estimated at £12,000 million annually (adjusted for inflation). At today's prices, more than £1,000 million per year is required to support the supply of contraceptives to low-income countries, but over the past decade family planning programmes have stalled and the actual support from international donors has declined to only £100 million per year. This is largely because of the example of the 2000–8 United States administration, which switched support to abstinence-only sex education programmes to deter its unwanted teen pregnancies. In Africa and Latin America, condoms are now the most popular method of contraception among the sexually active; in Africa alone the difference between the number of condoms needed and the supply is roughly 1.9 billion per year. Current decisions about international support for family planning will therefore influence whether global population in 2050 will reach the UN's projections of 7.8 billion, 9 billion, or 10.5 billion – an issue that many scientists fear will produce dangerous conflicts among states and regions over access to the earth's natural resources.[118]

Fertility rates among the 1.3 billion people living in fragile areas are some of the highest in the world. Parents in these parts choose to have large families as support for their future, but no country, with the exception of a few oil-rich states and parts of India, has risen from poverty while having high fertility rates. In this respect the UN Millennium Summit in September 2000 is considered to be a major event because world leaders agreed to set goals and targets for combating poverty, hunger, disease, illiteracy, environmental degradation and discrimination against women, as well as commitments to human rights, good governance and democracy. These are the Millennium Development Goals (MDGs; see Box 5.1).

Subsequently, the issue of population growth was included within these goals since indicators revealed that in low-income countries there were fewer girls than boys in primary, secondary and tertiary education; fewer literate women than literate men in the 15- to 24-year-old age group; a low number of women in waged employment in the non-agricultural sector; and a low proportion of seats held by women in national parliaments.[119] This 'feminization' of poverty was reflected in the preponderance of female heads of households among the hungry, and the lopsided impact of environmental degradation on women (time spent gathering fuel and hauling water).

Questions remain about the future realization of these development goals, but a failure to fulfil the MDGs will compromise human development strategies in less-developed countries.[120] As noted in Box 5.1, two of the key aspects of the MDGs relevant to this part of our discussion are the promotion of gender equality and the empowerment of women as crucial steps towards family planning. About 40 per cent of pregnancies in less-developed countries are unplanned; so the education of women and the recognition of the need for family planning by both sexes are essential for any development plan if the poorest in society are to stand a chance of being lifted out of the poverty trap. For decades this has been a focus of advocacy, research and coalition-building by the international women's movement. Other goals of equal

---

Box 5.1 The Millennium Development Goals

There are eight goals to be achieved by 2015 that respond to the world's main development challenges. The MDGs comprise the Millennium Declaration that was adopted by 189 nations and signed by 147 heads of state and government during the UN Millennium Summit in September 2000.

- Goal 1: Eradicate extreme poverty and hunger.
- Goal 2: Achieve universal primary education.
- Goal 3: Promote gender equality and empower women.
- Goal 4: Reduce child mortality.
- Goal 5: Improve maternal health.
- Goal 6: Combat HIV/AIDS, malaria and other diseases.
- Goal 7: Ensure environmental sustainability.
- Goal 8: Develop a Global Partnership for Development.

---

significance are improvements in primary education (fewer than 50 per cent of pupils complete primary level in sub-Saharan Africa) and eradication of extreme poverty (helping people who live on less than $US1 per day, especially in sub-Saharan countries and parts of South Asia where the numbers are rising). If the MDGs are to be achieved, the regulation of population growth is paramount. However, the fact that the MDGs have been formulated by the international community serves to illustrate that, when international structures are built around co-operative aims motivated by a wish to improve the lives of the most deprived, a consensus can be achieved, though a successful outcome remains in the balance.[121]

Rome 1996 and 2002, and food security

An inter-related issue is food security – the availability of food and access to it. A household is considered food secure when its occupants do not live in hunger or fear of starvation, and have physical, social and economic access to sufficient safe and nutritious food to meet their dietary needs and food preferences and sustain an active and healthy life. The World Food Summits held in Rome in 1996 and 2002, called by the Food and Agriculture Organization, renewed a global commitment to the fight against hunger. Yet today, serious concerns persist about food security. Worldwide around 850 million people are chronically hungry due to extreme poverty, while up to 2 billion lack food security intermittently owing to varying degrees of poverty. Natural disasters such as drought in Africa and Australasia and flooding in South-east Asia have pushed up world prices of grain and oil; agricultural land has been lost to residential and industrial development; biofuels have raised land values; and consumer demand in China and India has contributed to reduced world stocks of grain. These are just some of the factors that have resulted in food riots in many countries across the world and are aggravated by economic speculation in the world commodity markets.

Hitherto, food production has kept pace with population growth but 'business-as-usual' scenarios suggest future consumption rates will increase to well beyond the rate of population growth. Energy demand is also predicted to show a fivefold increase over the next 100 years and, as less-developed countries catch up, the numbers of people wishing to adopt a lifestyle and diet once limited to rich nations will rise.[122] This has produced a class of new consumers defined as 'an average four-member household who possess purchasing power parity of at least $10,000 per year'. So, while the average Chinese or Indian still consumes much less than the average North American or European, the combined class of 'new consumers' is larger than that of all western Europe – and growing![123]

A paradigm for policy-makers and consumers in the twenty-first century is sustainable consumption and production – 'continuous economic and social progress that respects the limits of the Earth's ecosystems, and meets the needs and aspirations of everyone for a better quality of life, now and for the future generations to come'.[124] In terms of food security, current agricultural practices in many countries are unsustainable. The amount of cultivated land supporting food production was 0.44 hectares (ha) per capita (person) in 1961; today it is about 0.26 ha; by 2050 it will be in the vicinity of 0.15 ha per capita. Modern agricultural techniques have damaged land productivity by enabling erosion, causing waterlogging and compaction of soil, and producing overgrazing, salination and pollution. The picture that emerges is that agricultural production has to change to more sustainable practices because if we continue to live off the capital rather than the interest, the present and future needs of an extra 2.5 billion people will not be met (see Chapter 9).[125]

The International Assessment of Agricultural Knowledge, Science and Technology for Development (IAASTD) has identified a widespread realization that 'despite significant scientific and technological achievements in our ability to increase agricultural productivity, we have been less attentive to some of the unintended social and environmental consequences of our achievements. We are now in a good position to reflect on these consequences and to outline various policy options.'[126] One example concerns agriculture's responsibility for about a third of GHG production through methane from the decomposition of anthropogenic organic matter in flooded rice paddies and from livestock, and nitrous oxide emissions from fertilizer breakdown and livestock manure and urine. A sustainable consumption and production paradigm would aim to reduce GHG emissions by an improvement in livestock diets, discouragement of slash-and-burn policies to provide for livestock production, better land management to enhance carbon sequestration by more effective erosion control, conservation tillage, reduced fossil-fuel usage by the judicious application of biofuels, and improved employment prospects to diminish vulnerability among poor farmers.[127]

Could the future lie in new technologies that bring positive effects to food security through reduced pesticide use and better carbon balances?[128] The recent IAASTD report has reservations particularly about the genetic modification of plants as a way forward in helping to feed Africa's poor,[129] and few believe that genetically modified (GM) crops will solve the problems of food insecurity or displace conventional plant breeding.

However, genetic modification can increase the range of options for the improvement of crop yields, disease resistance, storage properties of products, and the protection of farmers from exposure to large amounts of pesticides and herbicides. It could bring benefits to countries where the need is greatest and it is notable that China has just announced a massive increase in the budget for such applications.[130] The utility of GM crops will depend on the provision of entitlements to the most impoverished and it is in this regard that the IAASTD has expressed its concerns (see Box 5.2).[131] Consensus does exist in understanding that the conventional models for agricultural knowledge, science and technology advocated by earlier international summits are no longer suitable for sustainable development because 'business as usual' is no longer an option. A more intensive engagement across diverse worldviews is envisaged to enable agriculture to achieve a multifunctional response to the demands of attaining food security in the twenty-first century.[132]

Sticking points

Reducing inequalities

Polarization between the high- and low-income countries is reflected in 25 per cent of the world's richest people accounting for 86 per cent of private consumption. Low-income countries have a low national GDP, low GDP per capita and low life expectancy, with 15 per cent of the world's poorest accounting for only 1.3 per cent of private consumption (Figure 5.1). Globalization has made the richer states more prosperous and many of the low-income ones increasingly dependent on outside aid and it is forecast that the latter will suffer disproportionately from the impacts of global warming. But political leaders and

---

Box 5.2 International Assessment of Agricultural Knowledge, Science and Technology for Development*

Agriculture – the need for change (April 2008)

The way the world grows its food will have to change radically to better serve the poor and hungry if the world is to cope with a growing population and climate change while avoiding social breakdown and environmental collapse. That is the message of a major new report by over 400 scientists which is launched today.

The authors' brief was to examine hunger, poverty, the environment and equity together. Professor Robert Watson, Director of IAASTD, said those on the margins are ill-served by the present system: 'The incentives for science to address the issues that matter to the poor are weak ... the poorest developing countries are net losers under most trade liberalization scenarios.'

Modern agriculture has brought significant increases in food production. But the benefits have been spread unevenly and have come at an increasingly intolerable price, paid by small-scale farmers, workers, rural communities and the environment.

The willingness of many people to tackle the basics of combining production, social and environmental goals is marred by 'contentious political and economic stances. Specifically, this refers to the many OECD member countries who are deeply opposed to any changes in trade regimes or subsidy systems. Without reforms here many poorer countries will have a very hard time ...'

The report has assessed that the way to meet the challenges lies in putting in place institutional, economic and legal frameworks that combine productivity with the protection and conservation of natural resources like soils, water, forests, and biodiversity while meeting production needs.

*IAASTD, see <www.agassessment.org/docs/SR_Exec_Sum_280508_English.pdf> and <www.agassessment.org/docs/Global_Press_Release_final.doc> (both last accessed 9 January 2009).

---

governments in low-income countries need to root out corruption and large-scale organized crime, while those in richer countries need to have a better realization of the true costs of unsustainable practices. As political scientist Scott Barrett points out, 'the challenges are local and not only global'.[133] In this sense better indicators are required to inform citizens of the true rate of their economic progress and the associated environmental costs.

Figure 5.1 A graphic analysis of Japanese inequalities as seen by Professor Hiroshi Takatsuki (High Moon), Director of the Miyako Ecology Center, Kyoto. Note how materially fortunate most Japanese are. (From Cartoon Gomic, part 6, p. 2, courtesy of Professor Hiroshi Takatsuki.)

Costing externalities

Some economists argue that Gross National Product as a national indicator of performance and individual welfare is flawed because it does not include lifestyle costs; that is, the impact on the environment resource base or 'externalities'. Net national product is a more realistic assessment of sustainable income because it gives a better evaluation of the costs involved in generating a product and includes the depreciation of environmental resources.[134] The Index of Sustainable Economic Welfare adjusts economic progress according to a variety of social and environmental factors,[135] and other indicators include the Human Development Index of the United Nations, the General Happiness Index of Bhutan, and the Sustainable Net Benefit Index of Australia – all indicative of the multiplicity of attempts to find a more informative instrument for policy-makers and consumers alike. Now a new commission is being set up under Nobel Laureate Joseph Stiglitz to consider whether the time has come to drop GDP as the accepted international indicator.[136]

Perversities

The root causes of unsustainability and environmental degradation may not be at the level of consumption but rather market and policy failures that cause consumers and producers to ignore the full social costs of their decisions on the productive base. Direct production costs are artificially reduced by 'perverse' subsidies that can result in the consumer's excessive use of energy, water (see Chapter 10) and other natural resources. Depletion costs are ignored because property rights exist that result in degradation of forests, pastures, fisheries and water resources. Environmental costs are overlooked because of ineffective environmental policies that permit excessive discharge of pollutants and hazardous wastes. It has been proposed, therefore, that attention should focus not on capping levels of consumption but on changing consumption and production patterns through the promotion of full-cost pricing, social co-ordination of regional action, and overcoming market and policy failures,[137] aspects also addressed in the paradigm of sustainable consumption and production.[138]

Adaptation

Failure to adopt a broad collective response to global warming recalls Jared Diamond's account of social collapse that occurred when nations and civilizations failed to adapt sufficiently quickly to threatening scenarios.[139] This means that the creation of a better successor to the Kyoto Protocol involving 'carrots' and 'sticks' is imperative. It will have to focus on a low- or zero-carbon economy, build on the experience with the EU Emissions Trading Scheme, and create innovative carbon-pricing schemes that do not penalize low-income countries. It will need to carry a strong verification process, and evolve National Adaptation Programmes of Action. A recent poll showed some progress towards these ends. In the USA, 47 per cent believe global warming is caused by human activity;[140] in the EU, 59 per cent of consumers separate their waste, nearly half have cut down energy consumption, and 37 per cent reduced their water consumption in the past month.[141] Greater significance will attach to coalition building and the importance of public/non-governmental organization (NGO) partnerships (an NGO, for example Oxfam, is a legally constituted organization created by private organizations or people with no participation or representation of any government). In the Western tradition, ideas of co-operation have been represented by notions of social contract, where individuals (or groups) of the same rational self-interest would get together for mutual advantage. This occurred in the successful adoption of the 1987 Montreal Protocol for the phasing out of ozone-depleting agents (chlorofluorocarbons), a treaty which was motivated by a degree of self-interest as light-skinned populations would benefit more because of their greater vulnerability to skin cancer.[142] Within this perspective, success is measured by consensus formation and social justice, achieving mutual advantage for different parties.

Co-operation

The framing of co-operative efforts in handling problems such as climate change has received a mixed reception so far. The philosopher Martha Nussbaum criticized the view that moral equality should involve an equivalent power equality among individuals. Instead, principles of justice are not always compatible with mutual advantage, and their acceptability cannot be reduced to a narrow sense of economic advantage. Whenever great power asymmetries are present, notions of extended reciprocity are needed. In fact, in the case of international co-operation, Nussbaum noted that 'social contract theories take the nation-state as their basic unit. For reasons internal to the structures of such theories, they are bound to do so. Such theories cannot provide adequate approaches to problems of global justice, that is, justice that addresses inequalities between richer and poorer nations, and between human beings whatever their nation.'[143]

To solve these problems Nussbaum advocated greater effort in acknowledging the complex interdependencies that exist between citizens of different nations and the moral obligations that pervade relations between citizens, institutions and nations as part of a process of considering how public policy should be formed and enacted internationally. Given the problems of climate change politics, it is notable how far states have agreed to collate data and communicate with each other about their GHG strategies and Kyoto aspirations. Scientists have shaped this co-operation, making it difficult to argue that scientific uncertainty does not justify action to reduce emissions (see Chapters 2 and 3).

Ideologies and dogmas

Part of the moral sentiments that are needed for a more encompassing view of co-operation has its origin not simply in terms of human dignity but in how people relate to nature and to each other. Some interpretations of early Jewish and Christian texts implied that humankind has 'dominion' and is called to subdue the earth and all that it contains. However, another political scientist, Lynn White,[144] questioned the interpretation of such biblical texts, and more recently[145] the emphasis has been placed on the stewardship role of humankind. In Islam, the theory of environment also incorporates a deep respect for nature and acceptance of trusteeship for the earth by humankind, though the problems of environmental degradation in the Muslim world are just as acute as in the West.[146] But even this idea of stewardship seems too passive for the present crisis because the challenge, which may be beyond us, is to reverse the damage inflicted on the earth by our exploitative attitudes, to learn how to adapt to lifestyles dictated by a paradigm of sustainable consumption and production, and to preserve and conserve intrinsic biodiversity before it is lost for ever. A form of 'beneficial dominion' may be required, provided that it avoids the somewhat arrogant assumption that the whole earth and its contents were created for exploitation by humankind, a theology commonly associated with the emergence of the industrial revolution. Skills and talents are urgently needed to bring about benefit to all the earth's inhabitants, as counselled in Exodus 23:4, Proverbs 25:21–22 and Matthew 19:19; 5:44, as well as to the earth (Genesis 2:15).

Population numbers

The All Party Parliamentary Report from Westminster[147] found that 80 per cent of the least developed countries believed that their population growth was too high. Economist Partha Dasgupta emphasizes this view, arguing that high population growth in the world's poorest regions (South Asia and sub-Saharan Africa) 'has been the obstacle to the achievement of sustainable economic development in those areas. It is believed that people in those regions are, on average, less wealthy now than they were 35 years ago.'[148] Clearly access to contraception is one element that influences population growth rates but, as we have noted previously, the education of women is just as important, if not more so (see Chapter 6). Current forms of contraception leave much to be desired, since the coercive approach to family size adopted by China has little international appeal because of its serious implications for family structures and restrictions on individual autonomy. However, the prospects of improved forms of contraception are bleak, as medical validation of any future products will take at least 15 years to complete. Pursuit of all aspects of the MDGs remains the most promising search for social justice in disadvantaged communities.

Institutions

It is as important to achieve change in the attitudes of institutions responsible for promoting innovation and regulating risk as it is to change the public's attitudes towards the roots of unsustainability.[149] This is because the complex interplay of profit-motivated companies and the political interventions of governments have resulted in a suspicion of new technologies and trade barriers, respectively. The tension here means that there are lessons still to be learned about openness, transparency and sharing of knowledge if we are serious about less-developed nations benefiting from new technologies that could mitigate GHG emissions and/or feed more people.

The power of business is complex and in the area of climate change coalitions have been formed on the one hand to undermine action to reduce emissions and on the other to stimulate the emergence of 'sunrise' industries that recognize new opportunities in renewable energy initiatives. NGOs are courted to mitigate the impacts of global warming on the insurance industry.[150] We cannot, therefore, take a wholly negative approach to industrial and business practices because prosperity with a purpose is usually something to celebrate rather than to berate. When economic activity raises the standard of living of the population and relieves the distress of the poor it is a contributor to the common good. In this sense the creation of wealth by economic activity can be an important engine of progress and greater well-being in the modern age provided that it is coupled to the common good by suitable distribution of this wealth, bringing benefit to the most disadvantaged and supporting the environment.[151]

Among the source of solutions to unsustainability is the role of multinational corporations, which have grown considerably in the past five decades and contributed substantially to the growth of the world economy.[152] In issues to do with energy, food security and population growth, multinationals have access to considerable funds for investment, can bring in the best business and technical expertise, and can operate in those areas of the global economy where they find it most profitable. Of necessity, they are subject to the governance and legal force of host countries, since states have ultimate control over their territories and borders, and can seize assets and personnel if so desired.

The way forward

We have examined some of the international attempts to tackle the root causes of unsustainability and the extent to which they are driven by or associated with climate change, population growth and food security. The attempts have been interpreted in terms of the need for co-ordination based on self-preservation (climate change), codes of social responsibility (population), and systems aggressively promoted by self-interested multinational conglomerates (food). So far as climate change is concerned, there have been substantial achievements in serious international scientific co-operation, but there are worrying signs that the mitigation of GHG emissions will not meet internationally determined global targets. Much will hang on strong leadership at the Copenhagen Summit in 2009 and the ability to encompass humanitarian and religious value systems that encourage change in people's behaviour towards the preservation and conservation of what is needed for the success of this and future generations. We have noted how the outcomes of summits have not always been translated into success but these are not necessarily indicators of a general malfunction. Failures seen in the area of population growth derive from long-standing cultural dispositions and political and dogmatic ideologies that have shifted support away from the poorest in society towards political expediency. Food insecurity persists because of the complex interplay of institutions and deficient policies that have inadequately embraced corporate social responsibility or adapted to the unexpected consequences of bad policies, unprecedented events or recovered from the exigencies of self-interested media conglomerations and special-interest groups. The main implications for policy are clear: greater co-ordination and integration of actions and responsibilities through multilateral agreements and coalitions nationally and locally.

Our inability to grapple with problems such as these at an international level begs the question of how we should live life on earth faced with imponderable dilemmas. One of the fullest visions is the Judeo-Christian idea of sustainability, which is characterized by hope, joy and a world that is harmonious, fruitful and equitable.[153] The type of co-ordination necessary to achieve this scenario is described poetically in the Old Testament (for example, Isaiah 40—66). The fulfilment of such a vision was dependent on the relationship between God and people (see Chapters 8, 12 and 14), and the prophetic writings in Isaiah resonate uncomfortably with post-modern countries where the divine relationship is broken, the land despoiled by human behaviour, the poor excluded from basic necessities, and ecosystem services are unfit for purpose or for future generations (Isaiah 5:8–10; 24:4–6). While some would say that little should be done to redress the balance because the future is divinely prescribed, we should recall that God's original creative work made order out of chaos, and our calling is to work creatively and to make yet more order and co-operate with God's creativity as human beings made in his image.[154]

At the outset of this chapter, we noted Diamond's point that collapse of societies was circumvented in the past by the subjugation of individual rights and selfish intentions to group interests.[155] Indeed, some theorize that an ability to co-operate is one of the main reasons why humans have managed to survive in almost every ecosystem on earth.[156] They have excelled in large-scale projects such as transportation networks, energy networks, sending robots to Mars and mapping the human genome, where great co-operation is demanded. Tackling climate change demands strong reciprocal action internationally but for realists such collective action is difficult to comprehend, since they see states that are protective of their sovereignty engaging in political games that maximize their own advantage in co-operative ventures. For liberals, the prospects are more optimistic because international co-operation and régime building result in the transfer of information, building of trust to overcome 'free-loader' problems, and businesses that strengthen developments within and between states. To co-operate effectively we need to think more deeply about how to embrace value systems based on humanitarian beliefs and often informed by our religious values because of their significant role in defining fruitful scenarios for co-operation.[157]

6

Population matters: voluntary contraception for environmental sustainability

JOHN GUILLEBAUD AND PETE MOORE

Unremitting growth is the doctrine of the cancer cell.
(C. Tickell, 'Letter of support' (2004),
<www.ecotimecapsule.com>)

At Jesus' birth, world population was around 300 million (Figure 6.1). In 2009 it stands at about 6,800 million and humankind's use of fossil fuels, fresh water, croplands, fisheries and forests exceeds supply. Our species now appropriates the resources of virtually the entire planet. In addition, our population is increasing by 1,000 million every 12–14 years and is projected to reach 9,400 million in 2050. But while the human population is growing, the earth is not. It may be large, but much of its surface is virtually uninhabitable – three-quarters is covered by salt water, half of the rest by ice, deserts, mountains and (rapidly disappearing) rainforest.

This chapter argues that the human population has grown beyond our planet's ability to supply us with the necessities for life. This not only raises the possibility of irreversible damage to our life-support systems, but also risks extreme population collapse. We contend that even if rich countries adopt massive lifestyle changes and introduce radically more efficient technologies, unremitting population growth is simply not an option on a finite planet and that promoting contraception, ideally within married relationships, should be part of the solution.[158]

Seeking sustainable population numbers

Forecasting the future is always a dangerous art. Predicting the size of the human population requires guesses and estimates about life expectancies and new technologies, few of which can be certain. It

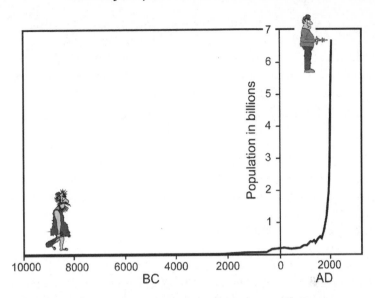

Figure 6.1 World population increase since agriculture first developed, which may be as early as 8000–9000 BC. Time to 1,000 million people: 10,000 years, reached in about AD 1830. Time to 7,000 million people: less than 200 years, expected in about 2012. (Image courtesy of Bob White.)

needs to acknowledge the wide diversity of lifestyles, and consequent rates of consumption, in different sectors of our population. It has to make room for personal and social desires to raise children and create a chain of inheritance. These factors may make the task complex, but even listing them highlights the need to address the issue seriously.

In 1996 Joel Cohen published *How Many People can the Earth Support?*, an important book that questioned many of the apocalyptical statements being made about the impact of human life on the planet. He pointed to all the uncertainties in the guesses, estimates and calculations, but even so concluded that a sustainable human population would be between 5,000 million and 10,000 million.[159]

Since then, many people have refined the data and models. Throughout the 1990s William Rees and Mathis Wackernagel developed an instrument known as ecological footprinting. Now used by the Global Footprinting Network (GFN), it played a key role in the 2006 *Living Planet Report*. This was based on 2003 data, the most recent available.[160]

Ecological footprinting accounts for income and expenditure in biological terms. 'Income' is seen as the planet's ability both to supply agricultural and forestry land, fish, water and energy, and to absorb all the waste that humans produce, including greenhouse gases (GHGs). It is often called the planet's total biocapacity and is measured in global hectares (gha). 'Expenditure' is defined as what humans actually use. Calculating this per head of population (per capita) is termed the ecological footprint of one individual.

The 2006 report estimated the earth's total biocapacity as 11,200 million gha; so, shared among the planet's 6,300 million human beings, in 2003 there were only 1.784 gha per capita. That same year, the mean global ecological footprint (48 per cent being due to GHG emissions) was 2.23 gha per capita; it had therefore already exceeded the 2003 biocapacity by 25 per cent. Thus the maximum sustainable (indefinitely supportable) population size appears to be less than it is at present and much less than that projected for 2050.

Such calculations are fraught with difficulties, but in 2004 an independent statistical analysis of 69 population-prediction studies concluded that, among the wide range of estimates of a maximum sustainable human population, the most likely size is 7,700 million.[161]

How many different-sized feet?

If we take the GFN estimate of 11,200 million gha for the maximum total biocapacity of the earth, Figure 6.2 shows that the question of maximum *sustainable* populations has different answers, depending on the mean ecological footprint of each person. Take, for example, the current mean ecological footprint of high-income countries: 6.4 gha. For everyone to live at 6.4 gha per capita, the maximum sustainable world population is 1,800 million people. To make room for 14,000 million people would mean each person could only have 0.8 gha, which is the average ecological footprint of inhabitants of the low-income countries including Uganda or Peru (Table 6.1). In between, around 6,000 million people (that is, less than the world total in 2009) could be supported by 1.9 gha per capita, which is the mean ecological footprint for middle-income countries such as Uruguay or Costa Rica. For people living in the rich West, the consequences of this are stark and few commentators believe that people in rich nations will willingly reduce their comfortable lifestyles to this degree. These figures signify maximum values; any drop in biocapacity through climate change (such as desertification and flooding) will reduce them.

Figure 6.2 also assumes that all current wilderness areas would be utilized by humankind, but many commentators find this completely unacceptable. For example, the GFN recommends that 30 per cent of biocapacity should still be available for wild species by 2100, even so adding the caveat that 'according to some ecologists, however, this is still not enough to stem biodiversity loss'.[162] Preserving that wilderness would bring the maximum sustainable population down to just 4,200 million, which means, alarmingly, that the optimum population for our species, in the interests of all life on the planet, has already by 2009 been comprehensively exceeded.

In reality, 96 per cent of the population increase will occur in the less developed countries. Many commentators remark that the impact of this will be blunted as these people will be low consumers of resources. But tolerating, almost welcoming, unending poverty is unacceptable. The mid-2008 estimate for the net annual population increase – all births (139 million) minus all deaths (57 million) – was 82 million.[163]

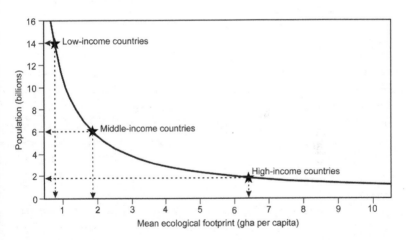

Figure 6.2 Plot of population number versus the mean ecological footprint per capita, in which their product always gives the GFN estimate of 11,200 million gha. This is the calculated *maximum* total biocapacity of the earth, though the *optimum* is less by at least 30 per cent to allow for biodiversity (see the text). Thus, for any given mean ecological footprint, a population number that gives a point lying above the curved line will be unsustainable or, for any given population number, a mean ecological footprint that gives a point above the line will also be unsustainable. The points on the line are at the limits of sustainable world population, if each country's mean ecological footprint per capita were that of the whole world. (Image courtesy of Martin Desvaux. Based on 2003 GFN data taken from World Wildlife Fund, *Living Planet Report*, 2006.)

Table 6.1 Mean ecological footprints in gha for selected countries and the world in 2003.

Country (in 2003)	Mean ecological footprint (gha)
USA	9.6
Australia	6.6
UK	5.6
Turkey	2.1
Costa Rica	2.0
Uruguay	1.9
Uganda	0.8
Peru	0.8
World	
Available	1.78
Utilized (i.e. overshoot)	2.23

Consequently, 1.5 million extra people need supporting each week. If they are to have a healthy future, that means building the equivalent of one new city each week. Even a slum uses land and inevitably further depletes habitats for other species. In addition, these 1.5 million people will seek lifestyles that are above abject poverty and become new makers of GHGs. Poverty cannot be alleviated anywhere without increased use of energy, derived at present mainly from burning oil, gas, coal or wood.

Many people have been born into poverty and should be assisted to rise out of their circumstances. In so doing, their global ecological footprint will have to increase. This brings us back to Figure 6.2 and to the big questions: for us in the developed world, how big a reduction in ecological footprint will we accept and, for the whole world, how many feet?

If the world were run by biologists rather than economists, our leaders would surely have known sooner what all species learn by experience: that increasing any population beyond the capacity of its environment leads to a crash. The *Living Planet Report* shows that humans are already overshooting the planet's total biocapacity and 'by midcentury humanity's demand on nature will be twice the biosphere's productive capacity'.[164] According to these data, the projected 2050 population of 9,400 million will be consuming at twice the rate that the planet can sustainably supply.

With no second planet available, surely the question should not be whether to stabilize our population, but how? Humanity could find itself facing a stark choice: *either* a gigantic cull by nature, quite possibly during this century, through escalating violence between and within countries and/or by mass starvation and disease (aggravated by climate change-related disasters such as hurricanes, monsoons, droughts and rising sea levels); *or* prioritizing now the necessary balance of population and resources, through properly resourcing the voluntary planning of fewer births.[165]

Impact of human numbers on the rest of creation

Today, of all the land-based vertebrate flesh (biomass), 97 per cent comprises human beings plus the biomass of our cows, sheep, pigs and goats: leaving just 3 per cent for all other animal species on land,[166] including all the big game animals of the African plains. An estimated 1 per cent of all species become extinct each year, and this rate is expected to increase. In addition, many invertebrates with crucial roles (from pollinating insects to the micro-organisms that maintain the carbon and nitrogen cycles) are at risk. By 2025 human beings will have eliminated an estimated 20 per cent of all the world's life forms – unlike the previous five established mass extinctions, this one has been triggered not by a natural disaster but by one species.[167]

Most of this destruction is not so much wanton as thoughtless. It occurs through competition from sheer numbers of human beings, leading (as they most understandably struggle to feed themselves and their families) to massive destruction of the habitats for other species, for example rainforests, wetlands, mangroves and coral reefs.

Seeking solutions

All solutions are either problematic, uncomfortable or raise controversy. The range of solutions can be grouped under just three headings.[168]

First, reduce mean per capita consumption/pollution. Everyone must evaluate and reduce their own consumption.[169] 'Let us learn to live simply, so that others may simply live.'[170] Start perhaps with food, specifically meat consumption: meat production accounts for a startling 18 per cent of world total GHG emissions, measured as CO_2 equivalents (see Chapter 2).[171] For those Christians and other concerned citizens who are not vegetarians, should meat now be a rare treat rather than an assumed constituent of one's daily diet?

Like meat, global per capita consumption of almost everything is destined to go up rather than down. Much of this is due to overconsumption by already affluent people, but some is rightly due to development, enabling the world's poorest citizens to fulfil entirely justifiable aspirations to leave poverty.

Second, devise better technologies. Humankind has proved successful because throughout history we have created tools that solve specific problems. We can now identify overconsumption of resources as a key problem and there is a need to promote new, more efficient technologies with far greater urgency. But technology is no 'magic bullet'.[172] A key issue is the supply of energy. No available alternative energy source has all the positive features of oil and gas. These fossil fuels have been created by millions of years' worth of solar energy being captured by plants and micro-organisms and compressed to form commodities that have high energy density. Humanity has guzzled for the past 200 years on this inheritance – a one-off bonanza. The immediate benefits have been huge. For a small energy input in terms of mining, refining and transport, we can deliver high-energy output. The energy is also in a form that is constantly available – it is not restricted by the intermittency problem of some renewables (for example, wind). It is easy to store and transport anywhere on earth. Its high-energy density has enabled air transport and it provides the raw material for essential chemical fertilizers and pesticides.[173]

'Greener' technology – for energy and most other environmental challenges (including lack of water, see Chapter 10) – is going to be indispensable. But the earth's finiteness guarantees it will never suffice in the face of unremitting population increase.

Third, achieve fewer humans doing the consuming. The need to keep a constant restrictive pressure on resource use is an inevitable consequence of the planet being finite. However, even if mean consumption per capita were to fall, it cannot reach zero. So the numbers of persons could never increase indefinitely, with no upper limit.

In any just world, the first solution cannot suffice because of the obligation for poverty relief – crucial for so many individuals – and relying on the second solution alone is a huge gamble. The third option means helping sexually active people to have choice in the number and spacing of their children. Voluntary, available and fully accessible contraception is not a substitute for reduced consumption per capita assisted by technology: it is just the much-neglected other side of the same coin (Figure 6.3).Yet both outside and within the Christian Church, this is a taboo subject for discussion: the 'elephant in the room that no one talks about'.

Critical questions

Coercion? Unacceptable and unnecessary

It is often assumed, by Christians and others, that 'any quantitative concern for population must be intrinsically coercive'.[174] This is in large measure a backlash against various coercive policies operated in 1970s India and the one-child policy introduced in China in 1979, which resulted in forced sterilizations, abortions and infanticides and a distorted sex ratio (an estimated 117 boys for every 100 girls).[175]

We need to recognize that compulsion in contraception, whether overt or covert, has always proved counter-productive (except uniquely

Figure 6.3 Environmental unsustainability: two sides of the same coin.
'The very greenest energy is the energy you don't use.' Not using energy, to some degree, is by individual conservation; but complete non-use is through contraception, since 'An absent human has a zero [carbon] footprint' (Chris Rapley, Director, Science Museum, London). (Image courtesy of Population and Sustainability Network.)

in China). Why consider so infringing human rights when around half of all conceptions are unplanned? Moreover numerous countries, as varied as Costa Rica, Iran, Korea, Sri Lanka and Thailand, each halved their TFR – the total fertility rate, defined as the projected mean total number of children born per average woman in her lifetime on current demographic assumptions, in short 'average family size' – primarily through meeting women's unmet fertility needs and choices.[176] Interestingly, it needed no more years for them to reduce their TFRs so dramatically than China required for the same outcome.

Social surveys in developing countries reveal much unmet need for contraception.[177] It is a myth that women in those settings will not accept birth planning: not only to space their babies, but also to limit the total to considerably fewer than the biological maximum. Women, particularly women in low-income households, are aware of the real health risks accompanying pregnancy. Over half a million women die annually as a consequence of pregnancy (one a minute). Indeed, the lifetime risk of dying through pregnancy for a woman in sub-Saharan Africa is at least 1 in 20, whereas it is about 1 in 30,000 in Sweden (where each labour is so much safer and family sizes are around two).[178] At least one-third of fatal pregnancies are unwanted at conception.[179] Regardless of its importance for the planet, therefore, affordable and accessible contraception is unquestionably 'pro' the life of many individuals; through reducing maternal mortality. It could also minimize the misery represented by the annual 50 million abortions.

We are failing to push at an open door marked 'women's choice'. Let us start with a target that every woman on the planet who wants a modern contraceptive method for use by self or partner has easy access to it.[180] Failing to resource such a choice-based approach with adequate services is surely coercive, since lack of this option regularly results in many women conceiving when they do not wish to. Furthermore, inadequately resourcing world contraception now will lead to relentless population pressure in the future and, inevitably, more governments legislating for coercive birth control.

Abortion?

Practically all Christians see abortion as an unacceptable method of birth planning.[181] Indeed, the choice by one of us (J.G.) to specialize in the field of contraception and reproductive health was in part motivated by the thought of 'making abortion history', through researching and promoting better contraceptive methods that would create the possibility, finally, of the disappearance of abortion from all societies.

Contraception, to the exclusion of other ways to help the poor?

Some people distrust talk of limiting populations as necessarily and intrinsically exclusive of many other key interventions such as social justice, fairer trade, poverty relief, better education, health care and improved child survival. But why should a caring person not have deep concern for all these as well? 'As well' can mean that, through reducing unintended pregnancies, there is an incremental reduction in average family size. With fewer to share the 'cake' of each family's and each country's resources, there is less extreme poverty.[182] As more children survive there is a growing acceptance of smaller family size, and ultimately less population growth. A well-known slogan is 'Development is the best contraceptive' – but this is misapplied wherever 'development' fails to incorporate the choice for all of affordable family planning services and supplies. Christians should advocate not only for increased investment in these services but also that they always (in conservationist Jonathon Porritt's words[183]) be supplied wisely, democratically and compassionately. Current world funding is just 10 per cent of that recommended at the UN's International Conference on Population and Development in Cairo in 1994.[184]

Hearings by the All Party Parliamentary Group on Population, Development and Reproductive Health in 2007 concluded that the UN's Millennium Development Goals, including both the eradication of extreme poverty and hunger, and the ensuring of environmental sustainability (see Chapter 5), 'will be difficult or impossible to achieve without a renewed focus on, and investment in, family planning'.[185]

The demographic transition

Fortunately, in most countries birth rates and average family sizes are declining. Yet world population increases annually by 82 million. Why? Because of 'population momentum', a consequence of the large population 'bulge' of previously born young people (2,500 million are under age 20).[186] Hence most of tomorrow's parents are already born; so numerous that even if their average family sizes were improbably to average 2.1, population growth (despite the ravages of HIV/AIDS) would not cease until a total of about 9,000 million was reached. This 2,500 million increase is more than the total population of the world in as recently as 1950.[187]

The classical demographic transition is depicted in Figure 6.4. In traditional societies, and over thousands of years, birth rates were high but death rates were also high. Therefore the TFR was around replacement – a little above two. With the arrival of modern medicines and effective public health (point A in the figure), the death rate especially of children always declines, so population growth accelerates dramatically. In many countries (but not yet in others), after a time lag the birth rate falls and eventually a new equilibrium is established (at B in the figure), with birth rates once again roughly in balance with death rates.[188]

Figure 6.4 remains a valid representation, but the driving mechanisms in successful countries have varied greatly.[189] Conventional economic wisdom says that couples in resource-poor settings actively plan to have many children, to compensate for high child mortality, to provide labour and income for the family, and to care for ageing parents. Often with cultural and religious endorsement, those factors certainly enhance the acceptance of large families.[190] Moreover, improved child survival and poverty reduction (if they occur, as both are inhibited by population growth) support fertility reduction. But most economists overlook the bewildering number of exceptions:

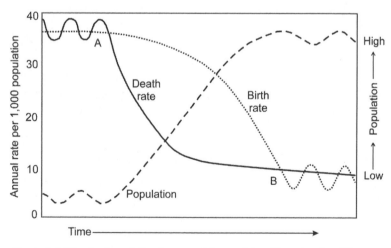

Figure 6.4 Classic view of the demographic transition. (For points A and B, see discussion in the text.)

countries where reductions in fertility began while infant mortality was still very high (for example, England in the late nineteenth and early twentieth centuries), or with no preliminary increase in wealth per capita (for example, Bangladesh, Kenya).[191]

Economists generally fail to take account of the basic biological fact that – in all settings – potentially fertile sexual intercourse is far more frequent than the minimum needed for intentional conceptions. Thus, for low-income groups, having a large rather than a small family is less of a planned decision (as in economic theory) and much more an automatic outcome of human sexuality. Something active needs to be done to separate sex from conception – namely, contraception.[192] But in resource-poor settings, access to contraception is often difficult. Barriers to women's choice are created through lack of empowerment and abuse of their rights by family members, or through the agency of religious authorities and some governments (for example, the Philippines) and, regrettably, sometimes even contraceptive providers.[193] Misinformation abounds: in Rwanda, for instance, rumours have spread that hormonal contraceptives cause permanent sterility and that condoms always have holes in them.

The evidence is clear that – without necessarily any improvement in education or wealth per capita,[194] or other presumed essentials – demand for contraception increases when barriers are removed and supply is fully resourced so as to be freely available, accessible, and accompanied by correct information about its appropriateness and safety; and when it is publicized in a matter-of-fact way.[195] However else countries may differ, these characteristics are shared by all the reduced-fertility 'success stories'.

In Iran, where the TFR declined from 5.5 to 2 (replacement) in just 15 years, the government requires all couples to learn about family planning as a precondition for marriage. (The main driving force may have been the implied 'official' blessing, promoting a new socially accepted norm.) Unequivocal endorsement by religious leaders (as occurred in Iran) or by celebrities like football stars (in the media) can be invaluable.[196] High rates of female education helped in Iran, as elsewhere, but men also need to be brought on board, and (re-)educated about the benefits of family planning for themselves and for local environmental sustainability, so they have full involvement in reproductive health initiatives. Young people must be appropriately targeted, given that no less than 43 per cent of the population of sub-Saharan Africa is under the age of 15.[197]

Education in all these issues should be by parents as much as schools, with a major contribution by the media. The Population Media Center, based in Vermont, USA, but working throughout the developing world, uses serial radio dramas or 'soaps'. Audiences learn from decisions that their favourite characters make, such as allowing wives to use contraception to achieve smaller and healthier families. In Rwanda, 57 per cent of new attendees at family planning clinics named a similar storyline in the radio drama *Rwanda's Brighter Future* as their reason for attending.[198]

A Christian response

Christians disagree on many issues, and that of the human global population raises many different responses. One influential strand of opinion among some non-Christians and some Christians alike believes that Judaeo-Christianity endorses unlimited procreation along with unbridled exploitation of nature. They point in particular to biblical passages such as: 'Be fruitful and multiply, and fill the earth and subdue it; and have dominion over the fish of the sea and over the birds of the air and over every living thing that moves upon the earth'(Genesis 1:28).

The first question is the nature of our 'dominion'. The Hebrew word translated 'subdue' (*kabash*) may also be used for working the soil and so can be interpreted as 'subduing' all that would get in the way of nature in its fruitfulness. 'Have dominion' or 'rule over' (*radah*) is used to describe the benevolent rule of a good Israelite king over his subjects (see Psalm 72).[199] Other Bible texts clearly show that humankind is being commissioned to stewardship with delegated authority from God over his creation.[200]

This commission or 'blessing' was repeated by God to Noah and his family in Genesis 9:7, without the word 'fill' but again without any clear suggestion of an upper limit to the multiplying. Furthermore, how should Christians as 'heirs' to Abraham interpret God's promise that the patriarch's descendants will be as numerous as the stars in the sky or grains of sand on the beach (Genesis 22:17)?

In the creation account, God says to the plants and animals on days five and six 'be fruitful and multiply'. However one reads Genesis, this clearly indicates God's intention and desire for non-human lives to thrive on the planet. God gave that commission to them before he created man. How could he have intended humankind to multiply to the present levels, which so seriously prejudice, by habitat destruction and predation, the fruitfulness of so many of his other creatures?

When God said, 'Fill the earth', it is reasonable to assume he did not mean us to 'overfill' it. God's earth is finite. On the basis of the numbers already present and sharing in its total biocapacity of 11,200 million gha (see Figure 6.2) and, since we are unlikely to accept an ecological footprint per capita that would dictate unremitting extreme poverty, the planet is 'full'. We face a dilemma. Non-human life is invited to flourish, and human life is invited to flourish. There is no indication that God intended either to impede the other – Genesis seems clear – God wanted both to 'be fruitful'.[201]

As for Noah, he was told to 'be fruitful and multiply' when, of course, there had just been a massive depopulation. He is depicted as the arch-conservationist of all history. Hence Genesis 9:7 can hardly be expected to mean multiplying to a level where one species threatens the survival of so many others. Moreover, within the early Genesis stories there is clear recognition that population and land are insep-arable and often have an unsustainable relationship: there is nowhere a suggestion that the people of Israel should bear children beyond the land's capacity to support them. There is also an understanding (for example, Genesis 6:1,13 and 13:6–7) that excessive population growth may lead to conflict due to scarcity of land and water. In summary, we need to be extremely wary of any claim that the Bible calls for or supports the current unprecedented growth of human numbers.[202]

How many children should a Christian have?

The Optimum Population Trust (a UK think tank) calculates that 'each new UK birth will be responsible for 160 times more GHG emissions . . . than a new birth in Ethiopia'.[203] Therefore having one birth fewer in a developed country makes an impressive contribution to tackling climate change. Should not rich Christian couples in any country (there exist rich Christians even in Africa), in a hungry, already damaged world, think twice about having a large family: which, for a given mean environmental footprint per capita, must always have a greater total footprint than a small one?

There is no definitive answer, but it might be salutary for couples to pray over a non-rigid replacement fertility guideline; that is, two children replacing two adults. This does not force everyone into the same family mould. A gradual decline in total population can be achieved by a TFR of 1.9 children, similar to that in the UK (2008). This is an average of 19 children in every ten families and clearly allows a few to have more than two children if counterbalanced by others who voluntarily choose to have one or none – as by happenstance is the case in the UK.[204]

Contraception and sexual ethics

Most Christians see medical technology as part of God's good provision for humanity – part of our God-given ability to serve the weakest in our community. As such, we accept a God-given role of intervening in human life and survival. Within that frame of reference, many Christians also see contraception as part of God's provision for humankind. Just as modern medicine has allowed human populations to grow rapidly by reducing death by disease, it is surely fitting to employ science to offer choice over the extent of that growth. Appropriately used contraception could then be seen not just as 'permissible' for believers, but as something for which to praise God:[205] a technology devised in the nick of time, for the better welfare of each child, as well as for the future sustainability of creation.

The Bible teaches that marriage was ordained because 'It is not good that the man should be alone ... Therefore a man leaves his father and his mother and clings to his wife, and they become one flesh' (Genesis 2:18, 24). Traditional Christian teaching sees this 'one-fleshness' resulting from making love, which is itself a gift from God. Indeed it is a 'sacrament', the highly pleasurable physical connection being an outward sign of what should be a deep inward psychological and spiritual bonding between the two life partners. The Bible indicates that this is to promote and maintain bonding, to establish and reinforce the Christian home. Within Christian churches there has then to be a debate as to whether the spiritual benefits of intercourse can be dissociated from the physical consequences – the birth of children.

Contraception within marriage

The separation by contraception of the 'unitive' and 'procreative' aspects of intercourse troubles many Christians, particularly within Roman Catholic and Orthodox churches. A key document here is Pope Paul VI's 1968 Encyclical. This states: 'The Church, nevertheless, in urging men to the observance of the precepts of the natural law, which it interprets by its constant doctrine, teaches that each and every marital act must of necessity retain its intrinsic relationship to the procreation of human life', and continued: 'Similarly excluded is any action which either before, at the moment of, or after sexual intercourse, is specifically intended to prevent procreation – whether as an end or as a means.'[206]

Though very widely disregarded by the laity, Roman Catholic authorities make clear their view that artificial contraception interferes with God's creative work. It is, however, worth noting that their appeal is to Natural Law rather than a biblical passage, and that Natural Law derives principally from the fifth-century theologian and philosopher Augustine of Hippo.[207] The Bible itself is almost silent on the issue and, specifically, nowhere does it state that the act of becoming 'one flesh' must on every occasion be linked with the possibility of having children. A purely biblical view of human sexual relationships does not rule out the use of contraception within marriage.

Once we accept contraception as legitimate for Christians, a responsible form of stewardship enabling us to maintain the marriage relationship and yet not overburden ourselves or the planet, we have made a far-reaching decision. Those of us who make use of contraception continue to see children as gifts from God, but believe he has enabled us to make responsible choices as to their number.[208]

Ethical considerations on the mechanisms of contraception

Couples can employ a wide range of different techniques to separate intercourse from conception. Again we enter an area where Christians disagree, the issue this time being when a human life comes into existence. Many Christians turn to biblical texts such as Psalm 139, when claiming that human life starts when a sperm and egg meet and join – at fertilization. For Christians with that view, there is still a range of contraceptive options which, when they are successful, are so because of preventing fertilization: namely, consistently taken combined oral contraceptives, injectable or implanted chemical contraceptives, condoms, male and female sterilization, and natural family planning (the fertility awareness methods).[209]

It is worth noting that while the psalmist clearly says God created him and knew him right back in his mother's womb, the psalmist does not (indeed in those days could not) clarify precisely when his personal history started.[210] He leaves open when this was, during the nine-month-long process of being 'knitted together'. Many Christians now take a view that conception is a process, one that is not complete until implantation of the early embryo in the mother's womb. For them, there are other acceptable contraceptives that may sometimes prevent implantation of an early embryo, as a back-up to their main mechanisms of action that block fertilization. These include intra-uterine devices and intra-uterine systems, pills containing only progestogen hormone, and emergency contraception.[211]

Sex and contraception outside lifelong relationships

One of the understandable fears expressed by Christians in these discussions is that contraceptive methods can be, and often are, used for 'recreational' sex without commitment, by people who disregard the creator's intention for their bodies and minds. This frequently causes much grief, to them and to others. The arrival of effective contraception came alongside the 'sexual revolution' in the 1960s and facilitated intercourse outside marriage. There was nothing new about this, but the availability of the contraceptive pill made it altogether easier and more prevalent. The legitimate fear is that making contraception available could encourage ever greater sexual activity outside marriage. But what is wrong is the sexual sin itself, not the use of contraception per se. Christians may, without any compromise, help couples to have control over the number of their children by encouraging the threefold message: abstinence ('saving sex') until marriage, faithfulness within marriage, and therein the use of contraception to enable sustainable families.

A holistic perspective

In 1992, James Grant of UNICEF stated that 'Family planning could provide more benefits to more people at less cost than any other single "technology" now available to the human race.'[212] Grant here stresses the value of family planning, but note he does not claim that it can ever solve everything. This chapter has argued that its unavailability, as an option for many multitudes over the years, continues to be one of the root causes of environmental unsustainability. Available and appropriately used contraception is necessary if the world is to have a halfway decent future. Yet it is not sufficient. It is now too late for family planning alone; too many people are already here. A considerable body of data indicates that we already have more people living on the planet than it can sustain at reasonable levels of living, and population momentum is bound to increase the number in this century.[213] Many commentators believe that this could have been an avoidable tragedy if the issue had been appropriately prioritized earlier. But compassionate contraception can still help, by reducing potentially hundreds of millions of new arrivals into future suffering; and their absence can only help to lessen collective GHG emissions.

There are grounds for some optimism. The UN reports that the TFR of all the less-developed countries has come down from 5.4 in 1970–5 to 2.9 in 2000–5. This has been achieved despite a derisory investment in family planning services. There is a distinct potential for Christians to advocate for greatly increased resources and to call for these services to be supplied wisely and compassionately. The greatest need is in the least developed – mainly African – countries whose TFRs (five or more) are much higher than the current mean and whose populations are set to more than double by 2050.[214]

When the camel collapses with a broken back, it is important to remember that the last straw did not really do it. It was the fault of all the straws. To achieve environmental sustainability, everyone must be involved. This means multitudes of individual good decisions for the conservation of energy and other resources, and (as we argue here) to have relatively small, 'replacement' families. But when push comes to shove, a common and understandable response is, 'Why should I bother to do the right (often inconvenient) things to promote sustainability, when no one else seems to?' Much is encapsulated in the sayings: 'My car is my car – everyone else's car is traffic!' and 'My baby is my baby – everyone else's baby is "overpopulation".'

Jesus said, 'Love your neighbour as yourself' (Matthew 22:37–40). The Brundtland Commission (see Chapter 5) stated that we should meet 'the needs of the present without compromising the ability of future generations to meet their own needs'.[215] We join with those who say Christians should put these together: love is about both horizontal and vertical equity. In this assessment, horizontal equity is to love and provide for the multitudes of our deprived overseas neighbours, and vertical equity is about loving our future neighbours. Can we do that without doing our bit to ensure that there are not altogether so many future neighbours that God's earth, in all its beautiful complexity, is damaged beyond repair?[216]

7

Natural disasters:
acts of God or results of human folly?

ROBERT S. WHITE

First the earthquake, then the disaster.
(Graffiti written after the 1994 magnitude 6.7 earthquake
in Northridge, CA, USA)

We live in a world where the same natural processes that make it hab-
itable can also turn round and bite us. They cause natural disasters that
may kill thousands or even hundreds of thousands of people. We may
blame God for those. But more often than not it is human actions that
change a natural process into a natural disaster – and our patterns of
unsustainable living are contributing to that.

So-called natural disasters may shake the foundations of the beliefs
of people of religious faith, including Christians, as well as pose serious
questions for atheists and agnostics. Every time there is a massive disaster, such as the 2004 Boxing Day tsunami or a large earthquake in a
heavily populated area, our quite proper reaction is horror that so
many people have suffered or died. For many Christians, an immediate
question that then arises is, 'How can an all-powerful, all-loving God
allow such things to happen?' For all of us, including those with no
particular faith, disasters that affect more and more people every year
challenge the hubris that assumes that humans can control their
environment at will – that our cleverness can keep us from suffering.
Natural disasters pull us up sharp and make us face head-on the hard
questions of life and death. For Christians they bring into sharp focus
the relationship between the creator God, his creation and human
beings made 'in his image' (see Genesis 1:27).

Natural disasters affecting huge numbers of people are one of the
most visible results of persistent unsustainable living by humankind:
it is likely that before long there will be a disaster that causes over

1 million deaths. Of course earthquakes, floods, volcanic eruptions, droughts and disease are not generally caused directly by human agency. But often human actions contribute to the likelihood of events such as floods and famines; in others to causing (or not preventing) more fatalities than might otherwise have been the case, as happens when proper building codes are not followed in earthquake-prone areas; and in yet others by allowing an increase in suffering and death in the aftermath of a natural event by insufficient or inappropriate care for survivors.

Global climate change is an example where the lifestyles of people in some parts of the world and their production of so-called greenhouse gases (GHGs, see Chapter 2) may cause global warming, which impacts directly on environmental conditions throughout the rest of the world, both now and for many decades into the future. Inevitably, it is people in the areas where income is low, living closer to the threshold of environmental disaster from crop losses, storms and flooding, or drought, heatwaves and disease, who are least able to cope with rapid climate change and who therefore suffer most.

I outline, in this chapter, the scientific understanding of natural processes that contribute to human disasters, and then discuss a Christian understanding of God's relationship, and ours, to the natural world. God's first commandments to humankind in Genesis 1:28 and 2:15 were that we should care for his creation, which together with Christ's injunction that we should love our neighbours leads directly to an imperative to adopt sustainable lifestyles. A consequence of such an attitude would be a huge reduction in the number and impact of natural processes that develop into disasters.

The science of natural disasters

Natural disasters occur when the normal processes of the earth interact with human populations to cause loss of life or injury. There is nothing disastrous to humanity about an earthquake, a volcanic eruption or a flood if it happens in an area where no one lives, nor about the 'greenhouse warming' that occurs naturally as a result of the water vapour and other GHGs that are present in the atmosphere, quite apart from (and preceding) human activity. Indeed, without these processes the earth would be a sterile, dead place, unfit for human habitation. For example, natural GHGs create a thermal blanket around the earth that keeps its surface at an average temperature of about 14°C: without this greenhouse warming the earth would average an icy 18°C below the freezing point of water, the planet would be permanently encased in ice, and life as we know it would be untenable. Regular floods irrigate and spread sediments rich in nutrients across flat-lying areas, which makes agriculture and animal husbandry possible in those regions – the cycle of annual floods in ancient Egypt was essential for maintaining soil fertility, and when the floods failed it was a disaster often resulting in famine. The movement of large regions of the earth's crust (plate tectonics) and the accompanying earthquakes and volcanic eruptions recycle to the earth's surface the minerals and nutrients vital for life. Natural processes of atmospheric and ocean circulation, weathering, erosion and volcanism keep in balance the atmospheric concentrations of carbon dioxide (CO_2) and water which are such crucial components for maintaining a climate conducive to life.

Disasters occur when humans decide to live in areas that are susceptible to extreme natural events. Ironically enough, areas of high risk from earthquakes, volcanic eruptions and floods are often the same areas with the highest population densities, and so are prone to great loss of life. The reason is easy to see: settlements and cities develop where there is access to water, in river valleys or at the feet of mountain ranges and where there is easy communication, again in valleys or by the sea. Yet such places are often particularly vulnerable to natural disasters. The need for fertile land for agriculture often leads people to settle in areas nourished by rich volcanic soils or on deltas or in valleys where the soil is replenished by frequent floods. Again, the very factors such as volcanic eruptions and floods that make them fertile are the same that make them dangerous places in which to live.

There are four other factors that make it more likely now than in the past for natural disasters to cause huge casualties. The first is the exponential growth in the number of people living on this planet (see Chapter 6). The second is the global movement of dispersed rural populations into concentrations in cities and megacities (cities with a population of over 5 million), many of which are located close to sea level. These people are especially vulnerable to global sea-level rise and may suffer enormous fatalities if struck by flooding or an earthquake, not only in the initial event but also in the aftermath as basic services break down. Third is the fact that the recurrence time between extreme events in any particular location, be they floods, storms, volcanic eruptions, earthquakes or tsunamis, may be on a scale of centuries and therefore often much longer than human timescales. For example, the last tsunami of a size similar to that of the 2004 Boxing Day tsunami in Indonesia that killed more than 220,000 people was 600–700 years earlier.[217] Put simply, the knowledge that a particular place is potentially dangerous is lost because nothing has happened for generations, and so the inhabitants fail to make adequate preparations. This is not to say that all disasters are infrequent. In some areas, such as Bangladesh and parts of China, serious flooding is a recurrent event every few years or decades and the people are well aware of that, but still vulnerable because they have nowhere else to live. Fourth, the impact of rapid global climate change with associated changes in rainfall, in storm patterns and in sea-level rise, is likely to make flood plains and coastal areas much more vulnerable to large-scale disasters, often exacerbated by major land-use changes.

Fatalities from natural disasters since the mid-twentieth century can be divided approximately equally between those caused by geo-logical factors (such as earthquakes, volcanic eruptions, mudslides) and those due to severe weather (such as droughts, floods, storms, heat-waves).[218] There is no reason to believe that geological events are occur-ring at a different rate now from that in the recent, pre-human past. But there is no doubt that climatic changes are occurring more rapidly than the earth has experienced since human beings first walked on this planet, and that the global temperature is now higher than it has been since long before humans were present. The fact of global warming is unequivocal (see Chapters 2, 3 and 5).[219] The main cause of global warming is very likely (that is, more than 90 per cent certain) to be human activity, and in particular the burning of fossil fuels – coal, oil and gas – and changes in land use. The consequences of global warming are likely to be rapid changes in weather patterns to which static human populations may be unable to respond quickly, since people are often tied to particular regions by national, political or ethnic boundaries. This will probably lead to increased suffering and mortality from extremes of weather including droughts, floods and heatwaves, from shortage of clean water, and from increased suscepti-bility to disease.[220] Statistics for the past 50 years, excluding mega-disasters where more than 10,000 people perished, show that the underlying trend of the global rate of deaths from climatic effects is increasing even faster than the global rate of population growth.[221]

Volcanic eruptions

Though volcanic eruptions are spectacular and often highly visible phenomena, they are actually much less dangerous than most other natural phenomena, including the weather. This is because there are almost always warnings before a major eruption on land. Modern monitoring systems can detect molten rock moving towards the surface before it actually erupts, both by the seismic signals it creates and by deformation of the surface above it. This usually allows time to evacuate people. Even in earlier historical times, there are many instances of people leaving the danger zone before a major eruption. This was the case for one of the biggest known historic eruptions, that of the Aegean volcano of Santorini in 1628 BC. Santorini blasted 60 cubic kilometres of rock to heights of more than 35 kilometres, equivalent to removing to a depth of 40 metres (130 feet) across a circle of radius 22 kilometres (14 miles), the whole of Greater London, together with its population of 7.5 million. The Santorini fallout buried the Minoan town of Akrotiri and caused a tsunami that swept through the eastern Mediterranean. It may even have contributed to the famines of Egypt and the surrounding area recorded in the Bible during the time of the patriarch Joseph.[222] Yet Akrotiri and the island of Santorini were apparently evacuated before this major eruption, as witnessed by the fact that all the jewellery and tools had been removed from the houses and the only skeleton found was that of a pig.

There was a less happy outcome from the violent eruption of Mont Pelée in Martinique on Ascension Day 1902, which was the worst volcanic disaster of the twentieth century, killing some 26,000–36,000 people (Figures 7.1 and 7.2). Although there were warnings of the eruption beforehand, with earthquakes and ash falls, the local papers asserted that there was nothing to worry about. The governor's official line was that people should stay because elections were due. In the event he and his wife died, along with all the inhabitants (except two) of Saint-Pierre, the largest city, in the space of just a few minutes when a burning plume of ash at about 1,000°C swept through the city. One of the two survivors, Ludger Sylbaris, was a convict in the deepest cell of the prison with no windows. He was found seriously burned, but still alive, four days later and was given a pardon. He eventually died a natural death in 1929. With more than two weeks' warning of the final cataclysmic eruption, this was a case where many more people could have been evacuated had the

Figure 7.1 Graveyard of Marigot with dense smoke rising from Mont Pelée eruption in 1902. Stereo card was printed by Keystone View Company, Meadville, Pennsylvania, with the caption "'Tis now the very witching time of night: When churchyards yawn, and hell itself breathes out contagion to this world (W. Shakespeare, *Hamlet*, Act 3, sc. II)".

Figure 7.2 Town of Saint Pierre, Martinique after the Mont Pelée eruption, seen from the Morne d'Orange. (Photo from A. Heilprin, *The Eruption of Pelée: A Summary and Discussion of the Phenomena and their Sequels* (printed for The Geographical Society of Philadelphia (Philadelphia: J. B. Lippincott Co., 1908)).)

precursors been heeded – as it was, many individuals ignored official advice and decided for themselves to flee, with steamers crowded with people leaving the island before the eruption.

Deaths from volcanic eruptions are more commonly a secondary effect – for example from lahars (fast-moving mudslides), such as those that buried the town of Armero in Colombia in 1985, killing 20,000 of the 29,000 inhabitants,[223] or from famines that are a result of crop failure or animal deaths, caused by the noxious gases and ash. The Tambora eruption of 1815 threw such a huge amount of ash into the atmosphere that there were spectacular sunsets round the world for three years (sunsets which may have contributed to the striking contemporary watercolours painted by William Turner). The depressed temperatures resulting from the ash and atmospheric haze gave rise to such poor weather that 1816 became known as 'the year without a summer' in the northern hemisphere, and ultimately an estimated 90,000 people died from famine, many of them in Europe, far away from the site of the eruption.

Another example of a famine induced by a volcanic eruption is the infamous Haze famine of the winter of 1773–4, which followed the 1773 eruption of Lakagígar in Iceland. It killed 76 per cent of the horses, 50 per cent of the cows, 79 per cent of the sheep and eventually 25 per cent of the people. Subsequently it was found that fluorine from the volcanic gases had polluted the grass and the animals had died of fluoride poisoning. Yet the initial volcanic eruptions and lava flows had not killed any people.[224] This again was an example where lack of aid from outside was a material factor in the eventual enormous death toll. The fact that there had been a large natural disaster in Iceland was well known in Europe, and indeed Benjamin Franklin, then American ambassador in Paris, lectured and wrote a scientific paper about it in 1784.[225] It is not difficult to find direct contemporary analogies for the failure of rich nations to supply sufficient aid to distant nations facing famine. To this extent a natural event developed, unnecessarily, into a 'natural' disaster.

Earthquakes

Unlike volcanic eruptions, the exact location and timing of big earthquakes cannot be predicted, and there are usually no precursory warnings. So they are much more dangerous than volcanoes. Nevertheless, with 60 years of mapping earthquakes using global seismometer networks, there is now a good understanding of the areas most at risk.

Death tolls from earthquakes can be enormous. In the People's Republic of China, an earthquake in Shaanxi in January 1556 killed about 830,000 people (though numbers are hard to confirm from so long ago), and another in Tangshan in 1976 killed an estimated 650,000 people. Despite our scientific understanding of earthquakes and our technological expertise, the number of deaths they cause has continued to rise dramatically over the past millennium (Figure 7.3). The reason is simple – the number of cities containing more than 5 million people continues to increase as population rises. And many of these large cities are located in seismically active areas (Figure 7.4).[226]

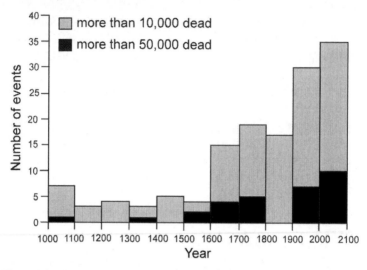

Figure 7.3 Histogram of the number of earthquakes per century killing more than 10,000 or 50,000 people. Current century extrapolated from rate in the decade to 2007. (Data from J. Jackson, *Philosophical Transactions of the Royal Society* (2006) **364**: 1911–25.)

Our understanding of earthquakes is now sufficiently good that, although we can not prevent them happening or predict exactly when and where they will occur, we can take steps to mitigate their effects. The shaking caused by earthquakes is generally well understood, and buildings can be constructed to withstand it without catastrophic failure. It is even possible now to use automatic earthquake detection systems that recognize and locate an earthquake within a few seconds of it happening and then immediately send out automated alarm warnings to areas at risk. Although seismic waves from earthquakes travel at several thousand metres per second, the warnings can be sent electronically at the speed of light (300 million metres per second), thus in many cases giving a vital few seconds or tens of seconds warning of the impending arrival of the seismic waves – this is sufficient for a prepared population to take cover under reinforced furniture, or to run away from buildings. Such warning systems are already in place in California and Japan.

Most earthquake fatalities are from collapsing buildings. So failure to build properly is a major contributor to the death toll. A poignant

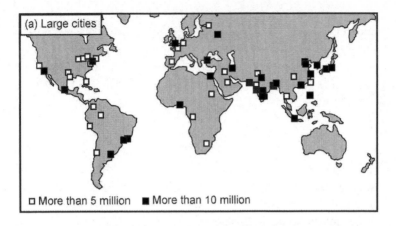

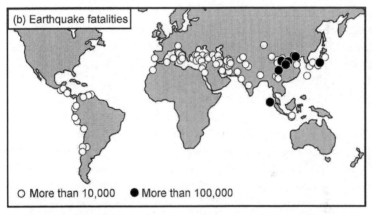

Figure 7.4 (a) Cities with more than 5 million or 10 million population. (b) Earthquakes of the past 1,000 years known to have killed more than 10,000 or 100,000 people. There are 115 earthquakes in this figure, many of their symbols overlying each other. (Data from J. Jackson, *Philosophical Transactions of the Royal Society* (2006) **364**: 1911–25.)

example is a magnitude 6.9 earthquake that caused at least 25,000 deaths on 7 December 1988 in the Spitak region of Armenia. Most people died as a result of the collapse of poorly built apartments and other buildings constructed during the premiership of Leonid Brezhnev. Less than a year later, on 18 October 1989, an earthquake of identical size in Loma Prieta, California, USA, killed only 57 people, most of whom were trapped in their cars beneath a collapsed bridge due shortly to be strengthened against earthquake failure. In other earthquake disasters, adequate building codes were in place, but builders had cut corners for selfish gain to save money during construction, and the inhabitants paid the price when those buildings collapsed. Such was the case in the 1999 magnitude 7.6 earthquake in Izmit, Turkey, when an estimated 17,000–40,000 people died in collapsed buildings and half a million were left homeless.

Floods

It is often not realized that floods are the most devastating natural disasters, having an effect on more people than do all other causes combined. For example, on 13 November 1970 over half a million people died in floods in Bangladesh. More recently, in May 2008, an estimated 130,000 people died and 2.4 million people were affected when the Irrawaddy delta in Burma was inundated during a tropical storm. In 1887 (when population densities were much lower), floods on the Yellow River in China left an estimated 0.9–2.0 million people dead, while in 1931 more floods in the same area caused 1.0–3.7 million fatalities. By 2025 it is estimated that half the world's population will be at risk from storms. Today 100 million people, mostly with low incomes, live within 1 metre of mean high sea level. It is they who will lose their homes and their livelihoods, maybe even their lives, when the sea level rises as a result of global climate change.

Floods disproportionately affect low-income countries and their people. In Britain we can build the Thames Barrier higher and the Dutch can enhance their sea defences to keep out rising sea levels; but people living in a deltaic region in Bangladesh simply do not have that option. So there is a clear moral issue here: rising sea levels are caused by global climate change resulting from the burning of fossil fuels in high-income countries. But people in high-income countries are not usually the ones who suffer the worst consequences – the people most affected played little part in causing the problem in the first place, and have the least resources to cope with it.

The way in which floods most severely affect poor people is, however, also apparent when disaster strikes high-income, technologically advanced nations. In the floods following the breach of the levees in New Orleans as a result of Hurricane Katrina in 2005, more than 1,000 people lost their lives – they were disproportionately the infirm and the poor who had no cars and could not leave the city as the storm approached.[227] And loss of life is not the only consequence of such a disaster. For many of the poorest who lost their houses and were resettled elsewhere, that one night caused long-term and often permanent disruption of family and community ties, of the relational social fabric on which their lives had centred. Despite our technologically rich world, the poor remain vulnerable.

Heatwaves

In summer 2003 a heatwave in Europe caused at least 20,000 additional deaths.[228] It was mostly the very young and the very old who died – and almost all the deaths could have been prevented by prompt medical care. But it happened to be August, and many doctors and nurses were on holiday. In the same year in Andhra Pradesh, India, there were 27 consecutive days above 46°C, which claimed over 1,600 lives. A similar disaster occurred in Chicago, USA, in July 1995, when an estimated 600 additional deaths, again mainly among the very old, occurred over a five-day spell of unusually hot weather. The deaths were from reasons as mundane as old people being scared to open windows for fear of crime, or not being able to afford to run air conditioning.

An increase in average global temperature and an increase in weather extremes are both consequences of human-induced (anthropogenic) climate change. The 2003 summer temperature in Europe is likely to be regarded as 'normal' by 2050 and cool by 2100 if we continue our present level of production of GHGs. So the occurrence of the heatwaves and the inability to deal with the consequences both have human factors that led to these disasters.

Famines

Famines have caused an estimated 70 million deaths during the twentieth century alone. They are also one of the disasters most readily averted by intervention from others who have food and resources available. There are numerous examples throughout recorded history of the exacerbation or even the causation of mass starvation by government actions, such as the 3.5 million deaths in Bengal in 1943, which were at least in part the result of well-meaning but inappropriate government policies, with peak death rates occurring at a time when rice yields had actually increased.[229] Other examples are the 3–5 million fatalities in the Ukraine famine of 1932–3, which, it has been argued,[230] resulted from Joseph Stalin's rural collectivization policies, and the estimated 20–40 million excess deaths in China during 1958–61 as a result of Mao Tse-tung's attempts to modernize the economy in the 'Great Leap Forward'.

In contrast, there are also many examples of the prevention of famine by appropriate preparations, starting with the biblical report from the region around Egypt early in the second millennium BC when Joseph, acting as Pharaoh's steward, laid up grain reserves during the years of plenty and was able to distribute them during the succeeding years of famine (Genesis 41:53–56). Indeed, that can be seen as God's providence because Joseph was only in a position to do this because his brothers had tried to get rid of him many years earlier – and as Joseph pointed out to them when they came pleading for aid, 'Even though you intended to do harm to me, God intended it for good, in order to preserve a numerous people, as he is doing today' (Genesis 50:20).

In recent decades the number of deaths from famines has decreased, at least in part as the global news media have brought the plight of the starving into the living-rooms of people in high-income countries, prompting widespread giving for aid. Nevertheless, it is still a shocking statistic that as recently as 1984 nearly a million people died of famine in Ethiopia. Famine remains a culprit in over 6 million deaths annually of children under 5 years old, with over 850 million people, or 16 per cent of the world's population, being undernourished in 2001–3.[231] It may come as no surprise that the regions most vulnerable to famine coincide almost exactly with the regions where global climate change is predicted to cause the most extreme variations in climate: so the 30 per cent of the population in sub-Saharan Africa who are at present undernourished live in precisely those areas that in the coming years and decades will be most prone to crop failure as a result, ultimately, of human influence on climate.

Cultural and religious views often play a large part in the policies, or lack of them, put in place to prevent or to deal with famines. For example, the missionary Timothy Richard, who was present in China during the great famine of 1876–9 that killed an estimated 9.5 to 13 million Chinese, saw the intellectual literary traditions of Confucianism as part of the problem. He considered that 'the Christian religion, education, science and invention and investigation ... [and] better means of communication and distribution' would lead to 'the relief of the poor from starvation'.[232] He was also instrumental in one of the first great appeals for overseas aid by the China Relief Fund, from which I show an illustration in Figure 7.5.

BODIES LIE DEAD ON THE ROAD, AND THE LIVING STRIVE
TOGETHER FOR THEIR FLESH.

Figure 7.5 Picture from *The Famine in China* (1878). The original text read 'The dead died because they could get no food, and the living seek now to prolong their lives by eating the dead. Would you have them die rather? What will not famine compel men to do?' (From Committee of the China Famine Relief Fund, *The Famine in China* (C. Kegan Paul and Co., London, 1878).)

115

However, Christian nations didn't necessarily do any better than the Chinese. During the Great Potato Famine of 1845–55 in Ireland, about 1 million people died and another 2 million were forced to emigrate. The Whig minister Sir Charles Trevelyan described the famine as 'a direct stroke of an all-wise and all-merciful Providence', which, he wrote in 1848, laid bare 'the deep and inveterate root of social evil' in Ireland. He considered that the famine was 'the sharp but effectual remedy by which the cure is likely to be effected . . . God grant that the generation to which this great opportunity has been offered may rightly perform its part.'[233] As a consequence of this sort of thinking, the government did nothing to restrain the mass evictions that accompanied the famine. Trevelyan's attitude exemplified the notion that the suffering of the Irish was a direct result of their sinful behaviour, and underpinned the lack of serious action in responding to it. As I discuss in the next section, the notion that individual suffering is always a direct result of an identifiable sin does not appear to be in accord with the thrust of scripture. Nor does the muted response to the Irish famine appear to embody the Christian imperative to take action to offer succour to those in need and to seek to implement changes through society, politics and technology that prevent or at least minimize the impact of such disasters.

Why does God allow suffering?

It is not possible to discuss natural disasters without acknowledging the problem they raise of the suffering of apparently innocent people. The conundrum of how an all-powerful, all-loving God can allow or, worse, can cause such suffering is a central issue that has occupied much Christian thinking for two millennia. There is not space here to survey the wide range of Christian responses, so instead I offer some brief personal reflections.

First, it is important to remember that what we call 'nature' is not a force separate from God. Nature is one of the ways God works in this world. And earthquakes, volcanoes, storms and floods have occurred on this planet since long before humans first walked on it. Indeed, as discussed earlier, if it were not for these 'natural' phenomena, this world would not be the fertile, fruitful habitat that allows all life, including humans, to flourish. They are part of the very fabric of creation. But it is also clear that often it is the greed and selfishness of human beings, or more generally our failure to be good stewards of God's creation, that has exacerbated the number of deaths and the degree of suffering from these natural phenomena (see Chapters 8, 9 and 12). In the example given earlier of two similar-sized earthquakes hitting cities in California and Armenia, the death toll in the former was less than 0.025 per cent of that in the latter, almost entirely as a result of the way buildings had been constructed. The Armenian death toll from the earthquake was an avoidable disaster for which the blame can be laid on human shoulders. Similar analyses can be made of almost all other natural disasters.

However, this is not an entirely satisfactory answer to the problem of suffering because most of the people who died when the buildings collapsed had not themselves been responsible for the shoddy building, and probably had no realistic alternative places in which to live. Furthermore, although human failings, deliberate or otherwise, contribute in large part to the scale of suffering and death in disasters, it remains the case that some suffering and death still occur even when all practical precautions have been taken to minimize them. We cannot give tidy reasons that will completely satisfy our desire to understand why any particular person suffers.

One thing that is clear from the Bible is that we should not infer that there is always a direct link between the suffering a person experiences as a result of a disaster and their own sin. That much is made clear in the Old Testament story of Job (Job 1:16–18). Though Job was a righteous man, he suffered terribly, losing his wealth, his health and his family. He lost his sheep to one natural disaster, and his seven sons and three daughters were all killed in another when a freak wind blew down the house in which they were living. His three friends Eliphaz, Bildad and Zophar thought of all sorts of things Job might have done to make him responsible for his own misfortunes. They were not true, it did not help Job at all, and finally, when Job was restored, God had nothing good to say about those unhelpful friends who thought they knew all the answers. But neither does God give Job nor us a philosophically complete and tidied-up account of the mystery of suffering and evil. Rather, he commends Job, who had endured his suffering and maintained his trust in God despite his doubts and confusion, and reminds us forcefully and in beautiful imagery in Job 38—41 of his own power and fruitfulness in creation, of his sovereignty over all that he created, and of his ultimate power over evil.[234]

The Bible does suggest, however, that suffering in the world is ultimately the result of humankind's disobedience to God the creator. The Apostle Paul reminds his readers that God, in his sovereign rule, allows people to make the choice of rejecting their creator God's rightful call on their obedience and allegiance, and hands them over to the consequences: a broken world, where suffering often seems severe and arbitrary, and where the wicked prosper at the expense of others (Romans 1:28). This combination of the free-will choices that God allows people to make with a structural sinfulness in the way humans order and rule their societies can go far to explain the majority of deaths and suffering that are caused by disasters, and especially their disproportionate impact on the poor and disenfranchised.[235]

The biggest disaster, the Bible says, is not physical death itself, since that is what everyone in this world should expect, but the eternal disaster of dying alienated from God. The very brokenness of this world, including the disasters that are such a recurrent feature of it, act as a reminder of the broken relationship between the creator God and the people he created. Jesus made a similar point, reported in Luke 13:4–5, when commenting on the contemporary disaster at Siloam that killed 18 people when a building collapsed on them. The only ultimate answer to the suffering that humankind experiences is the fact that God himself has taken decisive action to deal with evil through the life, death and resurrection of Jesus. The suffering Christ on the cross is the basis for the hope that is embodied both in Christ's victory over death and the promise of the new creation where there will be no more death or mourning or crying or pain (Revelation 21:4; and see Chapters 16 and 17).

Some biblical principles

In this section I suggest four principles for how we ought to interact with the environment that follow from a Christian perspective governing the relationship between God, his people and the created order.

God cares for his creation; so we should

The universe was created by God. He shows his commitment to the material world by becoming incarnate within it (John 1:14; Hebrews

1:3; Colossians 1:16–17). God glories in his creation, and his creation in turn reflects something of his glory and character. 'The heavens are telling the glory of God' says the psalmist (Psalm 19:1), and the Apostle Paul comments that God's invisible qualities can be clearly seen from what has been made (Romans 1:20). The volcanic eruptions, earthquakes and seasonal weather cycles are all part of the material creation made and upheld by God. Neglect, abuse and despoliation of the world damage something that is precious to God and also are an indirect, sometimes a direct, cause of much of the death and suffering that people endure.

God commands humankind to care for his creation; so we should

God's first command to humankind was that we have a responsibility to care for his creation (Genesis 1:28, 2:15). This suggests that people are to work at ruling and ordering creation as good stewards, without abusing it for their own selfish ends. By caring for the earth properly, it is enabled to be fruitful and to play its intended role in giving glory to God. Since we are people made in God's image (Genesis 1:27), human beings are given the privilege of carrying out the mandate of delegated dominion in a way that reflects the character and values of God's loving and compassionate kingship (see Chapter 13). It is in part the failure of humankind to show proper and consistent care for creation that often allows natural phenomena to develop into catastrophic disasters.

Our care for our neighbour is an expression of our love

Those who live in high-income nations including Europe, North America and Australia, with high standards of living achieved partly through the selfish and unsustainable use of natural resources, have a particular responsibility to care for others affected by global climate change. As already discussed, global climate change is a major factor in exacerbating many disasters, including floods, heatwaves, droughts and famines. Christians should care for our unborn successors and for the stranger and the foreigner (Leviticus 19:33–34; Jeremiah 22:3; Matthew 25:35–45) even if they live out of sight on the other side of the world but are affected by our actions.

The promise of a new creation gives hope for the future

One day the cosmos will be renewed and re-created in the 'new heavens and new earth', to which both the Old and New Testaments look forward (Isaiah 65; Revelation 21; and see Chapters 16 and 17). That will bring the fullness of life that God intended for his creation: a place where God will dwell with his people, and where both they and the whole of creation will give him glory. Scripture speaks of both the discontinuity and the continuity of the new creation: passages such as 2 Peter 3:10–13 highlight the need for God's judgement and the radical newness of the new creation, while others such as Romans 8:19–22 are reminders that it remains fundamentally the same creation in which we now live that finds its freedom and fulfilment in future redemption. Since there will be no more death in the new creation, never again will natural processes turn into disasters. They will instead form part of the beauty and creativity of God's created order.

C. S. Lewis commented that 'the Christians who did most for the present world were just those who thought most of the next ... Aim at Heaven and you will get earth "thrown in": aim at earth and you will get neither'.[236] We ought to do all in our power to alleviate the sometimes disastrous impact of natural phenomena on human populations. This includes looking to ways in which our own unsustainable patterns of consumption may exacerbate problems such as global climate change, as well as seeking through scientific, technological, educational and aid channels to mitigate their impact or to help adaptation to the natural environment in which people have to live (see Box 7.1). That is the practical outworking of Jesus' command to love the Lord our God and to love our neighbour as ourselves (Luke 10:27).

Box 7.1 Practical responses to natural disasters

- When disasters happen, reach out with humanitarian aid and compassion. That is a practical way of showing love for one's neighbour, even if they happen to live on the other side of the world.
- Before disaster strikes, support can be provided through education, through prayer and giving to agencies such as Tearfund that aim to bring practical assistance alongside the gospel to help people adapt to changing circumstances and the lack of things we take for granted.
- Consider carefully our own use of resources, and how that affects others.*
- Work for social justice, for a fairer use of this world's resources. One way to do so is through lobbying our government and our elected representatives over issues such as debt relief for poorer countries, the removal of unfair trade tariffs, the implementation of ethical purchasing and investment policies, provision of medical aid and drugs, and of taking seriously our responsibilities for mitigating climate change and famine.
- Assist vulnerable communities to prepare for disasters through implementation of appropriate building codes for earthquake protection, building flood defences, typhoon and tsunami shelters, and to adapt to changing circumstances, for example by developing drought-resistant crops and planting trees to contain floods.
- Ensure that provision is in place for rapid response teams to assist when disaster does strike, and be alert to the threat of developing catastrophes such as drought, disease epidemics and famine so that aid can be provided before it is too late.

*A number of suggestions for practical responses at individual, community, national and international levels is discussed in N. Spencer and R. White, *Christianity, Climate Change and Sustainable Living* (London: SPCK, 2007).

8

Just food: a biblical perspective on culture and agriculture

ELLEN F. DAVIS

However much we might think of ourselves as post-agricultural
beings or disembodied minds, the fact of that matter is that we
are inextricably tied to the land through our bodies – we have to
eat, drink, and breathe – and so our culture must always be sym-
pathetic to the responsibilities of agriculture. If we despise the
latter, we are surely only a step away from despising the former
too.

(Norman Wirzba, *The Essential Agrarian Reader* (2003), 5)

Eating is the most basic and essential of all cultural acts; every culture
organizes itself to meet that need. A just culture organizes itself to meet
it for everyone, and to do so safely over the long term – as far ahead as
we can imagine. Judged by that criterion, our global industrial culture
is unjust. Hunger is again on the rise worldwide, due largely to failures
of local economies and distribution systems. Even worse, our very ways
of producing food jeopardize long-term food security. According to
the United Nations (UN) Millennium Ecosystem Assessment, industrial agriculture may currently constitute 'the largest threat to biodiversity and ecosystem function of any single human activity'.[237]

We are eating dangerously, and increasingly we know it. On a nearly
daily basis, the news media bring us updates on such 'items' as:

- food riots, with prices for food staples rising worldwide;
- factory farming of animals, with the attendant hazards of meat
  contamination and pollution of air, water and soil;
- destruction of forests for cropland, most dramatically the conversion of a large portion of Brazilian Amazonia to 'Soylandia' (and
  see Chapter 11);[238]

- dead zones numbering in the hundreds or more, produced by agricultural run-off into ocean systems, from China to the Chesapeake Bay in the USA.[239]

If we take in just a fraction of this bad news, it disturbs our sanguinity. A recent poll of the American public revealed that only 15 per cent of that generally well-fed (or over-fed) populace considers their food supply to be safe.[240]

Surprisingly, the Bible speaks to concerns such as these, at least indirectly. In many places, and pervasively in the Old Testament, the biblical writers treat the theological significance of agriculture. If to most people in the pew (or for that matter, in the pulpit) the notion that agriculture has theological significance seems odd or incoherent, that is because contemporary industrialized culture is unique in world history for its failure to draw any connection between food production practices and our relationship with God. That very failure may itself lie at the root of a global food system that, we now see, is uniquely destructive of the created order. Therefore, as we seek a healthy and sustainable relationship with the soil and other natural systems on which all terrestrial life depends, it is wise to ask how the Bible may guide us in understanding that relationship as part of the life of faith.

Serving the soil

Although it is neither an ecological tract nor a farmer's almanac, the Bible consistently represents the care of arable land as a primary religious obligation. The seminal text is Genesis 2, which sums up the origins of humankind and the world as we know it in terms that are distinctly agricultural. It begins with a glance back to a time 'before any field crop had sprouted, because . . . there was no human being (*adam*) to work the soil (*adamah*)' (2:5).[241] The relationship between *adam* and *adamah* is elemental and essential for both, as is evident from the twin actions of God that, by this account, give shape to the world. First, 'The Lord God formed the human being, dust from the soil' (2:7), and, second, 'The Lord God planted a garden in Eden' (2:8).

The human and the arable land are made for each other. *Adamah* is the source of life for *adam*. The English word-play, 'human from humus', serves quite well to express the connection, but the Hebrew is more deeply descriptive. It evokes the particularity of the local landscape. Both *adam* and *adamah* derive from the word *adom*, 'reddish brown'; that is the colour of the thin layer of rich loam, *terra rossa*, which covers the hill country in which the Israelites settled. In the land of the Bible, people and land share a common skin tone; they are intimately related.

Further, care of land is represented as the original human vocation: 'The Lord God took the human being and set him in the garden of Eden to *work* [or, *serve*] it and to *keep* it' (Genesis 2:15). This statement of human vocation is as carefully worded as the preceding statement of human origin, and it suggests to the sensitive (Hebrew) reader that care of arable land is a distinctly religious vocation. The crucial point is that both the key verbs – 'work/serve' (*avad*) and 'keep' (*shamar*) – occur frequently in the Bible, in many or most cases with reference to human activity that is directed towards God. Thus they have a distinct religious resonance, although that resonance is much muted in the standard English translation, 'to till it and keep it'. 'Till' is an unambiguously horticultural or agricultural term, but the Hebrew verb *avad* refers in only a few instances (out of several hundred occurrences) to working the soil (Genesis 2:5, 3:23, 4:2 and 12). Generally it means to *work for* or *serve* a person or, by extension, to *serve* or *worship* God. The Bible unequivocally forbids humans to worship any creature, including the fertile earth, but nonetheless the religious resonance of the verb *avad* has some bearing here: humans are meant to serve God by working and serving the garden that God has planted.

The second verb, *shamar* ('keep'), reinforces the suggestion that the human vocation to the soil has a specifically religious dimension. *Shamar* occurs hundreds of times, most often with reference to 'observing' the ordinances of God (Leviticus 25:18), 'keeping' God's sabbaths (Exodus 31:16) – that is, to acting in accordance with the divine ordering of the world. Thus the whole statement of human vocation might well be translated: 'And the Lord God set the human being in the Garden of Eden to serve it and to *observe* it' and, equally, 'to *preserve* it'. Like Sabbath and the divine ordinances, the fertile earth is part of the fundamental ordering of the world. Its natural systems – which the biblical writers call 'the work of God's hands' – set limits on human action, which must be respected. We may work the soil and take sustenance from it, but only on the condition that we observe its special character and safeguard by our actions the soil from which comes all life, our own included.

As Israel understands it, then, humanity's service to God is grounded in service to the soil. Therefore, Israel's worship – its service to God in the narrower sense – is legitimate only when this essential grounding is remembered and enacted. The prescriptions for formal worship and daily religious practice, detailed in the four books of Torah that follow the foundational stories of Genesis (Exodus, Leviticus, Numbers and Deuteronomy), provide the basic framework for Israel's service to God through care for the fertile soil. A key instance is the offering of the first-fruits, incumbent upon each Israelite farmer – which is to say, nearly everyone – each year. The presentation of the basket of produce to the priest is accompanied by a confession of faith and self-obligation: 'I declare today to the Lord your God that I have come into the land that the Lord swore to our ancestors to give us' (Deuteronomy 26:3). The word 'give' echoes throughout the passage (vv. 1, 2, 3, 9, 10, 11), and always the subject is God. Dwelling in the land means accepting it fundamentally as gift, with grateful recognition that the fruits of the land are in truth the work of God's hands, and only secondarily our own. That understanding reveals the theological significance of the detailed prescriptions in Torah about the tending of arable land and fruit trees (for example, Leviticus 19:23; Deuteronomy 20:19), about protecting farm animals from injury and exhaustion (for example, Exodus 20:10, 21:33–36) and preserving the wild bird populations (Deuteronomy 22:6–7), and also about ensuring that the landless poor have a livable share in the fruits of the earth that God provides (for example, Deuteronomy 24:19–22).

An especially suggestive symbol of the connection between Israel's agricultural practice and its religious life is the altars of earth (*adamah*) or unhewn stones that the Israelites are commanded to construct when they enter the promised land of Canaan. Such altars were a mark of Israel's religious distinctiveness, for ancient Near Eastern temples normally had altars of dressed stone. The importance accorded to this instruction is indicated by the fact that it is placed immediately after the climactic moment of Torah, the giving of the Ten Commandments. Further, the prescription for the altar is framed as a recapitulation of the chief of the Commandments, the prohibition on idol worship:

> You shall not make alongside me gods of silver and gods of gold, you shall not make for yourselves; an altar of earth you shall make for me and offer sacrifices upon it . . . And if you do make

for me an altar of stone, you shall not build with dressed stones. For if you have wielded your tools over it, then you have profaned it. (Exodus 20:23–25)

The charge to worship God on an earthen altar is a call to *humility*, in the literal sense of that word, which derives from the same Latin root as *humus*. It is a call to a grounded life. The prohibition on stones dressed with metal tools, the advanced technology of the Iron Age, is an implicit reminder that technological innovations, though necessary for human thriving, should not be presumed innocent. Worshipping God, and not idols of our own making, entails a realistic acceptance of the limits that the earth itself sets on sustainable interventions into natural systems.

The altar of unhewn stones is a guiding symbol for Wes Jackson's project of Natural Systems Agriculture. A plant geneticist and agriculturalist, Jackson is working to develop agriculture that works like an ecosystem and is viable on a commercial scale. He and his colleagues at the Land Institute in Salina, Kansas, USA, are challenging the dominant model for agriculture as it has been practised for over 10,000 years: reliance on annual grain crops, grown in monoculture, which deplete the soil and leave it vulnerable to erosion. Their model mimics the natural growth of the tall-grass prairie, with perennial food grains grown in polyculture. This is in one sense high-tech farming: current knowledge of genomes allows these scientists to use innovative methods such as wide hybridization between annuals and perennials, and marker-assisted selection.[242] But it is science and technology disciplined by humility. That is to say, new technologies are applied in accordance with the recognition that our ignorance of how nature works vastly exceeds our knowledge; we have only hurt ourselves by trying to bully nature into doing our will. Now the only safe way forward is to learn from nature, accepting it as mentor and measure, and to work willingly and creatively within the constraints it imposes.[243]

The agrarian culture of the Bible

As the Bible tells the story of human origins and culture, there was no moment when we could obtain our food safely without observing limits. Even in Eden, God sets a limit: 'From the tree of knowledge of good and evil you shall not eat, for on the day you eat from it you shall surely die' (Genesis 2:17). Although the man and woman do not die on the day they eat beyond the limit God has set, they do 'fall' away from the possibility of growing and learning in harmony with God, each other and the non-human world, which seems to have been God's hope for them in Eden. As the biblical story implies, the limits most essential for our survival are determined by a finite reality whose full dimensions elude our comprehension and do not necessarily meet with our approval.

Modern industrial culture is unprecedented for the extent to which it has ignored or deliberately flouted the limits of a finite world. It will surely have no successor in this respect; too many resources have already been spoiled or consumed. Of all human industries, agriculture is the largest and most indispensable.[244] For 10,000 years or more, it has also been the arena for the most intense and consequential interaction between human beings and the larger created order. Not surprisingly, therefore, the most probing and imaginative critique of industrialism as we now know it comes from the perspective known as 'agrarianism'. The core agrarian insight is that healthy land and healthy human communities are inseparable phenomena, as any sustainable culture must recognize. Contemporary agrarianism, therefore, counters industrial culture precisely as a way of thinking and living based, not on money, but on the permanent wealth of fertile soil, clean water and air, and other material sources of life. Agrarianism is a set of commitments – personal, philosophical, economic and religious – and fundamental to them all is the conviction that everyone must have a livable share in the real wealth that is built into the created order. In order to preserve that wealth in perpetuity – to 'keep' the garden – humans must now choose to live (as do all other species perforce) within the limits of our particular time and place on earth.

The necessity and goodness of living within sustainable limits is a recurrent theme in the essays, poetry and fiction of Wendell Berry. Produced over more than 40 years, Berry's writings are the most influential body of agrarian literature in the modern era. Recently, he observed the beginning of a shift away from 'the doctrine of limitlessness', as our culture comes at last to the realization that 'we are not likely to be granted another world to plunder in compensation for our pillage of this one'. Berry offers encouragement to those who have abandoned the fantasy that propelled industrialism through the twentieth century, namely that any damage done by inappropriate uses of technology could be cured by more technology. More genuinely hopeful is our dawning self-recognition 'as limited creatures in a limited world', for

> it returns us to our real condition and our human heritage . . . Every cultural and religious tradition I know about, while fully acknowledging our animal nature, defines us specifically as *humans* – that is, as animals . . . capable of living not only within natural limits but also within cultural limits, self-imposed. As earthly creatures, we live, because we must, within natural limits, which we may describe as 'earth' or 'ecosystem' or 'watershed' or 'place'. But as humans, we may elect to respond to this necessary placement by the self-restraints implied in neighborliness, stewardship, thrift, temperance, generosity, care, kindness, friendship, loyalty, and love.[245]

Agrarianism is an ancient mindset. Indeed, ancient Israel's scriptures may well include the oldest agrarian literature in the world, as I shall discuss below, and they are altogether the richest body of agrarian literature in existence. Throughout, the Old Testament represents the condition of the land as the best index of the health of the relationship between God and humanity, or Israel in particular. When humans are obedient to God, the land flourishes and 'yields its increase' (Psalm 85:12; Hebrews 13). When they turn away, the land loses its fertility, and people may lose their land as the penalty for sin. From an agrarian perspective, there is nothing arbitrary about the fact that the disobedience in the garden is followed immediately by the cursing of the soil, which then sprouts 'thorns and briars' – that unproductive growth which, in the Mediterranean landscape, is a sure sign of eroded and desiccated land. Because human beings, God and land are bound together in a threefold relationship that the Bible terms 'covenant' (see Chapters 12 and 13),[246] distortion in one aspect of the relationship necessarily deforms the whole.

A fragile land

Several of the contemporary agrarian writers look to biblical images and stories to guide their search for healing in our own distorted relationship with the land.[247] Their instinct is right: in many places the

Bible offers ways of viewing the human relationship with arable land that seem surprisingly apt to our situation. Yet it is fair to ask, is this more than fortuitous? Can there be any real points of cultural similarity between ancient Israel and contemporary society, such that we can and should rely on scriptural insights as we face the crisis of modern agriculture? Or to put the question in more historical terms, what is the source of the biblical writers' agrarian sensitivity? As Wes Jackson, President of the Land Institute, once put it to me, 'How come they always get it so right?'

It is not enough to answer that most ancient Israelites were farmers, for that in itself does not distinguish Israelites greatly from their neighbours in Egypt or Mesopotamia, the great agricultural empires that dominated the cultural horizons for centuries. Those empires produced literature in abundance, yet on the whole it lacks the keen sensitivity to matters of land care that pervades Israel's scriptures. A more adequate answer is that Israelites acquired their agrarian insight by the grace of God and from the particular place they occupied: a small and exceedingly fragile land that is only marginal for farming. Mesopotamia and Egypt developed elaborate irrigation systems, but Israelite agriculture was rain-fed – and three or four years out of ten are drought years in that semi-arid land.[248] Moreover, with steep slopes and small valleys, and a thin layer of topsoil easily eroded by the strong winter winds and rain, the uplands of Canaan (later the sibling kingdoms of Israel and Judah) allowed little or no margin for bad farming.

Although Mesopotamian soil suffered permanent and, in some areas, drastic salinization from over-irrigation, the full effects of that damage were evident only after centuries of abuse. By contrast, the small plot of an Israelite farm family could easily be ruined within a generation or two, if carelessly treated. This is the scenario envisioned by the sage of Proverbs:

> I passed by the field of an indolent person,
> > and by the vineyard of one lacking sense.
> And here, all of it was overgrown with nettles,
> > its face covered with weeds
> > and its stone fence wrecked.
> I saw it myself and took it to heart,
> > I looked and took it as a lesson:

A little sleep, a little napping,
   a little folding the hands to rest –
and your poverty comes prowling,
   and your want, like an armed man.
             (Proverbs 24:30–34)

From the fragile ecological niche they occupied, Israelites learned the necessity of observing limits. In order to leave an inheritance for which their children would bless them, farmers had to serve their own small plot of land well, to be vigilant in guarding its fertility. This was a family obligation and, at the same time, a religious obligation, for Israelites understood that God, too, was invested in the health of their land. The greatest biblical preacher of land care is Moses in Deuteronomy. The book presents Moses' peroration, delivered in the wilderness, just at the edge of the promised land of Canaan. There he draws the contrast between the flat, Nile-watered land of Egypt – a farmer's dream – and the more challenging landscape the Israelites now face: 'But the land (*eretz*) that you are passing over [the Jordan] to possess is a land of hills and valleys; by the rain from the sky it drinks water. It is a land over which God keeps watch; always the eyes of the Lord your God are upon it, from the first of the year to the end of the year' (Deuteronomy 11:11–12). That is a brilliant piece of agrarian rhetoric, an oblique but powerful exhortation to land care. Thus the hearers – Israelites and all subsequent readers of the Bible – are encouraged to regard their precious and vulnerable place on earth as God does, and respond to it with gratitude, affection and wise use (Figure 8.1).

If the agrarian sensibility of the Bible is instructive for us, that is *not* because a return to Iron Age agriculture is a viable alternative to the currently dominant practices of 'catastrophic agriculture'.[249] Rather, its peculiar relevance to our present situation is that the whole world is now vulnerable and intolerant of neglect; it requires work and service, as did the land the Israelites knew. The Hebrew word *eretz*, so frequent in Moses' speeches in Deuteronomy, denotes both a particular land and (elsewhere in the Bible) the earth in its entirety. Therefore, by legitimate extension, we might hear Moses saying to us that God keeps watch over planet earth and expects us to join in the vigil.

Some 70 years ago, American soil conservationist Walter Clay Lowdermilk drew such a connection between the fragility of the land of the Bible and the vulnerability of the whole earth. Moved by the soil

Figure 8.1 This original papercut by Diane Palley illustrates verses found near the end of the Torah, in Deuteronomy 30. The central image, The Tree of Life, refers to the famous words, 'I have put before you life and death, blessing and curse. Therefore, choose life' and emphasizes the Jewish tradition of valuing and celebrating life itself. (Copyright © 2007 Diane Palley.)

degradation he witnessed on a visit to Palestine, he formulated the so-called Eleventh Commandment:

> Thou shalt inherit the holy earth as a faithful steward, conserving its resources and productivity from generation to generation. Thou shalt safeguard thy fields from soil erosion, thy living waters from drying up, thy forests from desolation, and protect thy hills from overgrazing by the herds, that thy descendants may have abundance for ever. If any shall fail in this stewardship of the land thy fruitful fields shall become sterile stony ground and wasting gullies, and thy descendants shall decrease and live in poverty or perish from off the face of the earth.[250]

The Eleventh Commandment reflects the particular features of the land of the Bible and the damage that resulted largely from centuries of economic exploitation of the rural population, first by Israelite kings and then by colonial powers, ancient and modern. Nonetheless, his Commandment addresses people everywhere. Coming to Palestine in the wake of the American dust bowl, Lowdermilk 'read' the land of Israel in a way congruent with the larger meaning of Israel's scriptures. In its particular sanctity, the holy land of Israel/Palestine epitomizes the sanctity of the whole earth, and likewise its vulnerability to abuse.

The prophetic witness

The fact that the Old Testament bespeaks an agrarian sensibility does not mean that the culture of ancient Israel was friendly to farmers. Much more likely, the very opposite was the case, for Exodus, Leviticus and Deuteronomy all include detailed legal stipulations that aim to contain the linked evils of indenture, debt slavery and land loss (see Exodus 21:2–11; Leviticus 25:13–35; Deuteronomy 15:1–18). Thus the Bible attests obliquely to the fact that, like most economically and stratified societies throughout history (including the modern industrialized world), Israel was plagued by persistent problems of rural poverty and injustice. Exorbitant taxes kept many farmers deep in debt. So they sold their sons and daughters into servitude and put up their small landholdings as collateral for their debts – the heritage that was meant to belong to every Israelite family in perpetuity. When they had forfeited their land, heads of family sold themselves in order to feed what was left of the household.

Earliest Israel (twelfth century BC) seems to have been a more or less egalitarian society of small farmers. The Bible upholds the original, decentralized agricultural economy as divinely ordained; the book of Joshua sets forth the system of tribal and clan allotments that was meant to guarantee each family permanent access to the means of subsistence. Micah, one of the earliest of the prophets, articulates that ideal: 'And everyone shall sit under his own vine and fig tree, and no one shall terrify [them]' (Micah 4:4). But in fact, by Micah's time (the eighth century BC), the decentralized economy was more an ideal than a current reality. Agriculture in Israel and Judah was largely a state-controlled operation. Agents of the crown (including priests at state sanctuaries) extracted wealth from the people and their land in the form of exportable commodities – grain, wine and oil – and meat for the feasts of the powerful, while farmers sold their bodies and those of their children to stay alive.

It is against this social background that the prophetic movement seems to have gained a firm hold on Israel's religious imagination.

Downtrodden farmers are the poor of whom Amos speaks in this oracle of doom, addressed to the king's agents:

> Therefore, because you trample upon the poor and exact from them the grain tax – though you have built houses of dressed stone, you shall not live in them; you have planted delightful vineyards, but you shall not drink their wine. (Amos 5:11)

Amos (himself a farmer or herdsman) was a true agrarian, as were his near-contemporaries, Hosea, Micah and Isaiah (see Chapter 12). Like the modern agrarian writers, these ancient prophets spoke into the teeth of an exploitative agricultural economy, one that they recognized to be destructive to human communities and the land itself. Further, they perceived that those who set themselves against God's generous provision for all finally guarantee their own demise and the collapse of the devouring economy. Hosea (5:7) fiercely warns: 'A single month will devour them, along with their portion of land.'

The agrarian sensitivity of the biblical prophets may help us to face the gravity of our own situation. There are obvious differences, of course, between the crown-controlled agriculture of Iron Age Israel and the corporation-controlled food system that now dominates our whole planet. Nonetheless, we may find a strange aptness to the prophetic insight that a society which misuses land and abuses those with the skill and passion to care for it stands in fundamental opposition to God. For never in its 10,000-year history has agriculture accomplished such extensive damage to natural systems and human culture as it does now. We are destroying topsoil that is replaceable only in geological time and seed stock that represents the genetic and cultural heritage of millennia. Likewise, we are destroying a way of life on which virtually all human beings depend, even if they never set foot on a farm.

Independent farming constitutes the weakest sector of the industrial economy; workers within the food production system are among the most endangered – physically, economically and legally. Many older farmers and most of the young are bailing out, if they have the choice, but many do not. So, worldwide, farmer suicides are several (or many) times higher than the societal norms. We are losing skilled farmers, just at the time when we most need to be redeveloping an alternative to industrial agriculture as it has been practised. For we have reached the end of an era of cheap oil and of resources that even seem to be expendable. Ready or not, we are reaching 'the end of food' as our current system can deliver it.[251]

Organizing for hope

Every culture is fundamentally characterized by the way it organizes how (and how much) people eat. I have argued that the Bible helps us to judge our dominant food production practices, and thus our global industrial culture, as unjust on that account. Does the Bible also point the way forward – not back into the Iron Age – to new ways of farming and eating that are wise and genuinely hopeful? And, if so, what action can the Church take to promote sustainable agriculture in our larger culture?

Any answer must begin with the observation that, from a biblical perspective, possession, management and care of arable land belong to the vocation of a whole community – indeed, of every community. Land care is an ineluctable vocation that is given by God, and at points it seems nearly coextensive with being human: *adam* formed from *adamah*. Because land care is a function of a healthy community, improper land use leads to the destruction of community. Indeed, it requires such destruction, as is exemplified in the story of Elijah's confrontation with King Ahab over the expropriation of a vineyard belonging to Naboth the Jezreelite (1 Kings 21). The Israelite king builds his vacation palace (not coincidentally) in the heart of the richest agricultural district in the land, and then proceeds to pit the elders of the rural community against one another in order to facilitate his land-grab. At royal instigation, Naboth, the elder who upholds the traditional Israelite system of small family landholdings, is 'legally' murdered by his neighbours.

Israelite farmers suffered for centuries under the centralized agricultural systems instituted by their own rulers and continued under various colonial powers, yet the biblical writers never cease to insist that God intends something else for Israel. Repeatedly in the Old Testament and on into the New, we catch glimpses of another kind of society, characterized by social stability, a non-exploitative economy, and a system of decentralized land care, in which many or most members of the community exercise responsibility. Therefore we should be wary of overspiritualizing Jesus' blessing of the lowly, that they 'shall inherit the earth' (Matthew 5:5). It may be a key to understanding the kind of action the Church should now be taking and endorsing.

Jesus is quoting from Psalm 37, where the phrase 'inherit *eretz*' ('land' or 'earth') appears five times (Psalm 37:9, 11, 22, 29, 34). The psalm is a wisdom teaching for 'righteous' farmers like Naboth, whom 'the wicked . . . seek to kill' (Psalm 37:32). In that context, the repeated assurance should be translated: 'The poor [or, "the vulnerable"] will possess *land.*' When Jesus repeated the promise of the psalm, he was speaking to Galilean peasants pressed hard by the extractive economy of the Roman Empire. Drawing one familiar phrase from a psalm that is replete with agrarian imagery, he evoked for them a vision of a community of good neighbours sustaining itself on the land. 'The righteous' may have little enough, but they share what they have, with the aim that a community that lives wisely and generously on the land they possess may 'live on it for ever' (v. 29).[252]

What should this vision of the poor possessing land, a vision upheld by both Testaments, mean for us today? We might well hear Jesus and the psalmist urging us to claim a share in the agrarian vision and commitment that is now emerging widely, in both rural communities and cities throughout the world. It is essentially a vision of eating and farming in community, and protecting arable land, so that all who eat may share responsibility for how their food is grown and how the land is tended. In both North America and Europe, some of the most hopeful work involves various forms of land trust, or property laws that prohibit development that will permanently change the character of the land and its 'natural uses', thus recrafting the public understanding of what it means to own land. The biblical ideal of small-scale ownership of arable land may in many cases be the best way to preserve its health, while also maximizing its productivity. Worldwide, small diverse farms produce more food per unit area than industrial farms, and by a factor of 200 to 1,000 per cent.[253]

A vision for decentralized agriculture, horticulture and marketing is assuming a variety of concrete shapes and sizes: membership farms (Community Supported Agriculture or CSA, see below), farmers' markets, farming and marketing co-operatives, small urban groceries, urban farms in backyards and on derelict lots. In some cities, such as Detroit, USA, urban farming, begun ad hoc by the poor, is now organized city-wide, with a high level of civic involvement. The general tendency of decentralized farming is towards low use of chemical and petroleum inputs, and local and regional consumption. A high priority is placed on preserving and sharing traditional knowledge, skills and material resources – seed and animal stock, soil and water – within living communities, while also developing new strategies and appropriate technologies to maximize their use. In some cases the scale of change has been large and the rate of change rapid, as with the 'Campesino a Campesino' (farmer to farmer) movement that swept across Mexico and Central America in the 1980s and 1990s, or Cuba's 'cold-turkey' shift to organic farming after the US oil embargo was imposed. In Kerala State, India, land reform policies have been abetted by programmes in education and literacy, health and sanitation, and by peasant associations and laws that protect farm workers even in a very poor economy.[254]

In my own area, and at the other end of the size scale, some churches are starting gardens and finding that they are a magnet for urban children who had no place to go after school and no way to get their fingers in the earth, for youth who previously had no interest in church and no job skills, for older gardeners and farmers whose skills had long been overlooked. At the same time, the North Carolina Council of Churches is working on both public education and agricultural policy, in order to preserve family farms, provide health care and legal services for farm workers, and relieve urban and rural hunger. Even more significant is the observable fact that our local farmers' markets and CSAs are increasing yearly in size, number and diversity of their produce, as more and more consumers embrace decentralized agriculture as a community value and a source of personal health.

Most of these efforts were a response to immediate urgent need; all of them proceed from a recognition that we have been eating foolishly in our global culture, and we must change now, while there are still good choices to be made. Large and small, they are all pieces of a wiser and more just culture of eating. Thus they are part of the fulfilment of Jesus' blessing in our own time, in our dangerous circumstances: 'Blessed are the humble – those who are grounded – for they shall have a livable share in the fertile earth.'

9

Unsustainable agriculture and land use: restoring stewardship for biospheric sustainability

CALVIN B. DeWITT

One out of every three people on earth is in some way affected by land degradation. Latest estimates indicate that nearly 2 billion hectares of land worldwide – an area twice the size of China – are already seriously degraded, some irreversibly. This . . . reduces productivity, disrupts vital ecosystem functions, negatively affects biodiversity and water resources, and increases vulnerability to climate change.

(Food and Agriculture Organization,
Fact Sheet AI559/E (2008), 1)

No longer can we take sustainability of the biosphere and its ecosystems for granted. Humankind has become a major biological and geological force, and is now challenging the very sustainability of the biosphere upon which our and every other living creature's lives depends. Our crisis of changing global climate, worldwide loss of biodiversity, and degradation of land and soils requires that we better understand the biosphere as the system that sustains us and all life and the human institutions that guide and shape our thoughts, actions and enterprise.

Understanding the biosphere and the biospheric economy

The biosphere – the earth-enveloping life-support system upon which we and all living things depend – is dynamically created and sustained by vibrant exchanges, transfers and connections of energy, materials and information. The awe and wonder it generates continues to inspire every human being that takes the time to behold and ponder it; it is a great gift – a gift given and yet not owned by all who receive it. This gift is also a giver of gifts; it gives life through a myriad provisions. While many of these provisions have been appreciated for millennia, others remain to be discovered. They have come to be called 'ecosystem services'. Joined with other provisions – like our star's energetic provision of a broad spectrum of light and our moon's provision of gravitational attraction – ecosystem services help to develop a sense of provenance and providence in the world, and an awesome realization of a dynamic sustaining system of systems that supports and fosters the abundant life of earth.

Ecosystem services, such as those summarized in Figure 9.1 below, are most often dealt with individually; however, each operates not as a soloist but as a vital contributor within a kind of 'biospheric symphony', joining in harmony and intonation with the others. Separable for reasons of study, they are inseparable in performance. Each gains from the dynamic integrity and symphonic gifts of the others, even as each makes its particular contribution. Much as the performance of a symphony cannot be adequately predicted from hearing a single instrument or seeing musical notation, so also the biosphere. Both the biosphere and a symphony display 'emergent properties' not fully predictable by examining its parts or knowing the score.

Emergent properties increase in scope and service at increasingly higher levels in the biosphere. Investigation of the forests, biomes and biosphere finds that ecosystems are nested (like a Russian baboushka doll) within ecosystems. Below the level of ecosystems are still more nested systems such as molecules, atoms and subatomic particles. The beauty of the biosphere – including its social, religious, cultural and financial aspects – emerges from its all-embracing integrity and wholeness. As nested systems within the biosphere stand in relationship to the larger system of which they are part, 'reciprocating systems' relate to others within a particular level. Reciprocating photosynthesis and respiration, for example, use carbon dioxide to assemble carbon skeletons, build cells, tissues and whole organisms, and these, after productively passing through food webs and chains, are disassociated and returned for reassembly. In the biosphere's hierarchy of nested systems, each component satisfies its own needs as well as the needs of the larger system of which it is part. If any system satisfies its own needs but fails to meet the needs of its enveloping system, it is in peril and may also imperil the larger system. It is also imperilled if it serves the needs of its enveloping system at the expense of its own integrity. What this means for agricultural systems is that growing crops and raising live-stock 'without regard to ecological relationships' is not sustainable.[255] Not surprisingly, the living fabric of the biosphere and its all-pervasive and systemic beauty – with its nested and reciprocating systems – makes sustainability and unsustainability difficult and challenging to assess. Even more so when human beings work in discord with its biospheric services.

Physical chemist and social scientist Michael Polanyi helps us to understand these systems and their integrated complexity and variety.[256] He observed that every component system has its internal control, even as it is controlled by the system of which it is part: photosynthesis has its own internal controls, but is also controlled by the chloroplasts. The chloroplast, with its own controls, is controlled by the cell within which it operates, and so on to leaf, plant and biome. This dual-control relationship continues up through tissue, organ, organism, ecosystem, biosphere and solar system levels, and beyond. Each system is constrained from being anything other than what is by being held in concert within the larger enveloping system.

When our impact upon or investigation of things is done without considering the controlling levels above, it is necessarily 'reduced' in scope. This is often done intentionally to allow discovery and study of internal controls of the system being studied. And while this is a con-venient 'fragmentation', it also often leads to a corresponding reduction in the scope of investigation. While this helps us to understand specific systems, it also reduces our view of its context within the larger whole. Such fragmentation might persist and be mirrored in the classes we teach and the structuring of our colleges and universities, as these are divided and subdivided into disciplines, sub-disciplines and special-ties. Disciplinary fragmentation is often mirrored in the structure of the practical institutions we create that produce the products bought and sold in business and industry. Ford Motor Company, for example, largely restricts itself to the production of cars and trucks – intention-ally reducing its scope to highway motor vehicles; Ford perceives itself as being primarily in the motor vehicle business, not the transportation business. By contrast, BP – formerly British Petroleum – has expanded its disciplinary scope 'beyond petroleum' to include the wider energy business, and now is also a major producer of solar panels. Whether more fragmented or less, the arrangements we make for shaping car production, energy technology and all other human action in the world brings us to the topic of 'institutions', and it is to understanding them in relationship to society and biosphere that we now turn.

Understanding institutions

Global changes that contribute to unsustainability at all levels – including weather events, degraded ecosystem services and regional public health issues – require understanding not only of the biosphere, but also of institutions, for it is these that produce and can correct the various social drivers of unsustainability. 'If the world fails to meet the challenge of a transition to sustainable growth in agricultural production, the failure will be at least as much in the area of institutional innovation as in the area of resource and environmental constraints' wrote the distinguished international development economist Vernon W. Rattan.[257] And so, what is meant by 'institutions' and 'institutional innovation'? Rattan and other institutional economists define 'institutions' as the sets of rules, conventions, arrangements and framework that form and shape human actions in the biosphere.[258] Institutions shape human relationships within the world, both in support of the way the biosphere works and contrary to it.

Institutions are the social constructs that frame human action in the world, whether that be at the level of Ford, BP, national governments or the Worldwide Fund for Nature. From the perspective of institutional economics – universities, hospitals, courts of justice, non-governmental organizations (NGOs such as Christian Aid), and food and agricultural organizations (like the United Nations' FAO) are themselves not institutions, but are embodiments of institutions. These organizational embodiments incorporate particular rules and arrangements that define and determine what and how things are accomplished. Institutions are determined by beliefs about society and the wider world and are 'external manifestations' of these beliefs. These beliefs, wrote economist and Nobel laureate Douglass C. North, are 'internal representations' of the world.[259] These internal representations taken together form our worldview, which includes ourselves and what we believe makes for good personal character and wholesome relationships within our families and communities, what we believe to be our purpose in life, and what we believe about everything beyond ourselves – the rest of human society and culture, our view of our biosphere from outer space, our biogeophysical world, the biospheric economy, and our planet's ecosystem services. Together, institutions form the 'institutional structure' that reflects 'the accumulated beliefs of the society over time'.

North emphasizes that our internal representations can displace the 'rationality' of market economics, maximization of profit, and attempts that might be made to disconnect the present from culture and history. The 'uncritical acceptance of the rationality assumption', North warns, 'is a major stumbling block in the path of future progress', and its currently wide acceptance 'forecloses a deeper understanding of the decision-making process in confronting the uncertainties of the complex world we have created'.[260] There is of course another warning needed, and that is the falsehood that the human economy 'trumps' the biospheric economy. The uncritical acceptance of this assumption may prevent ongoing recognition of increasing unsustainability, such as is represented by eight of its signs presented in this chapter, and may foreclose the critically necessary decision-making and urgent action that is required within our institutions and institutional structure.

What this means for addressing the root causes of unsustainability is that institutions and institutional structure must be developed and maintained to match the changing complexity of the biosphere, biospheric change and the broadening 'reach' of human actions that affect the biosphere and its ecosystem services. It also must be matched to human values and aspirations for a world of justice and vibrant human life and culture. Otherwise institutional decay and ineffectiveness results. In the systems language of the management of business, as developed by cybernetician W. Ross Ashby (1903–72) and business management professor Stafford Beer (1926–2002), the necessary 'match' of the institution to the complexity and variety of the system it mirrors is the institution's 'requisite variety' – the required dynamic variety that needs to be created and sustained within the institution so that it corresponds to the 'variety' or dynamic complexity of the system within which the institution operates.[261]

As institutions change to mirror better the economy of the biosphere and human values – including their complexity and variety – they will also shape and reshape human relationships with the biosphere. As institutions mirror and complement the world within which they operate, they must mirror not a world compartmentalized into specialties and disciplines but a world of dynamic and ordered complexity and variety – a necessarily ethical world – that we have helped to create and have embedded in the symphonic system of systems we call the biosphere.

With this introduction to institutions and institutional structure, and their critical importance for achieving sustainability and avoiding unsustainability, we now can turn to pursue some signs of unsustainability, particularly with regard to agriculture and land use. From these we will identify some of their associated institutional deficiencies. Once identified, these deficiencies can provide a base for appropriate institutional refinement and reform.

Signs and drivers of biospheric unsustainability and institutional deficiency

Degradation of ecosystem services

The current human challenge to biospheric sustainability now extends to disrupt and diminish the very ecosystem services upon which all life depends. This is the finding of the Millennium Ecosystem Assessment, established in 2001 to assess 'the consequences of ecosystem change for human well-being and to establish the scientific basis for actions needed to enhance the conservation and sustainable use of ecosystems and their contributions to human well-being'.[262] This first effort by the scientific community to describe and evaluate the services provided on a global scale identified a wide array of vital ecosystem services, some of which are illustrated in Figure 9.1. Of 24 ecosystem services for which the Millennium Ecosystem Assessment found sufficient information available for analysis, about 60 per cent (15 out of 24) were found to be degraded or used unsustainably.[263]

Institutional deficiency: services by the biosphere are not returned sufficiently with services of our own, thereby failing to assure their continuance and fruitfulness. Institutions fail to incorporate dynamically more than one or a few ecosystem services, much less the biosphere and the dynamic biospheric economy, and therefore are not sufficiently robust in their dynamic variety to match the dynamic variety of the systems within which they operate.

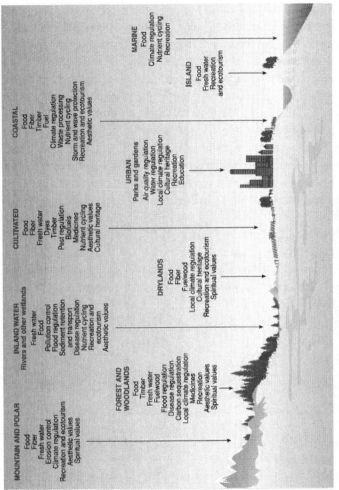

Figure 9.1 Ecosystem services as identified by the Millennium Ecosystem Assessment and classified into nine major categories. (Courtesy of Millennium Ecosystem Assessment, from <www.millenniumassessment.org/en/BoardStatement.aspx>.)

MOUNTAIN AND POLAR
Food
Fiber
Fresh water
Erosion control
Climate regulation
Recreation and ecotourism
Aesthetic values
Spiritual values

FOREST AND WOODLANDS
Food
Timber
Fresh water
Fuelwood
Flood regulation
Disease regulation
Carbon sequestration
Local climate regulation
Medicines
Recreation
Aesthetic values
Spiritual values

INLAND WATER
Rivers and other wetlands
Fresh water
Food
Pollution control
Flood regulation
Sediment retention and transport
Disease regulation
Nutrient cycling
Recreation and ecotourism
Aesthetic values

DRYLANDS
Food
Fiber
Fuelwood
Local climate regulation
Cultural heritage
Recreation and ecotourism
Spiritual values

CULTIVATED
Food
Fiber
Fresh water
Dyes
Timber
Pest regulation
Biofuels
Medicines
Nutrient cycling
Aesthetic values
Cultural heritage

URBAN
Parks and gardens
Air quality regulation
Water regulation
Local climate regulation
Cultural heritage
Recreation
Education

COASTAL
Food
Fiber
Timber
Fuel
Climate regulation
Waste processing
Nutrient cycling
Storm and wave protection
Recreation and ecotourism
Aesthetic values

MARINE
Food
Climate regulation
Nutrient cycling
Recreation

ISLAND
Food
Fresh water
Recreation and ecotourism

Agricultural land and soil loss

Among the signs of unsustainability in agriculture and land use are that, during the latter half of the twenty-first century, nearly one-third of the arable lands worldwide were lost to erosion and taken out of production. In Asia, Africa and South America, annual soil loss was about 31 tonnes per hectare (ha), and in the USA and Europe about 15 tonnes/ha – losses that contrast sharply with annual soil formation rates, which average about 1 tonne/ha.[264] Soil erosion and degradation is rampant (Table 9.1). These losses are compounded by associated reductions of water infiltration, soil water-holding capacity, topsoil thickness, soil carbon sequestration (capture), organic matter and nutrients, soil biota and productivity and also by associated increases of water run-off, surface water overfertilization, silting up of rivers and streams; and by reduction of hydroelectric capacity by silting up of reservoirs.[265]

Institutional deficiency: services by soils to soil formation and sustaining food production are not sufficiently returned with services of our own to assure replacement of soil losses and sustained productivity. As a result, land is made unproductive and in time abandoned for food production.

Table 9.1 Estimates of the global extent in millions of acres (hectares in parentheses) of land degradation.

Type	Light	Moderate	Strong plus extreme	Total
Water erosion	847 (343)	1,302 (527)	553 (224)	2,702 (1094)
Wind erosion	664 (269)	627 (254)	64 (26)	1,355 (549)
Chemical degradation	230 (93)	254 (103)	106 (43)	590 (239)
Physical degradation	109 (44)	67 (27)	30 (12)	206 (83)
Total	1,850 (749)	2,250 (911)	753 (305)	4,853 (1965)

From L. R. Oldeman, 'The global extent of land degradation', in *Land Resilience and Sustainable Land Use*, ed. D. J. Greenland and I. Szabolcs (Wallingford, UK: CABI, 1994), 99–118.

Masking of soil degradation by unsustainable amendments

A particularly serious problem is the temporary compensation for loss of soil and soil fertility by the addition of chemical amendments or 'improvers'. While such amendments may be acceptable, they become deceptive when they mask the degradation and loss of soil by erosion and oxidation of soil carbon. Figure 9.2 shows how corn production can increase even as the topsoil is decreased.

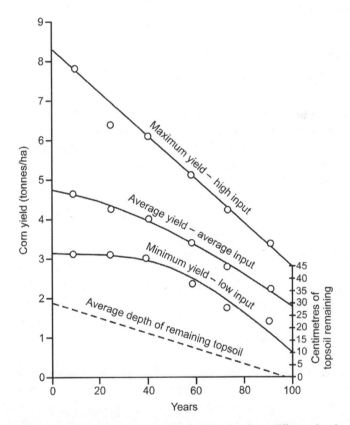

Figure 9.2 Decline of corn yield and topsoil under three different levels of management: high fertilizer and other technology, low fertilizer and other technology, and an intermediate case. (Graph based upon data for corn yield versus topsoil depth and technology input and data on loss of US topsoil given in D. Pimentel, E. C. Terhune, R. Dyson-Hudson *et al.*, 'Land degradation: effects on food and energy resources', *Science* (1976) **194**: 149–55, and adapted from, with permission, C. B. De Witt, 'The land entrusted to us', in *Earthkeeping in the Nineties: Stewardship of Creation*, ed. Loren Wilkinson (Grand Rapids, MI: Eerdmans, 1991), 19–67.)

Institutional deficiency: degradation of soils and soil structure are compensated for, not by processes of soil formation but by soil additives. As soil structure and intrinsic soil fertility are thereby diminished, the resulting soil serves primarily as an infertile root-holding medium that requires continued application of more soil additives and masks the degradation and loss of soils and soil structure. Current institutions diminish incentives to maintain inherent soil fertility and soil structure, failing to recognize that land produces not one but two crops: soil and plant material.

Conversion of farm land to urban uses

In the USA about 4.5 million ha of crop land are converted annually for development of residential areas and associated infrastructure, including commercial districts, roads, parking areas and highways.[266] On the global scale, losses of agricultural land to urbanization and other non-agricultural purposes are also under way as food and land are converted from subsistence uses into commodities that become accessible only to those with money. Labour-saving technology, increasing land values and undercutting of local food prices result in people migrating to cities, which in turn expand outwards to cover adjoining farmland. As urban expansion utilizes agricultural land, agricultural land area is reduced and this joins with population increases to drive intensification of agricultural production through fertilizers, herbicides, pesticides, higher-producing strains of crops and new genetically modified varieties (see also Chapter 6). Agrarian culture in time is displaced by agribusiness, and local stewards of the land are replaced by managers who administer industrialized crop production. Land as gift becomes land as commodity.

Institutional deficiency: prices and rent of land for agrarian uses are lower than for industrial agriculture and still lower than for residential, business and industrial development use. Institutions fail to create, develop and sustain means for keeping land affordable for agrarian purposes. Institutions fail to create, develop and sustain means of land ownership and tenure that allow and sustain earth-keeping by resident stewards of the land.

Deforestation

Deforestation reduces sustainable production of native forest products and support for indigenous human inhabitants, increases run-off, reduces recharge of the watersheds, increases flood peaks (storm flows) and diminishes drought flows (low flows). Deforestation reduces evapotranspiration of water from vegetation to the atmosphere, with consequent potential reduction in rainfall; increases exposure of soil surfaces to direct sunlight, with resulting higher ground temperatures and soil oxidation; and increases atmospheric carbon dioxide levels, with consequences for climate change (see Chapters 2 and 5). Deforestation also destroys the habitats of a wide diversity of forest-dependent creatures, fragments habitats that previously were connected, and increases the forest-edge and edge effects.[267] And increases in forest edge exposure lead to windfall of trees and in many areas of the world open access to roaming cattle, other non-forest animals and, particularly important for tropical forests, to hunters and poachers. One net result is a large loss of native plant and animal species, including extinction of some.[268] Losses to deforestation are greatest in the tropical rainforests, where around 8 million ha are destroyed each year.

Institutional deficiency: the costs and benefits of deforestation are determined primarily if not exclusively in terms of the immediate taking, in disregard and neglect of biospheric costs and benefits. Institutions fail to incorporate dynamically the wide range of benefits and services of forest ecosystems in the present and over the lifetime of forests, and therefore are not sufficiently robust in their dynamic variety to match the dynamic spatial and long-ranging temporal variety of the systems within which they operate.

Biogeographical and trophic restructuring of the biosphere

Climate change is now pushing plant and animal ranges 6 kilometres towards the poles every decade; almost a third of earth's arable land has been lost to erosion, biodiversity is being threatened by habitat destruction and toxification, and overexploitation of the world's major fisheries has caused most of them to collapse and this has led to an adverse restructuring of ocean food webs. Earth has come to be under human domination, and this means that human responsibility has thereby been extended to the whole biosphere. This requires a more robust stewardship that preserves intact biospheric systems, establishes the conditions for restoration and healing of degraded systems, and makes peace with creation through deliberate and determined reconciliation.[269] Restructuring of the biosphere creates ecological unsustainability.

Institutional deficiency: human responsibility fails to extend to the biogeophysical reach of human domination. Institutions fail to incorporate dynamically the full biogeophysical system to include the full reach of the consequences of human action in the world. Institutions are not sufficiently robust in their dynamic variety and biogeophysical reach to match the dynamic variety of the systems within which they operate. Institutions are not sufficiently robust to assure and support human responsibility and stewardship that reciprocates the ecosystem services of the biosphere.

Institutional decay

Institutional economist Daniel Bromley described instances of institutional decay in African agriculture from which he concluded that

> When law enforcement is indifferent or non-existent, and when the judicial system has fallen into disrepair (and disrepute), institutional coherence is lacking, and economic transactions are stifled. Farmers receive prices below those required to cover production costs, and those production factors of production.

If the livelihoods of rural citizens 'are to recover from years of institutional decay,' wrote Bromley, 'it will be necessary for national governments to create an institutional structure (the legal architecture) that will encourage productive initiatives on the part of individuals'. It will also be necessary for those governments 'to establish the means and the procedures for that institutional structure to be modified through time as social and economic conditions warrant'.[270]

Institutional deficiency: institutions fail to match the dynamic values and requirements of local, regional and global economies and their corresponding biospheric integrity, including education, the judicial system, law enforcement, ecosystem restoration, nurture of land stewardship norms and prevention of predatory undercutting of local economies.

Neglect of the agrarian majority

Where farmers and agrarian culture remain in the world – and this consists of 2.5 billion people whose livelihood is in farming – stewardship of land held in trust over the generations largely remains the cultural and ethical norm. However, external factors increasingly push these people to the margins, even going so far as eliminating these farmers and agrarian land altogether. Put on a shorter-term programme of agribusiness, agrarian culture is degraded and destroyed, and soil stewardship is maintained only in so far as it is required for present and immediate gains (see Chapter 11). Both local knowledge and local investment in land and soil are discarded, and the pleasure of living on the land, the wholesomeness of agrarian culture and the beauty of the earth are thereby diminished (see Chapters 8, 12 and 13). An article entitled 'Food is Gold' in the *New York Times* in 2008 announced such transformation of land from trust to commodity.[271]

> Huge investment funds have already poured hundreds of billions of dollars into booming financial markets for commodities like wheat, corn and soybeans. But a few big private investors are starting to make bolder and longer-term bets that the world's need for food will greatly increase – by buying farmland, fertilizer, grain elevators and shipping equipment . . . And three institutional investors, including the giant BlackRock fund group in New York, are separately planning to invest hundreds of millions of dollars in agriculture, chiefly farmland, from sub-Saharan Africa to the English countryside.

The article announced the 'ambitious plans' of Emergent Asset Management, UK, 'to invest in farmland in sub-Saharan Africa, where it plans to consolidate small plots into more productive holdings', explaining that Africa was chosen because 'land values are very, very inexpensive, compared to other agriculture-based economies'.

Institutional deficiency: many current forces create and shape institutions to create and sustain means for protecting the powerful and their actions in the world to the detriment of people who live and sustain themselves on land that supports them and their cultures over the generations. They may degrade and destroy human cultures and indigenous food production, allow for legal and illegal takings of land, genetic material, intergenerational soil investments, may redefine land and its life from trust to commodity, and may degrade and destroy the dignity of local people.

Matching institutions to the systems they serve

Unpalatable or distasteful as it might be, we must conclude that our institutions, as currently constituted, are driving biospheric unsustainability. Institutions need to be transformed so that they, individually and collectively as institutional structures, will shape society towards sustainability – of both human society and the biosphere. In summary, institutions must be sufficiently robust in their dynamic variety to match the dynamic variety of the systems they serve and shape. The requisite variety of institutions must be refined and transformed to match the dynamic variety of the systems they serve and shape, thereby to do a number of things. Theses should include: defining human duty, individually and collectively; indicating what must be done and what must not be done; defining human privilege, individually and collectively, indicating what may be done without interference from other individuals or groups; and defining rights and things for which there are no rights, including what individuals and groups can expect to do on behalf of others. They need to be enhanced to match the full and expanding reach of human impact and interaction with the biosphere. This will occur in part by necessity, for example as we see happening when some disabled economic entities are 'bailed out' by governments during times of serious economic recession. Beyond immediate necessity, it must also occur by design, particularly design that better matches new variety – both anticipated and unanticipated – as it emerges. What might and should this transition include, both by design and of necessity? For agriculture and land use it is institutional development and creation that critically addresses and corrects the eight drivers of unsustainability presented above. Beyond these are institutional changes and transformation of institutional structure that address more deeply the root causes of unsustainability. Of these causes, three are identified next.

Defragmentation of the disciplines

Our institutions have to address the pervasive problem of the fragmentation of the disciplines, and its transfer from academia into our communities, businesses, public policies and government. This reintegration and defragmentation needs to occur at all levels of human endeavour, with the economy of the biosphere and understanding this economy both as the trophic and biogeographical fabric that sustains us and all life as an essential starting point and also as the vital system in which every endeavour operates and derives its capacity to flourish. At the core of this transition is the vital need for developing integrative 'cross-disciplinary' institutions and education within the university and college. In agriculture and land use, for example, this might begin with retitling 'agronomy' as 'agricultural ecology' or 'agroecology' and extending this field to integrate within it agrarian cultures, agrarian economies and the ethics of agrarian sustainability and biospheric prosperity.

Re-connection of economics and the political economy

A century ago, economics and political theory were combined into an integrated approach to government. But, wrote Daniel W. Bromley,

> in the earlier years of the 20th century, when economics came to be defined more by its method (rational choice under cover of methodological individualism) than by its subject of inquiry (the economy), there emerged a felt need to differentiate the alleged 'science' of economics from the mere 'art' of governance and politics.[272]

He wrote further that 'Economics came to be about axiomatic models of rational choice, while government and politics remained concerned with interest groups, logrolling, power, and contested visions about the purposes of government in society.' This demarcation is divisive of government, and needs to be removed, thereby of which matches the variety of the system that government needs to govern. This would broaden the view of the economy to integrate political theory, politics, government – and the biosphere. Our institutions need to reintegrate economics and political theory again to be defined by the economy – the 'subject of inquiry' – including the economy of the biosphere (see Chapter 4). In the area of agriculture and land use this would include integration of agroecology and agrarian stewardship into the domain of core institutions. Its status would be transformed from a 'special interest' to a vital interest.

Desecularization of ethics and values

International law, and through it also the law of nations, has suffered from secularization – principally by being distanced from ethical concern. Theologian William P. George from the Dominican University (Illinois, USA) provided the analysis of this separation when he wrote, 'Over the past four hundred years, international law has increasingly distanced itself from the theological discourse that was once at its core.'[273] Particularly problematic is that natural law at the time of the foundation of international law by Hugo Grotius (1609) and others had not yet incorporated the later work of Charles Darwin (1859) that could be interpreted as allowing unbridled competitiveness and natural selection to operate within the human economy – in disregard of the incapacitated, the downtrodden and the meek.[274] It has now become necessary to address this separation in order to reinstitute 'a renewed and robust conversation between international law and theology' with this fully recognizing that international law has been arrogated to claim its exclusive basis in natural law.[275] In the area of agriculture and land use, this can include a 're-enchantment' of the land, an introduction of the spiritual into land stewardship, a restoration of neighbourliness, and the belief that sustaining land and soil as a gift from previous generations and gift to future generations is right for society and the biosphere. Institutions need to reinstate the moral compass that is at the core of religious institutions and thereby restore respect for theological discourse and public theology.

Paradigm and task

From the earliest written records, living and working in the garden is all about life. Gardening is 'guardening' – a service and safe-guarding that is returned to the land and its creatures in return for their service to their guards and guardeners. For centuries following Eden, farming was viewed as life, as full-orbed living. Farming was necessarily ecological because it is done 'at home' and in 'one's place'. In reflecting on this earliest reported garden, the French lawyer and legal scholar, Jean Cauvin – who studied law under pre-eminent legal scholars Peter De l'Etoile at the University of Orleans and Andreas Alciati at the University of Bourges – wrote in the year 1554,

The earth was given to man, with this condition, that he should occupy himself in its cultivation ... The custody of the garden was given in charge to Adam, to show that we possess the things which God has committed to our hands, on the condition that, being content with the frugal and moderate use of them, we should take care of what shall remain. Let him who possesses a field, so partake of its yearly fruits, that he may not suffer the ground to be injured by his negligence, but let him endeavor to hand it down to posterity as he received it, or even better cultivated. Let him so feed on its fruits, that he neither dissipates it by luxury, nor permits it to be marred or ruined by neglect. Moreover, that this economy, and this diligence, with respect to those good things which God has given us to enjoy, may flourish among us; let everyone regard himself as the steward of God in all things which he possesses. Then he will neither conduct himself dissolutely, nor corrupt by abuse those things which God requires to be preserved.[276]

Clearly, as the *New York Times* story mentioned above shows, land, farming and food production are now becoming competitive investments that line up absentee corporate owners from across sub-Saharan Africa to the English countryside. They need not know their land or its place; all that matters is profit – 'the bottom line'. Secularization, fragmentation of the disciplines and reductionism in academia here as elsewhere have helped to set the pattern for agriculture, land use, government, law and institutions. As in academia, this fragmentation poses difficulty for, and even prevents, engaging responsibility with the land and the wider biosphere with appropriate stewardship. The separations that alienate food from agrarian culture, nutrition from agricultural production and financial investments from farm and land stewardship are among many that establish and perpetuate the problem of unsustainability. The higher purpose for agriculture and land stewardship can be reinstated institutionally where it has been lost. There can even be a 'buying back' of what has been taken – a redemption of life and work to assure that it is driven by vocation rather than greed. This does not mean of course that what has been gained by professional study of agriculture is lost; instead, it is a repurchase of a real and full-orbed life, made worthy by doing grateful work and pursuing effective service to family, land and community, with the support of knowledge gained by research and stewardship experience.

Are there examples – paradigms – of what can be done within and through our institutions? Yes, and one of these is the subject of a comprehensive study by Jules Pretty, professor of environment and society at the University of Essex. With his colleagues, he studied 4,104 certified organic farms in the UK covering some 741,000 hectares.[277] And while these farms are not fully 'agroecological' they had to meet British standards for sustainable agroecological systems. They make up 'a defined and certified system of agricultural production that seeks to promote and understand ecosystem health whilst minimizing adverse effects on natural resources' and as such is 'a restructuring of whole farm systems'. The results of their study are presented in Table 9.2 in which the ecological and health costs of current agriculture were found to be far greater than they would if organic agriculture were adopted in its place. Pesticides and their adverse health effects would be reduced to zero, loss of biodiversity would be dramatically reduced, releases of so-called greenhouse gases (methane and carbon dioxide) to the atmosphere would be diminished greatly, along with water pollution, soil erosion and human disease. Clearly, agricultural practice can respect ecosystem services beyond mere food production in a programme of responsible stewardship. This study is but a beginning of the kind of assessment that illustrates the consequences of new institutions that identify the domain of agriculture to include ecosystem services beyond food production, moving agricultural practice developed in reciprocal service with the biospheric economy.

But will it 'feed the world?'

A serious question of course is whether an agriculture respectful of ecosystem services is sufficient for meeting food needs. In another study, Pretty and colleagues present encouraging results from a survey of 286 recent 'interventions' by agencies committed to increasing food production and reducing poverty.[278] Covering 37 million ha in 57 'poor countries' their study found that productivity increased on 12.6 million farms while at the same time improving ecosystem services. Average crop yield increases were 79 per cent and all crops used water more efficiently. Each hectare of land on average sequestered an average of 0.35 tonnes of carbon annually. For projects with pesticide data, 77 per cent had 71 per cent less pesticide use and 42 per cent increase in yields.

Table 9.2 The negative externalities of UK agriculture (year 2000).

Source of adverse effects	Actual costs from current agriculture (millions of £/year)	Scenario: costs as if whole of UK was organic (millions of £/year)
Pesticides in water	143.2	0
Nitrate, phosphate, soil and *Cryptosporidium* in water[a]	112.1	53.7
Eutrophication of surface water[b]	79.1	19.8
Methane, nitrous oxide, ammonia emissions to atmosphere	421.1	172.7
Direct and indirect carbon dioxide emissions to atmosphere	102.7	32.0
Off-site soils erosion and organic matter losses from soils	59.0	24.0
Losses of biodiversity and landscape values	150.3	19.3
Adverse effects to human health from pesticides	1.2	0
Adverse effects to human health from micro-organisms and BSE[c]	432.6	50.4
Totals	1501.3	371.8

Adapted from J. N. Pretty, A. S. Ball, T. Lang and J. I. L. Morison, 'Farm costs and food miles: an assessment of the full cost of the UK weekly food basket', *Food Policy* (2005) 30: 1–20.
[a] *Cryptosporidium* is a bacterium found as a contaminant in untreated domestic water supplies: it can cause gastric problems.
[b] Eutrophication here is the overfertilization of water caused by run-off of agricultural chemicals. It can cause growth of unwanted plant matter and poison fish.
[c] BSE is bovine spongioform encephalitis, often referred to as 'mad cow' disease.

The researchers concluded that there are grounds 'for cautious optimism that future food needs can be met' following similar interventions. Pretty and colleagues, however, emphasize that also needed is improved access by farmers to productive resource-conserving practices and technology. This depends upon institutional reforms from local to global levels. Important to reforms is recognizing that the phrase 'feeding the world' may divert our attention immediately from the local to global scale, and unwisely may indicate the need for a global solution. Yet this study shows that the 2.5 billion agrarian majority that need to benefit from institutional reform are local. Institutions that push these billions to the margins – even eliminating them – does not help to 'feed the world'.

Unsustainable agriculture and land use and other unsustainability bring humanity up against the challenge to transform any and all degrading and destructive institutions that support human domination into restorative and supportive institutions that in turn shape and sustain responsible stewardship from local places to the entirety of the biosphere. This is the task before us; this is the task of the institutions we develop, transform and create.

10

Water, water...

RICHARD C. CARTER

At the start of the 21st century unclean water is the world's second biggest killer of children . . . 'not having access' to water and sanitation is a polite euphemism for a form of deprivation that threatens life, destroys opportunity and undermines human dignity.

(United Nations Development Programme,
Human Development Report 2006, Beyond Scarcity:
Power, Poverty and the Global Water Crisis (2006))

This chapter is about a service and substance that most of us in the West take for granted, and which we use on demand, day or night, without worrying about its cost, its continuing operation, or whether or not it might be doing us harm. It is about the water that flows through our taps and underpins every aspect of our lives, producing our food and drink, contributing to all the goods we enjoy, and forming the basis of so many of our leisure activities. However, it is not so much about the water supply that I as the writer of this chapter and most of you as readers of this book enjoy; it is primarily about the experiences of those who may live only a few hours away by aeroplane, or worlds away in terms of lives and cultures, south of the Sahara.

The United Nations Millennium Development Goals (UN MDGs, see Chapter 5) include under goal 7 ('ensure environmental sustainability') the target to 'halve, by 2015, the proportion of the population without sustainable access to safe drinking water and basic sanitation'.[279] I am among those who would question why this particular target is placed within the 'environmental sustainability' goal (as opposed to say the poverty or child health goals); nevertheless its positioning there provides some justification for considering the important topic of water supply in this book. However, as I point out later, the challenges of bringing safe, sustainable drinking water to the poor, while undoubtedly having an environmental dimension, lie much more firmly in the arena of public investment and the management of infrastructure than in 'environment' in its usual sense. Water supply provision is concerned with the built environment, and its management is to do with human institutions and their effectiveness.

At the last count, just over half the world's people had a water supply piped into their home or backyard.[280] The rest either had to share an 'improved' but communal water point up to a kilometre or so from their home, or go to an unimproved source, possibly even further away. According to the World Health Organization (WHO) and the United Nations Children's Fund (UNICEF), an improved water supply is one that is protected from outside contamination, especially human or animal excrement. Improved or engineered water supplies are demanding in terms of management and maintenance, and their users have to pay for the service. At any one time, many are broken down, forcing their users to revert to more distant and/or contaminated and/or costly water supply options (Figure 10.1).

Figure 10.1 Ethiopian girl filling an insera (domestic water jar) from an irrigation canal, which is also used for animal watering, bathing and laundry. (Photo: R. C. Carter.)

Unimproved water supplies provide an even poorer standard of service to their users. They are often very distant from people's homes (several kilometres), and so carrying water home requires large investments of time and energy. The water is often contaminated with excrement and is therefore a cause of infectious disease. Such water points often dry up shortly after the cessation of the rains, necessitating an even longer journey to fetch water.

The consequences of poor access to safe and sustainable water supply are largely experienced in poor health, and excessive amounts of time and energy spent on hauling water. Although water supply failings affect all members of the household, in the low-income and least-developed countries domestic water supply and its management are mainly the responsibility of women and girls. Furthermore, it is infants and young children who tend to suffer the worst health consequences when water is contaminated, since their immune systems are relatively undeveloped, and immunity is often further compromised by malnutrition. It is estimated that 1.5 million child deaths due to diarrhoea could be saved annually by improved sanitation, designed to prevent excrement from contaminating soil and water.

As mentioned above, included in MDG 7 ('Ensure environmental sustainability') is the target to 'halve, by 2015, the proportion of the population without sustainable access to safe drinking water and basic sanitation'.[281] The base year for this target, as for the others, is 1990. The latest data show that the world is not on track to reach the sanitation target, and about 2.5 billion people still lack access to improved sanitation. As far as water supply is concerned, for the first time in 30 years the number of people in the world lacking a safe and sustainable water supply is reckoned to have fallen below 1 billion, and the world is thought to be on track to reach the water supply target. However, as is often the case, global totals, averages and trends conceal local challenges. Out of all the regions of the world, sub-Saharan Africa is making the slowest progress towards the drinking water target. Indeed, as I show later, there were more people in this region lacking a safe drinking water supply in 2006 than in 1990. At the present time one-third of the people lacking an improved water supply live in this region. Progress is taking place, but it is not keeping up with population growth.

In this chapter I discuss four areas of analysis, all in relation to what is arguably the most challenging and intractable region of the world, sub-Saharan Africa. First, I explore in greater detail the linkages between poor water supply, ill health and poverty. Second, I indicate the likely future trends in a number of factors that affect this situation. Third, I discuss the underlying causes of the problems highlighted. And fourth, I ask whether there are any signs of hope amid the challenges.

Setting the scene

Sub-Saharan Africa consists of 45 nation states and is home to 788 million people.[282] An additional 200 million people live in the six countries of North Africa. About two-thirds of the population of sub-Saharan Africa live in rural areas, the remainder being split between numerous small towns and fewer large cities. The region has 43 cities of 1 million or more inhabitants, the largest being Lagos (Nigeria) at over 10 million. More than two-thirds of the households in African cities are reckoned to live in slum conditions, described by UN-Habitat as lacking one or more of the five elements: access to improved water, access to improved sanitation, security of tenure, durability of housing, and sufficient living area.[283] Despite this, and in contrast to many developed countries, rural life in sub-Saharan Africa is generally perceived by the resident population to be inferior to life in towns or cities. In the rural areas, services and infrastructure – education, health, water supply, roads, energy supplies – are poor, and survival is a daily struggle. Fetching and carrying water is part of that daily struggle.

Compared to the rest of the world, Africa is underpopulated, dry and uses disproportionately less water, especially for irrigation (the most demanding use of water). Table 10.1 summarizes some key statistics, illustrating these points.

The domestic water supply statistics

A joint programme conducted by WHO and UNICEF, known as the Joint Monitoring Programme or JMP, keeps track of individual countries' progress in water supply and sanitation. The picture of water supply service in sub-Saharan Africa is as follows:[284]

- 81 per cent of the urban population enjoy either a piped water supply or an improved communal supply.
- 46 per cent of the rural population enjoy either piped water or another form of improved supply.

Table 10.1 Africa: land, people and water.

Variable[a]	Africa (%)	Comment[b]
Land area	22	Africa's total land area is 30 million km².
Population	14	Africa's total population (in 2004) was 868 million. Now it is about 1 billion.
Rainfall	18.5	Average annual rainfall for Africa is 678 mm; world average is 818 mm.
Renewable water resources	9	Renewable water resources per person 4,521 m³ per year for Africa compared to 6,859 m³ per year for world.
Water withdrawals	5.6	271 m³ per person per year abstracted in Africa compared to 599 m³ world average.
Irrigated area	4.8	In Africa only 6 per cent of the cultivated area is irrigated compared to a world total of 18 per cent.

Source of data: FAO Aquastat database, see <www.fao.org/nr/water/aquastat/main/index.stm> (last accessed 19 January 2009). Data are for various dates between 2002 and 2004.

[a]Note, all variables are represented as percentages of the equivalent world figures.
[b]One cubic metre = 1,000 litres.

- Overall, 58 per cent have a piped or otherwise improved supply.
- There is wide variation between countries, with some reporting coverage of around 40 per cent and others having already achieved 100 per cent coverage.
- Although the coverage (expressed as percentage of population served) has improved between 1990 and 2006 for most countries in the region, the increases in this coverage have mostly not been sufficient to keep ahead of population growth (but compare Figure 10.2).

Coverage and sustainability

Meeting the water needs of a growing population is challenging enough, but a further dimension of the problem soon emerges. We can spend money, construct systems and so accelerate coverage, but then it soon becomes evident that existing water supplies are falling into disrepair and not being repaired or maintained. It is clear that investment in

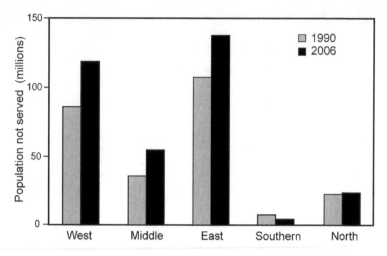

Figure 10.2 Progress in water supply coverage by subregion across Africa, 1990 and 2006. (From JMP, *Progress in Drinking-water and Sanitation: Special Focus On Sanitation* (Geneva: WHO/UNICEF, 2008).)

supply systems that fail within one or two years of construction is money wasted or misdirected. At the present time, the international agencies, national governments and non-governmental organizations (NGOs or charities) are so focused on increasing coverage, that the matter of sustainability is too often sidelined. This will have to change.

Water, sanitation, hygiene and health

The links between poor water supply, inadequate sanitation, poor hygiene practices and ill health are complex and numerous. Infectious diseases may be communicated by ingesting a disease-causing organism (or pathogen) directly from drinking water – as, for example, with truly waterborne diseases such as cholera. On the other hand, they may result from use of insufficient quantities of water for personal hygiene, leading to skin and eye diseases such as scabies and trachoma. Numerous infections are related to unsafe disposal of human excrement, allowing intestinal worms of various kinds to survive in the soil and be picked up through skin contact (as in the case of hookworm) or through direct ingestion of worm eggs from dirty hands.

Various attempts have been made to classify water- and excreta-related infectious diseases according to transmission mechanisms. The advantage of this approach is that it focuses attention on actions that can be taken to alleviate the situation. David Bradley and Richard Feachem carried out the groundbreaking work in this area in the 1970s and 1980s, but more recently, and in recognition of the identification of new pathogens since then, Duncan Mara has produced a comprehensive unitary classification of water- and excreta-related disease.[285] Table 10.2 summarizes some key features of this classification.

Because of the variety of disease transmission routes and causal factors, the preservation of health is not simply about having clean drinking water, but it is also about having sufficient water to practise good hygiene, and actually doing so. Furthermore, it is about preventing contamination of soil and water with human excrement. Consequently, improved water supply without corresponding improvements in sanitation and in hygiene behaviour has only a limited impact on health. Water supply, sanitation and hygiene have often been seen as the legs of a tripod stool.

Infectious disease related to poor water supply or sanitation may cause or contribute to diarrhoea, anaemia, malnutrition and numerous other debilitating symptoms. In infants and children who have not yet developed full immunity to disease, a vicious circle develops in which disease and malnutrition further compromise immunity, leading to more frequent or heavier infections. Nearly three child deaths per minute of every day are reckoned to be caused by diarrhoeal disease alone, caused by poor water quality and/or sanitation.[286]

Reference has already been made to the importance of water for food production. The cultivation of crops and the raising of livestock are inherently heavy users of water (see Box 10.1). In the tropics or subtropics the daily water demand of 1 hectare (ha) of a cereal crop, enough to feed a household in a good year, is about 50,000 litres, or the equivalent of the basic domestic water needs of 2,500 people. This water may come from rainfall (temporarily stored in the soil) or from irrigation. However, despite the widespread need for irrigation water (see Box 10.2), very little of sub-Saharan Africa's agriculture is irrigated (see Table 10.1, above). The water requirements of livestock in the region are generally significantly lower than those of industrial animal production systems in the wealthier countries, but they are nevertheless dominated by the water needed to produce pasture. The drinking water intake of animals is relatively insignificant.

Table 10.2 Key features of Mara and Feachem's disease classification.

Category	Description and example	Control measures
Faeco-oral waterborne and water-washed diseases.	Pathogen transmitted from human excrement (faeces) to mouth. Example of waterborne disease: cholera. In case of water-washed diseases, the problem is lack of water for personal (especially hand) hygiene. Examples in this case include various intestinal worms, amoebae and viral infections.	Improve water quantity (water-washed diseases). Improve water quality (waterborne diseases).
Non-faeco-oral water-washed diseases.	Infections that are exacerbated by poor hygiene, e.g. scabies, trachoma.	Improve water quantity and promote good hygiene.
Geohelminthiases.	Worm infections that can survive for long periods in the soil, e.g. hookworm, ascariasis.	Safe excrement disposal – sanitation.
Taeniases.	Beef and pork tapeworm.	Safe sanitation. Proper cooking of meat.
Water-based diseases.	Diseases in which part of the life cycle of the pathogen requires water. Examples: schistosomiasis, guinea worm.	Decrease contact with contaminated water.
Insect-vector diseases.	Diseases in which an insect carries an intermediate form of the pathogen, e.g. malaria, yellow fever.	Multiple measures to reduce breeding sites, kill mosquito larvae or insects, use of bed netting.
Rodent-vector diseases.	Diseases carried by rodents, e.g. leptospirosis.	Rodent control, hygiene promotion.

Summarized from D. D. Mara and R. G. A. Feachem, 'Water- and excreta-related diseases: unitary environmental classification', *Journal of Environmental Engineering* (1999) **00**: 334–9.

Box 10.1 The water footprint of a selection of goods*

It is possible to calculate the amount of water it takes to grow and/or produce various items that we commonly use or consume. The quantities involved and some of the comparative values are surprising. For example, it takes:

- 10 litres to produce a single A4 sheet of paper;
- 40 litres to produce one slice of bread;
- 70 litres to produce one apple;
- 120 litres to produce a glass of wine;
- 140 litres to produce a cup of coffee;
- 200 litres to produce one egg;
- 2,700 litres to produce a cotton shirt;
- 3,900 litres to produce 1 kg of chicken;
- 5,000 litres to produce 1 kg of cheese;
- 15,500 litres to produce 1 kg of beef.

*Source: Water Footprint Network, see <www.waterfootprint.org/?page=files/home> (last accessed 19 January 2009).

Trends

The situation with regard to water supply for both domestic needs and food production is challenging, and I explore some of the reasons for this state of affairs in the next section. Here though, I ask first whether things are improving or worsening, and, if so, why. I highlight six key aspects of the situation: population growth, urbanization, water pollution, land degradation, increasing water demands, and climate change.

Among projections of the future (all of which of course are inherently uncertain), one is more certain than most and it has important consequences. It is human population growth (see also Chapter 6). In simple terms, today's young adults are producing tomorrow's children now and so, barring major global catastrophes, population growth over the next several decades can be projected with some certainty. Figure 10.3 shows the projected population of sub-Saharan Africa, according to the UN's three alternative scenarios, known as the low, medium and high variants. To put these figures into context, recent concerns have been raised in the UK about possible population growth from 61 million to 70 million by 2050 (an increase of only 15 per cent over

---

Box 10.2 A little water makes all the difference in Zimbabwe

The requirements for irrigated land and irrigation water that can make a real difference to impoverished farmers are not to be measured in hectares and tens of thousands of litres per day, but a few square metres and correspondingly small amounts of water. The example of the Bikita Integrated Rural Water Supply and Sanitation Project in Zimbabwe is a case in point.* In a rural district, approximately 100 km east of Masvingo, a community-managed water and sanitation programme has successfully branched out into communal and family-owned productive gardens. Rains are unreliable in this area, and crops, most commonly maize and millet, may often fail if a reliable water supply cannot be secured.

The Bikita area has many boreholes of 40–60 metres depth, and wells up to 30 metres depth, all of which are equipped with the locally produced Zimbabwe Bush hand pump, and maintained within the community. The gardens at productive water points use these water sources to farm communal vegetable plots with groups of up to 50 people, growing a range of crops including ground nuts, maize, cabbage, onions, tomatoes, spinach and beans.

Gardens of 0.25 ha were allocated per household, giving the poorest and female-headed households the same amount of land as wealthier neighbours. Subsequent research in the area found that a good cross-section of the society had taken up and kept with the project, and many were selling a proportion of their produce to neighbours or at markets, to raise between $US2 and $US10 each per month. The project was found to be highly sustainable, with the communities working together for a common purpose.

The even-handed allocation of the plots meant that this groundwater project has been able to be very pro-poor, in that it does not discriminate against the smaller households or those with a female at the head. The food security and additional income allowed these individuals to help themselves out of poverty.

Although we do not know how much destruction or deterioration has taken place in the last two or three years in Zimbabwe, even if some of these gardens are still functioning, they will be more important than ever to their users.

*B. Mathew, 'Ensuring sustained beneficial outcomes for water and sanitation programmes in the developing world', Ph.D. thesis, Cranfield University, UK, 2004 (published by IRC as Occasional Paper 40; see <www.irc.nl/page/27612> (last accessed 14 January 2009).

---

40 years). The population of sub-Saharan Africa is almost certain to rise by 100 per cent over the same period. If a projected growth of 15 per cent is likely to put unacceptable stress on the world's eleventh wealthiest economy (in terms of Gross Domestic Product per person (GDP per capita), see Chapters 4 and 5), how much more so a growth of six times as much, in the world's poorest economies?

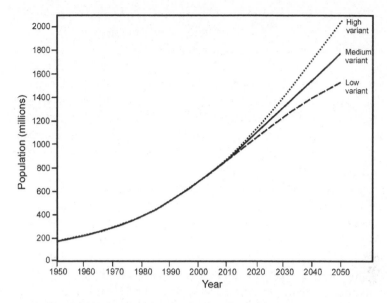

Figure 10.3 Sub-Saharan Africa: population 1950–2050. The variants represent
three of the scenarios used by the UN to project future population. The main difference
between the variants relates to assumed future fertility rates (children per mother).
(From UN Population Division, 'World population prospects: the 2006 revision';
see <esa.un.org/unpp/> (last accessed 14 January 2009).)

Second, the populations of the least developed countries, and those
in sub-Saharan Africa in particular, are rapidly urbanizing. Over the
period 2000 to 2050, rural populations in Africa are set to grow by
about 45 per cent, but urban growth will be much faster. It is estimated
that urban population in Africa will grow by a factor of four, that is
400 per cent, over the same period. Such growth will affect water in
three ways. It will lead to highly concentrated demand; it will lead to
increasing per capita consumption, so accelerating demand even faster;
and it will lead to increasing contamination of both surface water and
groundwater.

The discharge of raw or semi-treated sewage to watercourses,
dumping of industrial waste in or adjacent to fresh water, and diffuse
pollution of groundwater from agricultural fertilizers and pesticides,
are just a few of the activities that reduce the amount of fresh water in
circulation. The degradation of land and natural resources, caused
by rapid population expansion in combination with inappropriate
agricultural practices, adds to the pollutant load.

Demand for water rises over time, for two main reasons. First, population expands, so leading to increased overall demand. Second, as populations become wealthier and more urbanized, the demand per person increases. Put together, these two factors result in a demand for water that grows faster even than population. In 2006, the UN noted that water withdrawals had increased sixfold since the 1900s, at twice the rate of population growth.[287] The 'crunch' caused by rising demand and reducing quantities of fresh water (because of pollution) is serious, and it will increasingly push nations into water shortage and water scarcity over the coming decades.

Evaluation of the likely future impact of climate change on water resources and water supply is not straightforward.[288] Although there is reasonable certainty about the direction and magnitude of temperature changes (a rise of 3–4°C in Africa between the late twentieth and late twenty-first centuries was predicted by the Intergovernmental Panel on Climate Change),[289] the resultant changes in rainfall and other meteorological variables show more spatial variation, and their direction and magnitude are less certain. Furthermore, the relationship between rainfall and renewable water resources is not linear, and it depends greatly on soil properties and vegetation cover at a particular location. Both of these can and do change very significantly under population pressures and changes in agricultural practice and land use.

Causes

We turn now to address the question 'Why?' Why, in our globalized, twenty-first-century, socially aware world, does the situation described so far in this chapter exist and persist? Why, despite the efforts of numerous national governments, UN agencies and NGOs, do we seem so often to be moving backwards?

Of course these questions need to be addressed in relation to the much bigger context of global poverty and underdevelopment, and not simply one sector, water, important though it is (see also Chapter 9). And of course the answers are complex and interlinked. Let me attempt to address the larger issue through a small set of FAQs (frequently asked questions).

Is it a matter of technology?

First, it is highly unlikely that a 'silver bullet' technology is going to revolutionize the water supply to low-income countries in the way in which, for example, mobile telephones have transformed communications across the world. A recent global study for the Bill and Melinda Gates Foundation could find no prospect of this.[290] Nevertheless, choosing the right technology to fit the need and the context, and in particular to enable easy and inexpensive operation and maintenance, is important. For example, water supply systems that work by gravity are inherently easier to manage (and likely to be more sustainable) than those requiring diesel fuel and spare parts for pumps, especially in remote areas (Figure 10.4). However, no technology either functions in isolation from human management or continues to work in the absence of maintenance. Ironically, the more 'appropriate' the technology (in the sense of low cost and ease of management), the earlier and more frequent attention it is likely to need. The long-term effective functioning of water user organizations is crucial to the functional sustainability (whether or not it continues to work over time) of technology.

Aren't more and more countries experiencing water scarcity? Are we running out of water?

A recent review of global water scarcity (by the Internal Water Management Institute, IWMI) distinguishes between countries with little or no water scarcity (such as the UK), those with physical water scarcity (for example, the North African coast and Middle East), those approaching physical water scarcity (including some in southern Africa), and those experiencing economic water scarcity (nearly all the countries of sub-Saharan Africa that are the focus of this chapter).[291] IWMI's definition of economic scarcity is expressed as follows: 'water resources are abundant relative to water use, with less than 25 per cent of water from rivers withdrawn for human purposes, but malnutrition exists. These areas could benefit by development of additional blue and green water [*water abstracted for irrigation, and natural precipitation*], but human and financial capacity are limiting.' In other words, for this huge and predominantly poor region of the world, the limiting factor is not generally the quantity of water available, but the level of investment and the management capabilities of governments and others.

Figure 10.4 An imported water supply handpump, repaired locally in Sierra Leone. Spare parts supply for handpumps is a major challenge in many countries. (Photo: R. C. Carter.)

Does the key lie in establishing effective water user organizations?

It is certainly the case that rural community water supply systems (as opposed to those in urban areas, which are operated and managed by a public or private utility on the basis of water tariffs paid by the consumers) depend heavily on management by the water user community. The effectiveness of the user organization is fundamental to the ongoing operation and management of the system. But such organizations often fail because of internal conflict (often over money), or simply because committee members lose interest or find themselves too busy. At such times, outside support is needed, and this is rarely available.

Do we have the answer?

Is the answer, then, to develop stronger capacity among local governments or other support organizations? This is definitely part of the solution. If local government or some other permanent institution can provide the support that local communities need, they can be very effective. Local government itself is often weak in sub-Saharan Africa, for a variety of reasons, and this is an area that needs much more attention. However, there are good examples of effective support to user communities, including those provided by the local church (see Box 10.3).[292]

What are the prospects for a safe and sustainable supply?

But what prospects are there for bringing safe and sustainable water supply to all, in a reasonable period of time? What would it take to do this? First, there is the question of money. It is widely recognized that investment in water supply in sub-Saharan Africa is insufficient, especially in rural areas. But a number of issues arise here. Investment in sanitation (arguably even more important than water supply) has lagged badly behind even that made in water supply. Of course there are numerous other competing demands for limited government budgets. Also there is the matter of the ability of governments and NGOs effectively to absorb and spend increasing amounts of money. In many places the existing funds are not well spent, so increasing budgets may simply exacerbate this situation if the underlying causes of poor financial management are not tackled.

Box 10.3 More than two decades of service and sustainability in Uganda – some key findings from a field investigation*

The Kigezi Diocese Water and Sanitation Programme (KDWSP) has been working with communities and households in south-west Uganda since 1986. Three external evaluations carried out between 1997 and 2004 indicated that KDWSP has consistently performed well in terms of relevance, cost-effectiveness, wider impact and sustainability of services. KDWSP has demonstrated that it is possible to deliver sustainable water and sanitation services. Systems up to 16 years old were found to be still performing well, both technically and institutionally. This is in stark contrast to some other programmes in the district, in which two-year-old systems are in serious trouble.

The delivery of sustainable water supply services is about moving people from independence or near-total self-reliance on distant, unprotected, unreliable, contaminated water sources to a state of interdependence, in which they have an improved service but need to interact with an external support structure provided by diocese, local government, private sector, community-based organizations and NGOs, or some combination of all these. This point is crucial. Water and sanitation interventions need to reject the myth that technology can be transferred and community institutions set up, and the community can then be left to manage on its own with no further external support. This is the myth of perpetual motion – wind up the clock and it runs for ever. All systems run down in the absence of continuing inputs of time, energy, money and support.

The programme's success was attributed to (a) taking seriously the principles of community participation to which many other programmes pay lip-service, (b) paying as much attention to how it operates as to what it achieves, and (c) the underlying service-oriented values and ethos of the programme.

*Extracted from R. C. Carter and R. Rwamwanja, 'Functional sustainability in community water and sanitation: a case study from south west Uganda' (Diocese of Kigezi/Cranfield University/Tearfund, 2006); see <www.tearfund.org/webdocs/website/Campaigning/Policy% 20and%20research/Uganda%20Watsan%20final.pdf> (last accessed 14 January 2009).

Second, there is the matter of organizational capacity. The professional and organizational competence of governments, donors and NGOs needs to undergo a step-change. Individual professional and managerial skills, organizational management procedures and operating guidelines need to be of the highest standard, and although there are isolated islands of good practice to be found, they are relatively few.

Third, there needs to be real commitment from the highest levels of government to the alleviation of poverty generally, and a clear understanding of the fundamental place of water and sanitation in addressing poverty. Sadly, some governments in the region appear to lack the commitment and will to serve their people in this way.

Fourth, the voice of the public and its demands for improved services need to be better articulated and more loudly expressed. The most effective international NGOs, such as WaterAid, place high priority on their 'advocacy' role, part of which involves facilitating communities to express their demands for improved water and sanitation services.[293]

However, even given significant progress in all these aspects, we need to find solutions to a set of fundamental problems that are rooted in the cultures of communities and the organizations that are meant to represent and support them. We need to understand much better how to bring about rapid, fundamental and lasting changes in human behaviour (see Chapters 9, 12 and 13). Effective management of improved water supply and lasting changes in sanitation and hygiene reduce largely to changes in human attitudes and values, and the behavioural changes that ensue. The following 'behaviours' all demand changes in mind-set, which are not always fully compatible with existing cultures: willingness to pay a reasonable fee for safe and sustainable water supply; the integrity and accountability required to manage those funds; the willingness to invest time and resources in preventive maintenance on behalf of the community; a public-service attitude within external support organizations; the routine utilization of safe sanitation; and the practice of good hygiene.

Is there room for hope?

Having devoted 35 years of my working life to addressing some of the issues touched on in this chapter, I have to maintain a level of optimism that permits me to believe that change is possible. My intention is to spend at least the next 15 years pursuing that same goal, and to do that I must maintain hope that sustainable progress at an appropriate scale is achievable.

The evidence on the ground, however, is mixed. National and regional statistics suggest that many of the trends are going the wrong way, and fast. When one examines the situation in greater detail though, it is certainly possible to identify national governments that are highly committed to bringing about change, donor organizations and international agencies that have a sound understanding of the issues and are prepared to form long-term partnerships, and NGOs that are engaged at the grass roots and in it for the long haul.

When national and global political will and commitment combine with down-to-earth realism about the magnitude of the challenges and the time that will be needed to bring safe and sustainable water to all, then there will be progress (see Chapters 5 and 9). When that commitment and realism translate into the highest level of professionalism and integration among the wide range of different players in the sector, then there will be a step forward. When the external drive for poverty alleviation coincides with people's own aspirations and demands, then real change can start to happen. The signs of these changes are to be found in the many islands of success that exist across sub-Saharan Africa and the rest of the developing world. What we need to see is those islands growing, coalescing and combining to form a continent in which extreme poverty is a thing of the past. To achieve that, a concerted effort by all those involved, different in nature from, and far in excess of, those efforts represented in various international decades of action, even in the Millennium Development Goals themselves, is needed.[294]

11

Globalization, ecology and poverty

C. RENÉ PADILLA

The greatest challenge we face [at the beginning of the twenty-first century] is the growing chasm between the rich and the poor people on earth . . . more than half the world's poor people live on less than $[US]2 a day, and 1.2 billion people have to survive on half that amount.

(President Jimmy Carter, 2002 Nobel Peace Prize,
in *Our Endangered Values* (2005), 179)

Among all the critical problems that affect humankind today, the ecological collapse and poverty place a big question mark over the shape of the future of humankind on planet earth. The close relationship between these two global problems is clearly demonstrated by the devastating effects of climate-related phenomena, especially on the poor in Asia, Africa and Latin America, as well as on the low-income groups in the industrialized countries. In fact, there is plenty of evidence to prove that global warming is far more life-threatening in the southern than in the northern hemisphere.[295] For reasons that will become clear as this chapter proceeds, however, I intend to examine what I consider to be the root cause of both ecological collapse and poverty: the globalization of the capitalist economic system.

According to sociologist Leslie Sklair, the globalization of capitalism that emerged, as a result of a long historical process, in the second half of the twentieth century, is a 'particular way of organizing social life across existing state borders'. Its primary moving force is the transnational capitalist class – 'the major locus of transnational political practices' – comprising globalizing bureaucrats, politicians and professionals. This class derives its material base from the transnational corporations – 'the major locus of transnational economic practices' – and 'the value system of the culture-ideology of consumerism'.[296]

The ideology of consumerism, closely connected with that of market fundamentalism, is at the heart of today's global economic system. The role that it plays in this neoliberal system politically ruled by the transnational class and economically controlled by the transnational corporations cannot be exaggerated. It may be defined as the widespread assumption that, in total contradiction to Jesus' teaching, a person's life does consist in the abundance of his or her possessions (cf. Luke 12:15). Motivated by that assumption, which is generally taken for granted by the mass media, the aim in life for a large majority of people is to accumulate material wealth by every means possible. Work, science, technology, economy, business and so forth become means to attain the maximum short-term profitability for the sake of economic growth at any price. People as individuals, as groups, or even as whole nations are obsessed by a standard of living that is measured in terms of economic security and 'things' possessed – material prosperity – with very little, or no, concern for its ecological or social consequences. The massive accommodation of people (mainly but not exclusively in the wealthy countries) to the values of the consumer society is an unavoidable premise in today's corporate economic system.

My central claim here is that both the destruction of the ecosystem and poverty can be traced back to the global economic system dominated by the ideology of consumerism embedded in the transnational class and implemented by the transnational corporations. In order to substantiate this claim, I propose, first, to examine one very powerful global industry that is making a considerable negative impact on millions of people: the soybean industry. Second, after a description of this industry and its socio-economic and ecological consequences, I attempt to show that the production and trade of soybeans exemplify the way in which the global economic system functions for the benefit of the transnational class. Third, I endeavour to lay a theological basis for a Christian response to counteract the negative effects of globalization.

Before proceeding, a word on globalization would be appropriate here. I am well aware that this phenomenon also has a positive side to it and that the tendency in the wealthy countries is to emphasize its benefits while that in the developing countries is to underline its evil results. The People's Republic of China and several East Asian countries are often mentioned as good examples of the way in which globalization in terms of export-led growth can pull countries out of poverty. I do not have space here to explore this subject in depth. Suffice to say that, as the economist Joseph Stiglitz has demonstrated, these countries did not follow the policies dictated by market fundamentalism.[297] On the contrary, they both refused to open themselves to destabilizing speculative capital flow and took measures to make sure that the process of liberalization of the economy (including the neoliberal policy of scaling down government regulations) did not involve drastic changes along the way, and benefited (at least to a certain extent) not only the rich but also the poor. Everywhere else outside Asia, including Latin America – where the policies of the Washington Consensus[298] have been faithfully applied under the mentorship of the International Monetary Fund and the World Bank – globalization, as exemplified by the soybean industry, has had a very negative impact on God's creation as well as on the socio-economic situation of the poor.

The soybean industry

The soybean industry has in recent years grown to such an extent that it may be used as a paradigm of the concrete results of the global economic system, with its emphasis on maximizing gain, without regard for the increasing destruction of nature and the deepening disparity between rich and poor.

One example will suffice: the case of the soybean complex that includes the Department of Anta – the southern region of the Province of Salta and a part of the Argentine Chaco – which has been the object of careful research done by Chris van Dam of the Forest Stewardship Council.[299] This Department, the second poorest department in the country and located in 'the heat pole of South America',[300] became a sort of paradigm of the intensive agriculture strongly dependent on transnational investments that characterizes extensive rural areas in Latin America today.

Various factors contributed to the spectacular development of soybean production in this area – a region that for a long time had been subject to uncontrolled deforestation for agricultural and cattle-raising purposes, with resulting environmental degradation due particularly to the cattle. For a start, there was the low cost of land, which encouraged local and foreign investors to buy many thousands of hectares at ridiculously cheap prices. Then there was the volume of money invested in sophisticated agricultural machinery for the entire process of food production, from the preparation of the soil to the sowing and harvesting. An additional factor was the introduction of new agricultural methods, including direct sowing, which started in 1992 and in a few years became quite common, and the use of genetically modified seeds, a practice in which Argentina is now regarded a world leader. There was also a government policy of tax exemption to encourage development. All these factors made, and continue to make, high returns on the investments.

But serious account has to be taken of the negative consequences of agricultural modernization, both ecologically and socially. In fact, as far as ecology is concerned, direct sowing has involved vast deregulated deforestation – one of the main causes of greenhouse gas (GHG) emissions (see Chapters 2 and 5) – and the use of herbicides to control the growth of the weeds, under the stubble, caused by humidity (see Figures 11.1, 11.2). Alteration of the ecosystem results in new plagues and pests, control of which often requires great quantities of chemicals. Although the use of genetically modified seed cuts down to two the number of herbicides (RoundUp and 2–4-D), the required quantities of 2–4-D are high and affect both the health of the human population and much of the vegetation of the region, including the trees, groves and fruit trees of the city of Las Lajitas.

The social consequences of agricultural modernization for the sake of maximizing short-term gains are equally negative. Van Dam described the problem thus: 'At the beginning of the 1990s, the new agricultural policies imposed by neoliberalism introduce a polarization process, in which people who are able to keep up with the modernization of production survive and grow, while the small producers, financially and technologically [too] weak to compete with the strong, are eliminated.'[301] With the growth of demand, the cost of land increases drastically and becomes unavailable to the large majority of local farmers, who are forced to sell their own fields and sometimes to hire them back. Many thousands of hectares of agricultural land are thus under the control of a powerful elite.

In addition to this dreadful expulsion from their land for financial reasons, the peasants have suffered a dramatic reduction in employment because of technological modernization and direct sowing. The current model of soybean production requires only one worker for approximately every 200 hectares. This constitutes a loss of four out

Figure 11.1 **Bulldozer knocking down forest, making way for soybean cultivation 20 kilometres from Tartagal, Province of Salta.** (Photo: ASOCIANA, courtesy of Andrew Leake.)

Figure 11.2 **Lines of ashes left after felled trees are burned on the property of a Swiss businessman, close to Wichi aboriginal communities east of Tartagal, Province of Salta.** (Photo: ASOCIANA, courtesy of Andrew Leake.)

of five jobs in the fields. A tragic consequence is the impoverishment of the local people, especially in the urban centres. What used to be done by the workers is now done by machines. The few specialized workers needed for sowing, fumigating and threshing are almost always brought from elsewhere, and their technical training is taken care of by the companies (most of them foreign) that make agricultural chemical products or are engaged in the soybean trade: for example, Monsanto, Cargill, Dekalb, Continental, Pioneer and Zeneca. Landless and jobless, many peasants are forced to survive on the availability of temporary jobs or to migrate to marginal rural zones or to urban centres. The few who are able to survive do so by dedicating their land to a subsistence level of agricultural or meat production for their own consumption and for the local or regional market.

The conclusion reached by van Dam is that the soybean boom in the Department of Anta has produced a private-interest economy based mainly on foreign corporations and oriented towards extra-regional and foreign markets, ignoring local rural development. It is made possible through the control of many thousands of hectares of Argentine land dedicated to a corporate monocrop. It benefits the investors, but its ecological and social results are very negative for the whole region. It perpetuates both the degradation of the environment and injustice in the distribution of the land, the result being the impoverishment of the large majority of people living in the region.

Anta, however, is not a unique case. What happened with the soybean boom there also happens wherever the land is used for industrial and commercial purposes and the production process is under the control of large economic interests. Deforestation, which has benefited a handful of transnational class entrepreneurs, has continued in Anta to such an extent that, according to a study presented in January 2008 by ASOCIANA – an Anglican church foundation working there – this department has now been almost totally deforested.[302] The same destructive process is taking place in several regions of Argentina mainly for the sake of the soybean industry: it has been estimated that the average number of acres of woods lost to this country is 270,000 per year (109,080 hectares), 760 per day and 37 per hour![303] It is beyond the scope of this chapter to describe the way in which Brazil's Amazon jungles – 'the lungs of the world' and the largest reserve of water, plants and animals in the world – are also being devastated by deforestation.[304] No space is left for the care of natural resources – including the land –

and biodiversity, nor for human solidarity. The one dominating concern is the short-term maximization of economic gain.

Closely related to today's use of land is the present worldwide food crisis. According to the Food and Agriculture Organization (FAO), out of an estimated 860 million people that in today's world suffer from hunger, about 830 million live in the so-called developing countries – the countries on which climate change is making the greatest impact.[305] Many of the roughly 1 billion people living on less than $US1 a day spend 80 per cent or more of their income on food. Nevertheless, in Argentina wealthy landowners – members of the transnational class who benefit greatly from the high price of soybeans in the world market – staged a protest from mid-March to mid-July 2008 because they considered that the custom toll for exporting that product was too high. Paradoxically, at the same time, Egypt, Cameroon, Mali, Côte d'Ivoire, Nigeria, Sénégal, Burkina Faso, Indonesia, Madagascar, Mexico, Haiti, and many other countries were the scene of violent riots by hungry people who were protesting because they could no longer afford to buy bread. According to the FAO, between 2007 and 2008 food prices rose globally by 52 per cent.[306] As a result, an increasing number of people are now being excluded from the food market – the UN estimates that around the world this food price crisis has pushed 100 million people into hunger.[307] At the risk of totally losing control of food riots, many national governments are forced to make food security their number one priority.

In light of the devastating effects of the global food crisis, one cannot but sympathize with FAO Director-General Jacques Diouf, who, referring to the use of cereals in the production of bioethanol to allieviate the problems of climate change, stated that 'it is incomprehensible that $11 bn–$12 bn a year in subsidies and protective tariff policies have the effect of diverting 100 million tonnes of cereals from human consumption, mostly to satisfy a thirst for vehicles'.[308] Efforts to minimize the damaging ecological effects of the consumer society's addiction to fuel by replacing fossil fuels by biofuels throws into relief the power of the ideology of consumerism mainly in the wealthy world. The solution to the problem of climate warming is not a change in land use to produce biofuel rather than food. The solution is the exchange of the materialistic intemperance intrinsic to the current economic system for the moral temperance derived from the recognition of humankind's role as the steward of creation.

The global economic system and the resource curse

The major driver of political practices implicated in economic global-ization is members of the transnational capitalist class and upholders of neoliberalism. The major driver of the transnational economic prac-tices involved in globalization is transnational corporations. Under the control of the transnational class and the transnational corporations, God's creation is devastated and the poor are locked into poverty for the sake of unlimited economic growth.

Many of the so-called underdeveloped countries of the world are not materially poor but are very rich in natural resources: minerals, agricultural products, timber, land, water, oil, precious stones, medic-inal herbs, and so on. Why, then, are so many people in these countries poor or even destitute?

Poverty is a very complex problem – there are many factors that contribute to it – but the solution, often taken for granted in the West, is encapsulated in the word 'corruption'. Corruption may in fact be the most important cause of poverty in the majority of the developing countries. But whose corruption?

In 2001, Andrés Oppenheimer published a book entitled *Blindfolded Eyes: The United States and the Corruption Business in Latin America.* In an effort to understand why the long-standing free-market reforms have failed to improve the economic situation of the Latin American countries, the Argentine journalist engaged in a four-year investigation that included 300 interviews in five countries. His conclusion was that the main reason for the failure was that in these countries 'the public functionaries and their friends in the [private] corporate world have implemented [the free-market reforms] for their own benefit'.[309] According to him, quite often the emphasis is laid on corruption as a problem in the developing countries, but no attention is given to 'the role of the multinational corporations and the governments of the industrialized countries in the shocking corruption that has shaken the [Latin American] region'.[310] He rightly concluded that, in view of the complicity between national and international stakeholders, 'The fight against corruption will not succeed in the near future without changing the laws in the United States and Europe in order to exercise greater control over their corporations and banks.'[311]

The question is whether it is realistic to expect that the necessary changes will ever take place as long as, in both the industrialized and the developing countries, there is in the transnational class a substantial overlap between government authorities and big business chief executive officers. Is not the lack of political will – 'the main obstacle hindering the fight against corruption', according to Oppenheimer[312] – a sign of the way in which political and economic interests are intertwined so as to maximize the profits of the transnational corporations for the benefit of the transnational class?

Because of the way in which the global economic system functions, the natural resources of a country are used as the bait to attract big fish. The path to be followed by the corporations is well known: survey the market, decide on the investment, find local members of the transnational class with political power, persuade them (if necessary with financial incentives) on the convenience of the investment, sign up the business agreements, and get to work to exploit the resources, regardless of the effects that the methods employed in the exploitation may have on the local environment and the local population.

As the main focus for transnational economic practices, the corporations promote the global imperialistic outreach that makes possible a very high level of consumption on the part of the minority of the world's population that they represent. The ideology of consumerism fulfils its function by fostering a kind of 'guilty innocence' among the members of that minority, with the co-operation of the mass media and their power over the domestic market.

Evidently, the economic growth represented by industries such as the one described in this chapter is designed to benefit global corporations and a handful of local wealthy families, members of the transnational class. By contrast, for the large majority of people, especially in the Majority World (Africa, Asia and Latin America), the natural resources found in their country become a resource curse. Injustice is thus institutionalized on a global scale and the very survival of humankind on planet earth is in question.

Ecology and poverty in theological perspective

Michael S. Northcott has rightly described global economy as tyrannical. According to him, 'Its growing power over the planet involves systematic erosion of local sources of power and freedom as the well-being of human communities, and ecosystems are sacrificed to sustain "freedoms" of global corporations and wealthy consumers to accumulate regardless of the costs to others and the earth system'[313] (see also Chapter 14). Despite the catastrophic effects of the globalization of the neoliberal economic system, its advocates insist that the only hope for humankind to eliminate poverty lies in giving free rein to the free market all over the world. Free-market fundamentalism, tightly related to the ideology of consumerism, ignores the catastrophic consequences of the unilateral emphasis on economic growth and obstinately perseveres in following a course of action that leads to both ecological and human destruction.

From the neoliberal perspective of the transnational class, the state is considered to be the political institution responsible for promoting investments for the sake of economic growth, to protect rights to private property, to encourage production, and to make sure that the free market functions in an efficient and transparent way. Thus conceived, the government has no jurisdiction over economic relationships in society, which depend on the market. It is taken for granted that 'the invisible hand' of the market will regulate those relationships for the benefit of all. What generally happens in practice, as we have seen in the case of the soybean industry, is that the free market increases the wealth of the rich and the poverty of the poor. In economist E. F. Schumacher's words, 'Nothing succeeds like success and nothing stagnates like stagnation. The successful province drains the life of the unsuccessful, and without protection against the strong, the weak have no chance; either they remain weak or they must migrate and join the strong; they cannot effectively help themselves.'[314] Quite definitely, the agenda of current neoliberal economics does not include the common good, nor is it designed to function according to ethical principles on questions of human relationships or the ecosystem.

In contrast to the *laissez-faire* view of the state promoted by today's global economic system, Scripture points to the state as being responsible for ensuring that socio-political and economic justice are highly honoured in society. The fundamental premises are: that the main cause of poverty is oppression, that God is a God of justice, and that justice is the unavoidable condition for peace.

Oppression and poverty

The problem of poverty is not merely economic. It is a complex issue that cannot be understood without taking into account not only the economic but also the social, political, cultural and religious factors involved. When these factors are given due weight, it becomes clear that poverty is essentially a relational problem. Bryant L. Myers, reviewing writings by several experts on the subject, rightly affirms that 'Poverty is a result of relationships that do not work, that are not just, that are not for life, that are not harmonious or enjoyable. Poverty is the absence of shalom in all its meanings.'[315]

This diagnosis of poverty, which is applicable to both individuals and nations, coincides to a large extent with biblical teaching. As Thomas D. Hanks has demonstrated, from a biblical perspective the basic cause of poverty is the oppression of the weak by the powerful.[316] The brief analysis I have made of the way in which the rich relate to the poor in the soybean industry today shows the relevance of the biblical insight into oppression as the basic cause of poverty in a world dominated by the global free-market economic system. The widening gap not only between rich and poor countries but also between the high- and low-income groups within countries, including those belonging to the industrialized nations, clearly shows that the global capitalism represented by the transnational corporations benefits the rich minority – the transnational class – but locks the poor majority into poverty and imposes exorbitant demands on the environment.

The justice of God

That God is the God of justice is taken for granted in Scripture. In order to understand God as a God of justice, however, it is essential to overcome the common misconception of justice as an abstract ethical concept. Rabbi Abraham J. Heschel is correct in maintaining that very few ideas are so deeply rooted in the mind of the biblical writers as the idea that justice and righteousness are inherent in God's character. 'This is not an inference,' he says, 'but an *a priori* of biblical faith, self-evident; not an attribute added to His essence, but belonging to the idea of God. It is inherent in His essence and is identified with His ways.'[317]

Scripture leaves no doubt that, because God is a God of justice, on the human level justice has to do primarily with power relationships among people and the correction of any form of inequity that there may be in those relationships. In any uneven situation where power is misused and the powerful take advantage of the weak, God takes the side of the weak. Specifically that means that God is *for* the oppressed and *against* the oppressor, *for* the exploited and *against* the exploiter, *for* the victim and *against* the victimizer. Because God loves justice, he is 'a stronghold for the oppressed' and 'the needy shall not always be forgotten, nor the hope of the poor perish for ever' (Psalm 9:9, 18). But because God loves justice, 'his soul hates the lover of violence' and 'On the wicked he shall rain coals of fire and sulfur; a scorching wind shall be a portion of their cup' (Psalm 11:5–6). 'The Lord works vindication and justice for all who are oppressed' (Psalm 103:6). That is the sense of the expression 'God's preferential option for the poor', coined in Roman Catholic circles in Latin America.

Many people react against this way of speaking about God. Their objection is that, because God is just, God does not take sides but deals with everyone on an equal basis. I respond to this as follows. First, because God loves justice, God requires that justice be done not only by the rich but also by the poor, and not only to the poor but also to the rich. The judges in the courtroom are obliged to be strictly impartial. Any form of injustice on their part, whether it favours the rich or the poor, is unpleasing to God. God's retributive justice is impartial and therefore excludes any form of favouritism (cf. Leviticus 19:15; Deuteronomy 1:16–17, 16:19; Micah 7:3–4).

Second, precisely because God is impartial, he is on the side of the poor and intends to correct any kind of imbalance of power created by sinful – and therefore partial – human beings. The partiality present in any situation of injustice is not God's but ours, as is clearly seen, for example, in Deuteronomy 10:17–19. Aside from pointing to the relationship between God's impartiality and God's action on behalf of the orphan, the widow and the stranger – the poor and oppressed – this passage throws into relief what God expects of Israel in terms of the practice of justice to the poor. The provision of food and clothing is God's provision, given to God's people to satisfy the basic needs of the poor. God's justice to the poor is executed through God's covenant to his people. It has to do with the correction of every form of abuse of power or unjust economic distribution, every violation of human rights present in society. It is not restricted to the courtroom, but embraces every human relationship and seeks to abolish every manifestation of injustice. It is corrective, rectifying justice, and in that sense partial.

Third, God's preferential option for the poor was ratified in the person and work of Jesus Christ, who claimed to be anointed by the Spirit to bring good news to the poor, to proclaim release to the captives and recovery of sight to the blind, to let the oppressed go free, and to proclaim the year of the Lord's favour (Luke 4:18–19). While there is good reason to beware a socio-political reduction of his ministry, no proper understanding of the teaching of the New Testament is possible unless one sees Jesus' mission as the fulfilment of God's purpose to establish his kingdom of justice and peace. In anticipation of the end of days, the kingdom of God has come into history, the new era has started, and the basis has been laid to proclaim good news to the poor (see Chapters 15 and 16).

Scripture leaves no doubt concerning 'God's preferential option for the poor'. Because God loves justice, he is against every kind of oppression and he expects justice to be done to the poor. The cause of justice, therefore, is not optional for Christians – it is a cause inherent in their commitment to God, who takes the side of the poor (see also Chapter 8).

Justice and peace

God's justice provides the basis for the redistribution of social, economic and political power in society for the sake of *shalom* – peace in the sense of wholeness, well-being, prosperity, life to the full – for every human being. It takes for granted that every member of a community – and, by extension, every human group and every nation in the world – is of equal value and is therefore socially entitled to have a rightful share of power, benefits and goods. It is closely related to covenant commitment (*hesed*) – solidarity with one another – and to humility before God, as is shown in Micah 6:8, which may be regarded as the synthesis of Old Testament ethics: 'He has told you, O mortal, what is good; and what does the Lord require of you but to do justice (*mishpat*), and to love kindness (*hesed* – [*covenant commitment, solidarity with one another*]), and to walk humbly with your God?'

In line with this ethical perspective, the central task of the rulers of Israel, beginning with the king, is to implement God's justice, as is clearly assumed in the prayer which opens Psalm 72: 'Endow the king with your justice (*mishpat*), O God, the royal son with your righteousness (*tsedakah*).' If justice is to mark the polity of the community, the king has to use his power to do justice to the poor. In other words, he is obliged to prevent the strong from taking advantage of the weak for their own aggrandizement – to ensure that there is equity in the distribution of power, and that all have access to the resources of God's creation. In Walter Brueggemann's words, 'The visionary insistence of kingship is that faithful kingship mediates Yahweh's sovereignty precisely in the performance of the transformation of public power in the interest of communal well-being.'[318]

On the basis of that vision, very frequently the prophets of Israel address their message to the rulers, denouncing their injustice and reminding them that their power is not to be used for their own benefit but in the service of justice. Intolerant of the oppression of the poor, they speak up in resolute terms on behalf of those who cannot speak for themselves. Their passionate call for justice is expressed in terms of unparalleled eloquence. If space allowed, I could give multiple examples of prophetic denunciations of injustice addressed not only to kings but also to other leaders, including princes, priests, judges and landowners, as well as to all the members of the Israelite community (but see Chapters 8 and 12). Justice is regarded as an essential element of God's covenant with his people and, as such, obligatory for every person without exception. Although addressed to the judges, the motto, 'Follow justice (*tsedek*) and justice (*tsedek*) alone' (Deuteronomy 16:20) applies to the whole nation.

Returning to the prayer for the king in Psalm 72, one is struck by the connection that it makes between justice and *shalom* – 'peace', but not merely in the sense of absence of armed violence, but in the sense of wholeness in all dimensions of life, prosperity or harmony in one's relationship with God, with one's neighbour and with God's creation. Endowed with God's justice and righteousness, the king will exercise his power for the sake of the well-being of the whole community, including its most vulnerable members. The result of his rule based on justice and righteousness will be a communal experience of *shalom*: 'The mountains will bring prosperity (*shalom*) to the people, the hills the fruit of righteousness (*tsedakah*)' (v. 3); oppression and violence will be eliminated (vv. 4, 14); there will be political stability (v. 5) and abundance of food (v. 16). Furthermore, the blessings of his rule will extend to other nations: 'All nations will be blessed through him, and they will call him blessed' (v. 17). *Shalom* involves just relationships under the sovereignty of God mediated by the king – communal relationships based on justice, but also the relationship between people and their environment based on righteousness.

The same vision of the close relationship between justice and *shalom* is brought into relief in Isaiah 32, which opens with words of hope: 'a king will reign in righteousness (*tsedek*) and rulers will rule with justice (*mishpat*)' (v. 1), and each person will be trustworthy (vv. 2–4). With the establishment of this new rule of justice and righteousness, the fools and the scoundrels will no longer exercise dominion over the people (v. 5). As a result, the neglect of the hungry and the thirsty will be over (v. 6), and the plea of the poor and the needy will be heard (v. 7). Furthermore, the false security of complacent women will be replaced by trembling in the face of problems of food production: poor harvests (vv. 10–12) and 'a land overgrown with thorns and briers' (v. 13). The royal palace will be abandoned, the city will be deserted, and the watchtower will become animal dens (v. 14). This situation of desolation, however, will change radically when, under the government of God-fearing rulers and by the action of the spirit of God, justice is practised, the fertility of the land is restored, and *shalom* is enjoyed as a result (vv. 16–20).

The world here depicted is a world of *shalom*. *Shalom* represents the vision of God's purpose for humankind. It points to a world where people experience the abundant life in terms that Jesus Christ used to define his own mission when he said: 'I have come that they may have life, and have it to the full' (John 10:10). It provides the horizon for the practice of socio-political and economic justice – God's answer to the longing of the Christian heart expressed in the Lord's Prayer: 'Your kingdom come, your will be done on earth as it is in heaven'.

The root cause for two of the greatest problems affecting humankind today on a global scale – ecological collapse and poverty – is beyond doubt an economic system rooted in an obsession for economic growth. The pursuit of increasing material wealth is part and parcel of the transnational corporations, the main vectors of a globalization that benefits the transnational class but locks millions of people into poverty, especially in the Majority World, and threatens the survival of the planet.

In the face of the challenge that this type of globalization represents, people with a social and ecological conscience need to be reminded that this is 'a game as old as empire'.[319] The present-day empire is not the first in the history of humankind, and all empires, sooner or later, have fallen. This one will also eventually fall. In the meantime, we have to make sure that we are raising the right questions with regard to our relationships and lifestyle, our fears and expectations, our weaknesses and our hopes. There is no formula to redress the dismal situation created by greed and to change the global economic system, but we must recognize that in order to break away from slavery to contemporary 'corporatocracy' (in the words of John Perkins) we need first of all to turn away from the enticing values of consumerism. From a Christian perspective, this is a call to repentance, but a call that needs to be placed together with the good news of the kingdom of God, as it was placed in Jesus' proclamation: 'The time has come. The kingdom of God is near. Repent and believe the good news' (Mark 1:15).

Because the kingdom of God has come in Jesus Christ, we Christians cannot allow ourselves to be sucked into a system that is causing genocide around the world and threatening to destroy earth in the name of economic growth. I fully agree with Walter Brueggemann, that 'the central conflict with the gospel in our time has to do with socioeconomic, political practices which bespeak theological idolatry, and idolatry that has come to exercise sovereignty over most of our life'.[320] Over against the idolatry of consumerism, those of us who acknowledge that the earth belongs to God and that human beings are not owners but only tenants of the land (Leviticus 25:23) must commit ourselves to a simple lifestyle that reflects an economy of 'enough', and seek ways to promote in our own community a responsible stewardship of natural resources.

Furthermore, as 'those who hunger and thirst for justice' (Matthew 5:6), we must always be willing to take the side of the oppressed against the oppressor. In the political realm that means that we are willing to exert all the influence we can to ensure that the rulers of our nations do not expect the 'invisible hand' of the free market to do what they are supposed to do; rather, they make it their priority to fulfil their God-given vocation to do justice to the poor. What this involves in practical terms is spelled out by Joseph Stiglitz, who, in his watershed book *Making Globalisation Work*, has suggested a number of specific 'steps to global justice'.[321] The task of working for justice for the poor and a responsible stewardship of natural resources is the primary political responsibility of Christians everywhere, but especially in the wealthy countries.

In the midst of the hopelessness provoked by today's ecological collapse and massive poverty, we continue to believe that a better world is possible because the same Spirit that 'testifies in our spirit that we are God's children' (Romans 8:16) is active in history. Therefore we can look forward to the fulfilment of our hope that 'the creation itself will be liberated from its bondage to decay and brought into the glorious freedom of the children of God' (v. 21). Indeed, we look forward to 'a new heaven and a new earth, the home of justice' (2 Peter 3:13).

12

Justice for all the earth:
society, ecology and the biblical prophets

HILARY MARLOW

The planet and all its inhabitants and life forms are suffering in
large part because some members of the human community
have violated their right relationship with creation, tipped the
balance, and acted unjustly and unethically. When read in a contemporary socioecological context, the texts of the prophets . . .
offer readers a disturbing picture that calls for an ethical
response that can no longer be avoided.

(Carol Dempsey, *Hope Amid the Ruins* (2000), 88)

An internet search for the terms 'environmental justice' and 'ecological
justice' brings up two totally different kinds of website. The first term,
'environmental justice', leads to websites that address issues of justice
for human beings in the face of ecological disasters and abuses.[322] These
include the effects of pollution and toxic waste on human health, the
annexing of fertile cropland in the service of big business, and, more
recently, the impacts of global warming on struggling communities.
More often than not, it is the poor and marginalized who are the
victims of such environmental injustice, as they bear the consequences
of industrial and construction processes driven by political or economic interests. As the conservation organization Friends of the Earth
(FOE) puts it, 'everyone should have the right [to] and be able to live
in a healthy environment, with access to enough environmental
resources for a healthy life . . .' FOE add that it is predominantly the
poorest and least powerful people who are lacking these conditions.[323]
The focus in such sites is on empowering local communities to ensure
that living and working conditions are safe and healthy and, in the
words of one website, 'to investigate, expose and peacefully resolve
abuses'.[324] In the USA, campaigning for environmental justice is closely
integrated with advocacy for racial and social inclusion.[325]

By contrast, searching for the phrase 'ecological justice' leads to websites concerned mainly with the well-being of other species and ecological systems that are threatened by human development. At the most extreme, such sites adopt an anti-human stance, suggesting that 'ecosystems and individual species should be preserved whatever the cost, regardless of their usefulness to humans, and even if their continued existence would prove harmful to us'.[326] A more moderate definition of eco justice would be justice that seeks to 'preserve and advocate for just relationships among all living things'.[327]

These differences represent broadly the delineation within environmental theory and practice between anthropocentric concerns (prioritizing human needs over those of other species and ecosystems) and ecocentric ones (focusing on non-human species, with human beings often regarded as the villains). But such a demarcation can be questioned on both philosophical and theological/biblical grounds.[328] The theocentric orientation of the Old Testament presents an alternative perspective – one that is concerned with both human interests and those of the wider creation yet with neither as the ultimate goal. Within this framework, human relationships to God and to the natural world can be conceived of as a triangle of relationships, each affecting and interacting with the others (Figure 12.1).

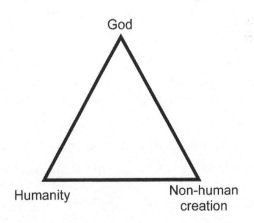

Figure 12.1 Diagram illustrating the triangular relationships between God, humanity and the rest of creation.

This relational model is used by biblical scholar C. J. H. Wright as a basis for investigating the relationship in the Old Testament between Israel's God Yahweh, his people Israel and the promised land, and subsequently developed in Wright's later books to encompass the wider context of God, humanity and the earth.[329] Reading the Scriptures with this triangular framework in mind brings new and sometimes surprising insights into God's interaction with all of his creation, both human and non-human, and particularly into the relationship between human beings and the natural world, which is often overlooked.

I use this framework here to examine the concept of justice in the Old Testament, in particular in some of the prophetic books. For a number of the biblical writers, justice is concerned with social relationships. The well-being of society and its future security depends, in part at least, upon Israel's maintenance of God's ethical standards – including the treatment of the more vulnerable members of the community (for example, see Deuteronomy 24:17–22). But is such well-being just limited to human culture and society? What is the relationship between social well-being and that of the land or earth (the Hebrew word *ha-'aretz* can refer to either)? How does social injustice affect the wider creation? Seeking answers for these questions from the biblical texts themselves offers new insights into the message of the prophets – insights that resonate with and are relevant to current environmental concerns. So the primary focus of this chapter is on a number of Old Testament prophetic passages where the concept of social justice is linked with the natural world, in oracles of either judgement or restoration. This provides the basis for suggesting ways in which the biblical text might be relevant in today's world, with its serious environmental issues, as well as instances where the worldview of the prophets differs from the contemporary Western perspective.

Justice in the Old Testament

In the Old Testament justice begins with God (Psalm 89:14) and is something that he gives to his people (Isaiah 33:5; Psalm 72:1). In the prophetic and poetic books of the Bible, a just and equitable order in society that reflects the just and righteous attributes of God is often described using the stock phrase 'justice and righteousness'.[330] In addition there are numerous other places throughout the Old Testament in which these two nouns are used in parallel sentences (parallelism is a stylistic device in Hebrew poetry, whereby one phrase repeats or elaborates the ideas of the preceding one; for example, Psalm 36:6, Amos 5:24.). This chapter concentrates on a few specific passages, primarily from the prophets, where ideas of justice and righteousness are clearly articulated, either by using the phrase 'justice and righteousness' or by means of parallelism, and which suggest a link between justice in society and the well-being of the natural world.

Justice and righteousness and the king

I begin with the royal Psalm 72, which depicts the ideal of a just king and offers a blueprint for the vision of society that the prophets develop.[331] The psalm begins with a petition for God to give his justice and righteousness to the king, and these opening words provide a summary of the whole prayer. The psalmist elaborates his request in the verses that follow as a series of attributes of the ideal monarch, each of which flows from the outpouring of God's justice and righteousness on his human representative. The outworking of this in society encompasses correct legal governance and equitable judicial decisions (v. 2) as well as their practical application in concern for the poor and the relief of oppression (v. 4).

The ideas in verses 2 and 4 frame a reference to the natural world in verse 3. Under the rule of a just king, peace (*shalom*) and righteousness will flow from the mountains and hills onto the people of his kingdom. What exactly this signifies is explained by a passage from Deuteronomy (33:13–17), which similarly links together the two terms 'mountains' and 'hills'. In this text, Moses' blessing on the tribe of Joseph is almost entirely concerned with the fruitfulness and flourishing of the land, including 'the finest produce of the ancient mountains, and the abundance of the everlasting hills'.[332] So too in Psalm 72, when the psalmist prays for peace and righteousness to flow from the mountains and hills, his request is for the flourishing of the natural world. Both the position of this verse in the psalm and its use of the vocabulary of justice and righteousness suggest a connection between the maintenance of divinely instituted order in society and the well-being of the wider creation.[333]

These ideas are repeated later in the same psalm (vv. 12–16) to complete the author's idyllic picture of a fundamental connection between human and non-human creation. If the king maintains justice and righteousness in human society, the fruitfulness of the land is guaranteed. As will be seen, this idea of cause and effect, whereby what happens in society impacts on the natural world, is also apparent in a number of prophetic oracles.

Justice and righteousness in the prophets

Micah 6

Justice in society is a prominent theme in several of the prophetic books of the Old Testament, most notably Micah, Amos and First Isaiah (Isaiah 1—39). The eighth-century prophet Micah epitomizes this when he proclaims:

> He has declared to you, O human, what is good,
>   and what the Lord requires from you.
> It is to do justice, love kindness
>   and walk humbly with your God. (Micah 6:8)

This simple statement, 'to do justice, love kindness and walk humbly with your God', encapsulates the Old Testament's vision for right relationships among human beings and between humankind and God (see also Deuteronomy 10:12–21). For the prophet Micah, walking wholeheartedly with God also involves responsibilities towards other human beings.

The wider context of this passage highlights three further points, which are also echoed by other Old Testament prophets, as we shall see. First, there is the hypocrisy of religion without justice. The words of Micah 6:8 are the prophet's answer to a question about the acceptable way of entering God's presence (v. 6). Micah rejects the idea that animal sacrifices and burnt offerings alone are sufficient to bring favour with God (v. 7). Neither the quantity of offerings ('thousands of rams') nor the extreme cost to the giver ('shall I give my firstborn') are what pleases God. Rather, says Micah, what matters is attitude and actions towards others.

Second, there is the central importance of social justice. Micah's somewhat unspecific charge to 'do justice, love kindness' in verse 8 clearly relates to behaviour towards the marginalized in society, as the rest of the chapter makes clear. In verses 9–12 the Lord condemns dishonest weights, ill-gotten gains, violence and deception – all wrongs perpetrated by the wealthy against the weak (v. 12a). Both the practice of selling with short measures and the attitude of greed and dishonesty are offences not merely against the victims but against God himself. Then, as now, abuse and exploitation of the poor by those in positions of power and influence represent serious moral failure.

Third, there are the consequences for the land. God's response to such violent and deceptive behaviour is to allow sickness (*chalah*) and desolation (*shamam*) to afflict those who have relied on their wealth and status (vv. 13–15). These words 'sickness' and 'desolation' denote the consequences of human wrongdoing, consequences that manifest themselves in people as moral and physical sickness, and in the land as destruction and loss of fertility. The punishment is not abstract; it is physical, affecting not only landowners but the well-being of their land, and is a direct reversal of the hopes and desires expressed in Psalm 72. Notice the idea of futility and failed expectations (vv. 14–15): eating yet not being full, sowing yet not reaping a harvest. The rich land-owners, who no doubt assumed the success of their crops, will be afflicted with famine and hunger.

The prophet Micah has seen an inextricable link between the way people worship God, their treatment of other human beings, and the welfare and productivity of their lands. This outlook is shared by a number of other prophets.

Isaiah 1

The opening chapter of Isaiah (1:11–15) uses the strongest of language to condemn the hypocrisy of the religious behaviour of the people of Judah (the southern kingdom of Israel). The outward signs of religious observance – multitudes of sacrifices, or zealous observance of religious festivals – are not pleasing to God. So long as the people's attitudes and behaviour towards others are harsh and unjust, their prayers, however fervent, will remain unheard and unanswered.

The prophet goes on to explain that the kind of behaviour God desires consists of repentance: 'wash and cleanse yourselves', followed by actions that demonstrate a genuine change of heart: 'cease doing evil, learn to do good' (vv. 16–17). What this means in practice is elaborated in the rest of verse 17 in terms of treatment of the marginalized: 'Seek justice, set right the ruthless; judge for the orphan, contend for the widow'. As in Micah, religious observance is meaningless when social injustice prevails.

There are other similarities between this chapter and Micah 6. Israel's rebellion against God is described as sickness of the body (Isaiah 1:5–6), and desolation and depopulation of the land (v. 7), in both cases using the same words as Micah 6, *chalah* and *shamam*. The idea of cause and effect, of connection between human actions and the well-being of the land, is amplified in verses 19–20, where obedience to the Lord is a prerequisite for eating the good of the land. One interesting addition to Isaiah 1 is the prophet's reference to the destruction of Sodom and Gomorrah in verses 9 and 10, which is a motif picked up by other prophets and one to which I shall return.

Amos 4

In Amos 4 the prophet begins by indicting the rich women of Bashan for their oppression of the poor and needy and their lives of opulent luxury (v. 1). Bashan was a fertile area to the east of the river Jordan, which was well known at the time for its lush grazing and fine livestock. Hence, the comparison with thoroughbred cattle, as well as being insulting, is an allusion to the richness and beauty of these women. They are guilty of abusing their privileged positions, and of indifference or arrogance towards others.[334]

A few verses later, Amos adopts a sarcastic tone to denounce the people's love of religious observance at two of their beloved shrines (vv. 4–5). Both their reliance on their wealth and their presumption that religious observance brings favour with God have aroused his anger. The prophet lists a series of calamities that the Lord has inflicted upon them, in a vain attempt to warn them against this behaviour (vv. 6–11). Some of these disasters concern the well-being of the land, as crops have been afflicted by drought, blight and pests (vv. 6–9), while others directly affect the human population – death by plague and injury (v. 10), and an earthquake reminiscent of the destruction of Sodom and Gomorrah (v. 11) (see Leviticus 26, Deuteronomy 28 and 1 Kings 8). The consequences of Israel's rejection of its God are felt in the cycle of harvest and fertility, but also expressed in terms of cataclysmic devastation. Each successive calamity is, suggests the prophet, an opportunity to repent; on each occasion, Israel has failed to heed the warning: 'And yet you did not listen.'

In Amos 5 and 8 the prophet repeats the message. Devastation in the natural world – both the failure of crops and wider cosmic disruption – are the result of the people's shortcomings, both in their worship and in their inability to practise justice and righteousness (5:4–15, 8:4–12). Like Isaiah and Micah, he sees not only a close link between worship of God and relationships towards other people, but also between how society operates and the fruitfulness of the wider world.

Social injustice in Sodom and Gomorrah

In a number of places, including Isaiah 1 and Amos 4, the biblical prophets draw an analogy with the destruction of Sodom and Gomorrah in Genesis 19. To understand why, we need to look a little more closely at this story. At first reading of Genesis 19 it might seem that the inhabitants of Sodom are condemned for their breach of the traditions concerning hospitality towards strangers, or for their homosexual inclinations, or both. However, in Genesis 18 it is immediately after God issues his mandate to Abraham: 'to keep the way of the Lord by doing righteousness and justice' (v. 19) that he expresses outrage over the sins of Sodom and Gomorrah (v. 20). This juxtaposition suggests that the reason for the destruction of these two cities may lie in their abuse of wider principles of justice and righteousness.

This interpretation is confirmed in another reference to Sodom in Ezekiel 16, where Judah is compared unfavourably with that city. Here the charges laid against Sodom are not sexual, but that 'she and her daughters had pride, excess of food, and prosperous ease, but did not aid the poor and needy' (v. 49). The prophet Ezekiel is explicitly stating what Genesis 18 implies – that Sodom's downfall is as a result of social inequity, arrogance and indifference to the plight of the poor. In Genesis 18 and 19 Abraham is held up as a model of justice and righteousness, while Sodom and Gomorrah are condemned for the opposite – oppressive and arrogant behaviour towards those powerless to withstand them.[335] In the story that follows, this manifests itself as uncontrolled and lawless mob violence.

These allusions to Sodom and Gomorrah in the prophetic books of the Old Testament are evidence of a longstanding Israelite tradition that regarded these cities as synonymous with evil. By comparing Israel and Judah with such wickedness, the prophets reinforce their message that violation of the standards of justice and righteousness is regarded as the most serious of offences against the Lord, punishable by utter destruction.

But this raises some questions about the nature of the judgement meted out in these prophetic texts, both for the poor and needy, who are ostensibly the recipients of the justice and righteousness advocated by the prophets, and for the whole of the natural world. The devastation of the land portrayed in these texts is undoubtedly catastrophic for the whole human population, not just the wealthy elite, as well as for the rest of creation. Are the poor not then worse off as a result of God's response to injustice? From an ecological perspective, God's judgement could also be said to adversely affect wider habitats and biotic communities. How does disruption of the land signify justice for the natural world? Is it divine wrath rather than justice and righteousness which triumphs – in human society and the natural world?

Justice for whom?

Although the prophetic denouncements described in these texts are addressed to political leaders or the wealthy elite, the effects of God's judgement surely impact on the whole population. Famine, drought and disease affect all levels of society, with the poorest arguably suffering the most (see Chapter 7). In the turbulent aftermath of natural disaster or war, it is the weak and vulnerable who are likely to get pushed to one side. The prophets' condemnation of the rich and powerful for their exploitation of the needy and the call for the restoration of justice and righteousness seem at odds with the comprehensive disasters which the texts depict. How can this apparent moral inconsistency be explained?

One way of looking at this is to explore more closely the exact nature of the social exploitation condemned by the texts. Several commentators suggest that, by the eighth century BC, a class of wealthy landowners had arisen in Israel and Judah who had been unscrupulous in forcing individuals and families from their ancestral lands (see also Chapter 8). The story of Naboth's vineyard in 1 Kings 21 is a good example of this practice. Similarly in the prophet books, the prophets take issue with this dispossession of the poor from their lands, as Hemchand Gossai suggests with regard to Amos:

> Now, the 'fruitful earth' is no longer providing for the poor, the 'people of the land', but is taken over by the powerful . . . The land, as a gift from Yahweh and as an element which is the right of every Israelite, now becomes the exclusive property of the rich.[336]

The failure of crops and the devastation of the land in so many of these texts are thus forms of judgement intended specifically to eliminate the rich and powerful by removing their means of economic support, and restoring to the poor the land from which they have been dispossessed. The prophets contrast wealth and poverty, gain and loss, to make their point in indictments addressed to those who have illegitimately acquired land and who will be deprived of it.[337]

Closely linked to this is the Israelite understanding of the land as sacred gift from God. With this gift comes a set of obligations – to the Lord, and to other members of the community (Deuteronomy 12:1). If the people obey God, he promises them blessings: health, peace, fertility and fruitfulness for both them and their land (Deuteronomy 28:1–14). If they are disobedient these promises will fail; instead both they and the land will be cursed (vv. 15–44). Even prior to the entry into Canaan, at the start of Genesis this sense of interconnectedness between the Lord, human beings and the earth pervades the text. This is particularly seen in the effect on the land of Adam's sin against God (Genesis 3:17–19) and of Cain's violence against his brother (4:10–13). It is echoed in the covenant following the flood, which is between God and all living things (a phrase repeated six times in eleven verses), not just with Noah and his family (9:9–17). The message of the prophets echoes that of Deuteronomy as they call the people to recognize the implications of God's goodness and gift for their behaviour towards him and towards others.

Justice for the land?

Not only does disruption of crops and desolation of the land potentially demonstrate injustice rather than justice for the poor, it also begs questions of how the prophets thought about the earth itself. Does it matter that the outpouring of God's judgement causes havoc to the natural world, and potentially damages his own creation? Some interpretations of these biblical texts, and indeed of the whole Old Testament, suggest that the biblical writers are concerned only with God's dealings with human beings. Hence the non-human natural world comes to have only instrumental value, and can be used or abused merely to further the human story. If this is so, then the Old Testament fits firmly in the category of anthropocentric environmentalism outlined at the start of the chapter, and has little to say to ecologists.

But this is not the whole picture. There are many instances in the Old Testament of a concern and interest in the whole natural world as part of God's creation, independent of human beings. Perhaps the clearest example is Job 38—41, where God's answer to Job's sense of injustice and pain is to draw his attention to the rest of creation. In a magnificent description of the physical universe, the text tells us how God challenges Job to reassess his perspective on life in the light of the whole created order, not just his own problems: 'Where were you when I laid the foundations of the earth?' he asks (38:4). In these chapters the natural world has value in its own right and is a reminder of human frailty and insignificance and a demonstration of the greatness and power of the creator God. In the end, all Job can do is humble himself before God and worship him (42:1–3). Likewise the whole of Psalm 104 is a hymn of praise to God as creator and sustainer of the world and a celebration of the wonder and diversity of his creation. Human life features briefly in this psalm (v. 23), but is not the predominant theme. Rather, human beings are just one among many creatures who look to the Lord for life and sustenance (vv. 27–30).

Isaiah 34

Similarly, the prophets' perspectives on the natural world do not always centre on its potential usefulness to human beings. The created order reveals God's name (Amos 4:13, 5:8–9, 9:5–6), and mourns as a response to human sin and God's judgement of the world (Hosea 4:3; Amos 1:2; Jeremiah 12:10–11). Likewise the judgement oracle in Isaiah 34 suggests that human beings should not presume upon their position in the world. The Lord's 'day of vengeance' in 34:9–17 is described as a series of disasters that have devastating effects on both the rural and urban landscapes, yet prove to be positive for wild animals at the expense of human beings. The text describes a number of physical changes reflecting environmental adaptations that might be observed by contemporary ecologists, not all of which is necessarily ecologically damaging.[338]

The judgement begins by describing the physical deterioration of the landscape (Isaiah 34:9–10). The land is burned, soil degraded and water courses contaminated, leading to long-term desertification and depopulation: 'From generation to generation it shall lie waste; no-one shall pass through it for ever and ever' (v. 10) (Figure 12.2). This makes way for an alternative ecology to develop as wild animals replace human beings (v. 11a). The next verses describe the destabilization of society, including the lack of leadership and eventual abandonment of the local city (vv. 11b–12). The vocabulary of verse 11 includes *tohu* 'formlessness' and *bohu* 'emptiness' – two words used in Genesis 1:2 to describe the pre-creation state, which may at first glance suggest that Isaiah 34 is describing the 'unmaking' of creation. However, here the devastation is not that of the whole created order, but only part of it, namely human civilization and society. The deserted and ruined buildings become overgrown with thorns (v. 13) and this paves the way for other species, both animals and birds, to colonize the former human habitation (vv. 14–15). Finally, verses 16–17 confirm that this habitat change has come about specifically as part of God's plan and purpose. The end of verse 17 repeats the phrases of verse 10 in order to stress the

Figure 12.2 'Thorns shall grow over it' (Isaiah 34:13). Thorn tree in Namib desert, Namibia. (Photo: Luca Galuzzi, used under the Creative Commons Attribution Share Alike 2.5 licence.)

permanent nature of this new habitat: 'They [*the animals*] will possess it for ever, from generation to generation they shall live in it.'

From a wider ecological perspective, the desolation and depopulation of the landscape has allowed another part of the created order apart from humanity to flourish. The ecological balance has shifted at God's behest in favour of the non-human creation, a change that warns against the assumption that human interests are all that matter to God. The power of the natural world, whereby settled land reverts to wilderness, and is colonized by wild animals, is a reminder, then as now, that human settlement and cultivation is not the default mode of the natural environment (see Chapter 13).

God's ways in the world

To a modern reader these judgement oracles might seem to offer a very simplistic understanding of the way the world works, in which human behaviour is the only criterion for the flourishing of the natural order. Even worse, they might suggest that God is behind modern-day natural disasters, such as the tsunami of Boxing Day 2004.[339] To respond to this, we need to recognize that the ancient view of the world was very different from our own, and it would be anachronistic to try to retroject our own scientific understanding of the working of the world and causes of natural phenomena into the biblical texts. Ecologists today realize that the world is not a static system in which natural processes operate according to a fixed, predetermined pattern, but one that is evolving in response to a complex range of variables.[340] The cycle of death and decay is necessary for life, and the processes that give rise to natural disasters are often essential to the functioning of the planet we call earth (see Chapter 7).

The ancient Israelite view of how God acts within his creation is described in a very directly causal manner, in which the wind is God's messenger (Psalm 104:4) and the eagle soars at his command (Job 39:26). For us, reconciling contemporary scientific understanding with belief in a creator God necessitates a rethinking of emphasis and vocabulary, as articulated by Vinoth Ramachandra:

> The creator respects the integrity of his creation. The relationship between creator and creation cannot be described adequately in the language of 'controlling' and 'ruling'. There is also

a 'letting-be', a willingness to let the creation unfold in its own way and according to its intrinsic character.[341]

In another respect, however, the writers of the Old Testament seemed to grasp some vital principles that we are often slow to understand in our modern world. They recognize the cyclical aspect of the world, whereby life operates around rhythms of sowing and harvesting, of birth and death, and where actions in one sphere can have far-reaching and often devastating effects in another. For them, justice is not an individual thing, but a communal responsibility. It is not to be equated with fairness, but rather a matter of maintaining divine order in the world. When this breaks down, a sense of balance, of *shalom* is lost, and the reaction is severe and drastic (see Chapter 11). Just as a pendulum swings widely in the opposite direction before settling, so the consequences of injustice shake the structure of their world to the core.

Restoration of justice

The prophets of the Old Testament are not exclusively concerned with messages of doom and judgement. They also offer hope of restoration to those who turn back to God, and they portray a vision of the world in which relationships are put right – between people and God, within human society and in the wider creation. A number of passages in Isaiah demonstrate that the prophetic vision of justice and righteousness encompasses restoration of the natural world as well as of human society, and provide an interesting and positive counterbalance to the messages of judgement. In Isaiah 29:17–21 the restoration of the non-human creation is portrayed as a return to fruitfulness of both field and forest (v. 17), and this is coupled with the end of injustice in society (vv. 20–21). Note the reversal of the 'sickness' described in Micah 6 and Isaiah 1 as physical healing figures alongside the coming of joy in Isaiah 29:18–19.

Similarly in Isaiah 30, when the Lord shows himself as the God of justice and righteousness (v. 18), the people turn from their idolatry, and the natural pattern of rainfall is restored. The result is abundance of crops in the fields (vv. 23–24) and spiritual healing for God's people (v. 26). In Isaiah 32 the outpouring of the 'spirit from on high' (v. 15) brings flourishing and fruitfulness to the wilderness as well as justice, righteousness and peace for the human population (vv. 16–17).

Such restoration is portrayed even more dramatically in Isaiah 35, which features healing of the blind, deaf and lame (vv. 5–6), as well as rejuvenation of the natural world, with the focus on wilderness rather than on the farmed land (vv. 1–2). Justice and righteousness are not specifically referred to but are implicit in the description of healing – in ancient society, as today, those with physical disability are very likely to experience abuse and injustice. Finally, moral wholeness is portrayed as the Way of Holiness (v. 8), which will bring those who walk it to a place of 'everlasting joy' in God's presence (v. 10). This chapter of Isaiah presents a picture of the exuberant and colourful restoration of barren and potentially hostile environments, as well as the renewal of human society, and of human relationship with God. In this passage as in the other restoration texts, the renewal of society and of the natural world, of human and non-human creation are inextricably linked.

Nowhere is this expressed more clearly than in the final text under consideration – the promise of the messianic king in Isaiah 11, which complements Psalm 72, which I discussed earlier. Here is an idyllic picture in two parts, in which a ruler from David's line ushers in a reign of justice and righteousness for the poor and judgement for the wicked (vv. 1–5), and where peace and harmony are established between predatory and poisonous animals and their prey (vv. 6–8). The ideal king is characterized, among other things, by 'the knowledge of the Lord' (v. 2) and this will also be the worldwide result of his coming (v. 10). Under his reign of justice and righteousness, not only will the wrongs in society be righted, but a fundamental change will occur in the whole of the natural world. This concept is obviously difficult to reconcile with contemporary scientific understandings of ecology and cycles of predation. But perhaps it is best to see it as dramatic picture language depicting the restoration of relationships and the coming of peace, *shalom*, in the whole of the created order, including the establishment of harmony between wild and domestic animals, and between wild animals and human beings. Just as the consequences of the Lord's judgement, as has been seen, often include disruption of the natural world, affecting the fertility of the soil and the boundaries between human and animal populations, so here the restoration of God's order under the banner of justice and righteousness represents a reversal of this process.

A prophetic message for today?

All these passages from the Old Testament prophets have much in common – both vocabulary and themes – which suggests that they share a common understanding of the relationship between social and natural spheres. For these prophets, just as the fate of the earth is inextricably linked with the punishment of human transgressions, so too the coming of justice and righteousness clearly encompasses more than human conduct in society.

The prophets' account of the relationship between justice in society and fruitfulness and stability in the natural world points to their fundamental belief in a divinely instituted world order. Such an order does not absolve human beings of their responsibilities. On the contrary, people, particularly those in positions of power or influence, are held accountable for both social and environmental breakdown. The well-being not only of the poor but also of the earth itself would appear to lie in their hands.

Despite the 2,500 years that separate these ancient prophecies from our current situation of global environmental crisis, their words have enormous relevance. If Amos and his contemporaries were proclaiming their message today, they would surely be talking about global warming and its impact on the poor and on the rest of creation. The oracles of these prophets remind us:

- of the capacity of we human beings to affect the well-being of our own environment and that of others, whether urban or rural;
- of the reality of cause and effect, whereby actions by one group of people produce consequences that affect others, often detrimentally;
- more specifically, that the actions and lifestyles of the rich and powerful may have serious and negative effects on the poor and marginalized and that overconsumption and greed threaten the long-term well-being and fruitfulness of the earth for all;
- that the theocentric perspective of the biblical texts presents a positive and holistic vision of the world that removes the need for demarcation between the ecocentric and anthropocentric positions held by environmentalists;
- that the assumption that the world should revolve around the needs of human beings is, in fact, presumption;

- that Christian worship of God, however fervent, is meaningless and even offensive to him unless it is accompanied by a profound change of heart demonstrated in just and righteous attitudes and behaviour – especially towards those those who suffer poverty and deprivation.

The biblical perspective differs from the current situation in one significant respect: it demonstrates a different understanding of the sequence of cause and effect. In the prophetic texts, it is neglect of justice and righteousness for the poor that results in the desolation of the land. By contrast, in today's situation neglect of the well-being of the earth (by overuse, exploitation and climate change) has a serious and negative effect on justice for the world's poor. But perhaps these are just two ways of saying the same thing: that the world is an interconnected whole and we ignore this at our peril. The prophets' call for social justice, although it comes from their own very different understanding, experiences and expectations, nevertheless calls us as Christians to examine carefully the impact our own actions have not merely on other human beings but on the rest of the natural world as well. To do any less than that is to make our worship of God into a hollow and meaningless charade.

13

Jesus, God and nature in the Gospels

RICHARD BAUCKHAM

As enfleshed, embodied in the soil like us, Jesus contains within
his humanity the whole evolving earth story.
> (Edward Echlin, *Earth Spirituality:*
> *Jesus at the Centre* (1999), 70)

None of the Gospels was ever meant to stand alone. Each explicitly pre-
supposes the Old Testament and presents its story as the continuation
and climax of the story of God, Israel and the world told by the Hebrew
Scriptures. Moreover, Christians read the four Gospels within the
context of the whole canon of Scripture. To read the Gospels well, we
need to understand them in that wider context of the biblical metanarrative.

A metanarrative or 'grand narrative' is a story we tell about the
meaning of everything, a story that sketches the total context within
which all the other stories we tell about ourselves or the world find
their meaning. In the Bible's case its metanarrative runs from creation
to new creation, from God's pre-historical act of bringing all things
into being to his post-historical act of renewing all things so that his
whole creation can participate in his own eternal life. There is a striking
symmetry between the first two chapters of the Bible, which portray
creation, and the last two chapters, which portray the renewal of this
same creation. Many of the documents included within this biblical
collection of books also refer back to creation and forwards to new
creation, but even those that do not can gain their full meaning only
when we read them within such a context.

The biblical metanarrative is all about the relationship between
God, human beings and the non-human creation. It has at least three
key participants, each of them a figure for more than one participating
subject. But, in the reading of Scripture, especially in the modern

period, the role of the third participant, the non-human creation, has been routinely minimized, degraded or forgotten altogether. The non-human creation has been seen merely as a stage on which the drama of the history of God and humanity has been played out – and a temporary stage, at that, due to be dismantled and removed when the story reaches its final climax. Even worse, too often Christians have thought of human embeddedness in nature as a fate from which we need to be liberated. But such religious disparagement of the non-human creation can scarcely be blamed on the Bible. The Bible is full of material about the relationship of humans to nature, partly at least because for people of biblical societies it was an inescapable, absolutely taken-for-granted aspect of human life lived close to non-human creatures. The problem is that modern readers of Scripture have usually failed to attend seriously to that material. They think of it as just part of the historical context, of the sort of lives people lived then, and they leave it aside when they reflect on the meaning of biblical stories, which they assume to be about human beings and God. Or they treat it as no more than poetic imagery deployed to tell us about human beings and God. Now that contemporary human society has once again woken up to the absolute seriousness of how we relate to the rest of nature, we must read the Bible with our eyes retrained to see that the Bible also takes our relationship to the non-human creation with complete seriousness.

If we think of that threefold relationship – between God, human beings and the rest of creation – as a triangle connecting each of the three with the other two, the Bible does have one limitation in how it fills out the triangle (see also Chapter 12). It is, of course, a book for human beings. About the side of the triangle that connects God directly with the rest of nature, it concentrates on the extent to which that relationship is relevant to us human beings. There is doubtless much about God's relationship with non-human creatures that the biblical writers never attempt to explore. But it is not a biblical idea that God and the non-human creation relate only via the mediation of humanity. The biblical writers refer to the direct relationships that God has with his non-human creatures of all kinds, even though they understandably focus on the other two sides of the triangular relationship.

The kingdom of God as the renewal of creation

The unifying theme of the gospel story, at least in the Synoptic Gospels (Matthew, Mark and Luke), is Jesus' messianic mission to proclaim the inauguration of the kingdom of God and to practise its presence. (In the Gospel of John, instead of the phrase 'the kingdom of God' used in the Synoptics we have 'life' or 'eternal life'.) The kingdom of God should be understood as the renewal of creation, the restoration of God's rule over his creation, in opposition to all that alienates, disrupts and damages, and the bringing of God's purpose for his creation thereby to its final fulfilment.

Two specific points involved in this understanding of the kingdom need to be stressed. First, the kingdom is holistic in character. It involves the healing of all aspects of human life in relation to God: spiritual, bodily, social, political and the human relation to the non-human creation. It does not concern only the human relationship to God, abstracted from other aspects of human life. It does not concern only the soul abstracted from the body. It does not concern only the human individual abstracted from human society. It does not concern only humanity abstracted from the rest of creation. It concerns human life in all its aspects and relationships, including human relationships with the rest of creation.

This holistic character of the kingdom is indicated by the signs of the kingdom that Jesus performs: the healings, exorcisms and other miracles. These are not just symbols, but actual instances of the coming of the kingdom in its various aspects, anticipating its coming in fullness at the end of history. Just as the miracles in which Jesus restores people to bodily health should not be reduced to symbols of a purely spiritual salvation, so the miracles that involve the non-human creation should not be deprived of their real reference, as signs, to the natural world. The nature miracles show that the healing of the human relationship with non-human nature belongs to the holistic salvation that the kingdom of God means in the Gospels.

The second point to emphasize is this: if the kingdom of God is the renewal of creation, there cannot be a kind of opposition between creation and salvation history, or between creation and eschatology (that is, the coming of the kingdom). The kingdom does not abolish or replace creation, but renews and fulfils it. Jesus' God is the Old Testament God of creation, especially the God who provides for all his creatures and attends even to the least of them (Matthew 5:45, 6:29, 10:29–31; Luke 12:6–7, 24), just as Jesus' God is also the God of Israel, and the God who is establishing his kingdom in all creation. The Jewish understanding of God as creator is something that Jesus could take for granted, but it was the necessary presupposition of his message that God is working to overcome the evil that mars creation and to bring his whole creation to perfection.

That the kingdom of God is the renewal of creation must be stressed because biblical scholarship in the modern period has not been immune from the influence of the dominant ideology of the modern West, in which human history has been seen as a process of emancipation from nature. This modern ideology imagined human beings as the omnipotent subjects of their own history, and history as a process of liberation from nature, so that, freed from a limited place within the given constraints of the natural world, human beings may freely transform nature into a human world of their own devising. This rejection of human embeddedness in nature and of the mutual inter-relations between human history and the rest of nature, in favour of an assumed independence of and supremacy over nature, is, of course, the ideological root of the ecological crisis. Its influence in biblical theology can be seen in a tendency to set history against nature and salvation against creation. The frequent assertion that salvation-history and/or eschatology are the key concepts of biblical theology – at the expense of creation – tacitly endorsed the modern understanding of history as emancipation from nature. The Gospel references to nature have been persistently understood from the perspective of modern urban people, alienated from nature, for whom literary references to nature could only be symbols or picturesque illustrations of a human world unrelated to nature. But once this modern ideology is questioned, as it has now been very widely, we shall not find it in the Gospels. The Gospels in continuity with the Old Testament tradition assume that humans are thoroughly embedded in nature and live in mutuality with the rest of God's creation, that salvation-history and eschatology – the kingdom of God – do not lift humans out of nature but heal precisely their distinctive relationship with the rest of nature. The goal is 'the renewal' (Matthew 19:28) of all things, not humans alone (*he palingenesia*, 'the renewal', is evidently used as a semi-technical term and therefore most plausibly refers to the new creation of all things).

Messianic peace with wild animals

In all three Synoptic Gospels Jesus spends time in the wilderness before embarking on his proclamation of the kingdom of God. The account in Mark's Gospel is briefer than those in Matthew and Luke, but Mark alone mentions the wild animals:

> He was in the wilderness forty days, tempted by Satan;
> and he was with the wild animals;
> and the angels ministered to him.[342] (Mark 1:13)

This account of Jesus in the wilderness follows Mark's account of Jesus' baptism, when he was designated the messianic son of God. The Spirit then takes Jesus into the wilderness for a task he must fulfil before he embarks on his preaching of the kingdom of God. Why must Jesus go into the wilderness? The wilderness is a richly symbolic notion in the biblical literature, but basic to the Jewish view of the wilderness was that it is the non-human sphere of the earth. So it is there that Jesus meets three categories of non-human being: Satan, the wild animals and the angels. He has to establish his relationship as Messiah to all three before he can embark on his mission in the human world, which fills the rest of the Gospel.

Brief as Mark's account of Jesus in the wilderness is, each part of it is important. The order of the three beings he encounters – Satan, the wild animals, the angels – is not accidental. Satan is the natural enemy of the righteous person and can only be resisted. Angels are the natural friends of the righteous person: they minister to Jesus. But between Satan and the angels, the wild animals are more ambiguous. On the basis of the common ancient and biblical perception of wild animals as a threat to human beings, we might expect them to be dangerous enemies, especially when located in the wilderness, the habitat that belongs to them and not to humans. But, on the other hand, since Jesus is the messianic king, inaugurating his kingdom, might we not expect his relationship to the wild animals to be appropriate to that kingdom?

In the prophetic expectation of the Messiah, his kingdom is a sphere in which the enmity between humans and the wild animals is turned into peace:

The wolf shall live with the lamb,
    the leopard shall lie down with the kid,
the calf and the lion and the fatling together,
    and a little child shall lead them.
The cow and the bear shall graze,
    their young shall lie down together;
    and the lion shall eat straw like the ox.
The nursing child shall play over the hole of the asp,
    and the weaned child shall put its hand on the adder's den.
They will not hurt or destroy
    on all my holy mountain;
for the earth will be full of the knowledge of the Lord
    as the waters cover the sea.

                      (Isaiah 11:6–9; see also Isaiah 65:25)

This passage has often been misunderstood by modern readers as a picture simply of peace between animals. In fact, it depicts peace between the human world, with its domesticated animals (lamb, kid, calf, bullock, cow), and those wild animals (wolf, leopard, lion, bear, poisonous snakes) that were normally perceived as threats both to human livelihood and to human life. What is depicted is the reconciliation of the human world with wild nature (Figure 13.1).

In the light of that prophecy, it seems likely that, in Mark's depiction of Jesus in the wilderness, whereas Satan is simply an enemy of Jesus and the angels simply his friends, the wild animals, placed by Mark between those two, are enemies of whom Jesus makes friends. Jesus in the wilderness enacts, in an anticipatory way, the peace between the human world and wild nature that is the Bible's hope for the messianic future.[343] Mark's simple but effective phrase ('he was with the wild animals') has no suggestion of hostility or resistance about it. It indicates Jesus' peaceable presence with the animals. The expression 'to be with someone' frequently has, in Mark's usage (Mark 3:14, 5:18, 14:67; cf. 4:36) and elsewhere, the sense of close, friendly association. Mark might have thought of the ideal relationship between wild animals and human beings, here represented by their messianic king, as the restoration of dominion over them or as recruiting them to the ranks of the domestic animals who are useful to people. But the simple 'with them' can have so such implication. Jesus befriends them. He is peaceably with them.

Figure 13.1 'Christ in the Wilderness' by Moretto da Brescia (Alessandro Bonvicino; c. 1498–1554). (Courtesy of the Rogers Fund, Metropolitan Museum of Art, New York.)

The context to which Mark 1:13 originally spoke was one in which wild animals threatened humanity, and their wilderness threatened to encroach on the human world. The messianic peace with wild animals promised, by healing the alienation and enmity between humans and animals, to free humans from that threat. Christians who read Mark 1:13 today do so in a very different context, one in which humans threaten the survival of wild animals, encroach on their habitat, and threaten to turn their wilderness into a wasteland they cannot inhabit. To make the point, one need only notice how many of the animals Jesus could have encountered in the Judean wilderness have become extinct in Palestine during the past century: the wild ass, the desert oryx, the addax, the ostrich and no doubt others. But Mark's image of Jesus' peaceable companionship with the animals in the wilderness can survive this reversal of situation. For us, Jesus' companionable presence with the wild animals affirms their independent value for themselves and for God. Jesus does not adopt the animals into the human world,

215

but lets them be themselves in peace, leaving them their wilderness, affirming them as creatures who share the world with us in the community of God's creation. Mark's image of Jesus with the animals provides a biblical symbol of the human possibility of living fraternally with other living creatures, a possibility given by God in creation and given back in messianic redemption. Like all aspects of Jesus' inauguration of the kingdom of God, its fullness will be realized only in the eschatological future, but it can be significantly anticipated in the present by respecting wild animals and preserving their habitat.

Messianic pacification of chaos

Where an ecological perspective on the ministry of Jesus is perhaps especially illuminating is in relation to the nature miracles, which are not to be reduced to symbols of something else, but are signs of the kingdom precisely in their engagement with non-human nature. The best example is the stilling of the storm.

In Mark's version of the story, he depicts Jesus and the disciples in a fishing boat on the lake of Galilee when a storm arises and puts them in serious danger. The disciples wake Jesus, and he, says Mark, 'rebuked the wind, and said to the sea, "Peace! Be still!" Then the wind ceased, and there was a dead calm.' The disciples' fear of the storm gives place to awe of Jesus, and they say to one another, 'Who then is this, that even the wind and the sea obey him?' (Mark 4:37–41).

The key to understanding this story is to recognize its combination of, on the one hand, a realistic situation and, on the other hand, strong mythical overtones. The situation of the disciples reflects realistically the hazards of sailing on the lake of Galilee, and also stands for the kind of quite frequent situations in which first-century people might find themselves in danger from the forces of nature. The mythical overtones of the story do not cancel out this realism but say something of religious significance about such a realistic situation.

The myth is a way of envisaging creation that is widely reflected in the Old Testament. It speaks of the primeval waters of chaos, the destructive powers of nature imaged as a vast tempestuous ocean, which God in creation reduced to calm and confined within limits so that the world could be a stable environment for living creatures. These waters of chaos were not abolished by creation, only confined, always ready to break out and endanger creation, needing to be constantly restrained by the creator. For ancient Israelites the waters of the myth ical abyss were not simply a metaphysical idea. In something like a storm at sea, the real waters of the sea became the waters of chaos, threatening life and controllable only by God. In the case of this story, a squall on the lake of Galilee (which, significantly, Mark here calls the sea) is enough to raise the spectre of elemental chaos.

When Mark says that Jesus 'rebuked the wind and said to the sea, "Peace! Be still!"', he recalls the most characteristic ways in which the Hebrew Bible speaks of God's subduing the waters of chaos. The 'rebuke' is God's powerful word of command, as in Psalm 104:7: 'at your rebuke the waters flee'. The word that silences the storm occurs, among other places, in Job 26:12: 'By his power he stills the sea', again referring to the creation myth. It is the creator's rebuke to chaos, then, that Jesus utters, and the peace of the creation secured against chaos that Jesus restores. This is why the disciples ask, 'Who then is this, that even the wind and the sea obey him?'

By telling the story with these mythical overtones, Mark invites us to see the event as presaging God's final elimination of chaos from the natural world, when, as the book of Revelation has it, there will no longer be any sea (Revelation 21:1). This is how the event functions in the Gospel story as a sign of Jesus' inauguration of the kingdom of God. It goes to the heart of the hostility between human beings and nature, promising that the destructive rage of the forces of chaos still active in the natural world against living creatures will in the end be pacified by God.

The disciples' question with which Mark's narrative leaves its readers – 'Who then is this, that even the wind and the sea obey him?' – points to the divine identity of Jesus, since the power of the creator over the cosmic forces of nature was generally agreed to be uniquely divine. Jesus does not, in this story, instantiate a general human possibility, but acts in a uniquely divine way.

When we read this story in a contemporary context, we should recall that the great scientific technological project of the modern world aimed to accomplish what is here ascribed to God. Instead of accepting our helplessness before the vast forces of nature, modern humanity aimed to eliminate the danger by harnessing and controlling nature. A lot was achieved, although, as the 2004 Asian tsunami and subsequent natural disasters have brutally reminded the world, nature retains destructive power of a kind we can scarcely imagine controlling

'). Climate change illustrates how human attempts to
can easily end up releasing powers of nature inimical to
this case it is humans who have unwittingly unleashed
symbolically appropriate that one of these effects is that
s now seem certain to submerge whole areas of inhabited
land (see Chapters 2 and 5).

The story of Jesus' pacification of the storm reminds us that control
of nature is godlike and humans may rightly participate in it only as
creatures, dependent on God and nature, respecting the givenness of
the created world.

Messianic lifestyle

One of the themes of the teaching of Jesus in the Synoptic Gospels with
which modern readers have found it most difficult to cope is that concerning material possessions and material needs. Jesus appears to
require his disciples not to accumulate material possessions, not to lay
up treasures on earth, and at the same time to live without the anxiety
that drives people to secure themselves materially by acquiring possessions. Instead, his disciples are to live by radical faith in their heavenly
Father's day-by-day provision of the basic necessities of life. This theme
is succinctly expressed in one of the petitions of the Lord's Prayer: 'Give
us this day our daily bread' is the expression of trust in the Father's
provision, not of affluence but of basic necessities and only on a
day-by-day basis. The prayer is designed to undercut the motives for
acquisitiveness and materialism. Its radical character appears especially
when we realize that Jesus is using the model of the day labourer, who
was employed and paid only one day at a time. The insecurity of such
a way of life made it peculiarly undesirable. Jesus evidently expects his
disciples to live like the day labourer, but to find security in their trust
in God's provision.

A fuller account of this approach to material needs and possessions is found in Matthew 6:25–34 (and similarly in Luke 12:22–32),
which is also a very significant instance of Jesus' indebtedness to Old
Testament creation theology.[344] When Jesus cites the example of the
birds that God feeds (Matthew 6:26),[345] he alludes to a familiar Old
Testament theme: the creator's provision of food for all his living
creatures:

Matthew 6:26:   Observe *the birds of the air;*   (Luke 12:24: *ravens*)
they neither sow nor reap nor gather into barns,
and yet your heavenly Father *feeds them.*
Are you not of more value than they? . . .[346]

Psalm 147:9:   He *gives* to the animals *their food,*
and to the *young ravens* when they cry.

Psalm 104:10:   You make springs gush forth in the valleys . . .
     11: giving drink to every wild animal . . .
     14: You cause the grass to grow for the cattle,
and plants for people to use,
to bring forth food from the earth . . .
     21: The young lions roar for their prey,
seeking their food from God . . .
     27: These all look to you
to *give them their food* in due season;
     28: when you give to them, they gather it up;
when you open your hand, they are filled with
good things.

Job 38:39–41:   Can you hunt the prey for the lion,
or satisfy the appetite of the young lions,
when they crouch in their dens,
or lie in wait in their covert?
Who *provides for the raven* its prey,
when its young ones cry to God,
and wander about for lack of food?

Psalm 145:15–16:   The eyes of all look to you,
and *you give them their food* in due season.
You open your hand,
satisfying the desire of every living thing.

In these passages[347] God is envisaged as himself directly providing food
for his creatures: the lions seek their food from God, the young ravens
cry to God, all creatures look up to God to provide for them, and he
opens his hand to provide them with food. The writers are of course
speaking of the ordinary natural ways in which animals and birds get

their food, but they see these as very directly the creator's provision for his creatures. Jesus speaks in the same way.

In the great creation Psalm 104, notable for its depiction of human beings as one species among others in the community of creation for which the creator cares, human beings are included among the living creatures who all look to God for food (vv. 27–28). The same words are echoed in Psalm 145:15. Here the psalmist is concerned primarily about God's care for human beings who turn to him in need. He refers to God's provision for all living creatures in order to assure humans of God's provision for them. In Matthew 6:26 Jesus does the same.

Jesus uses a 'how much more' argument, a form that is typical of his teaching, as also of rabbinic style:[348] 'your heavenly Father feeds [the birds]. Are you not of more value than they?' This gives formal expression to the connection between God's provision for other living creatures and his provision for human beings that can already be seen in Psalm 145. It would denigrate the value of the birds only if it meant that God is likely to let the birds starve in order to provide for humans. But the argument is quite different: because God so evidently does value the birds and does provide for them, he will certainly also provide for humans.

Jesus strengthens the lesson from the birds by observing that 'they neither sow nor reap nor gather into barns, and yet your heavenly Father feeds them'. There have been two main kinds of interpretation of the force of this statement. Some have supposed that Jesus contrasts the birds, who do not work, with people, who do. The argument then is: if God feeds even the idle birds, how much more will he provide for people, who work hard for their living! Others have thought that Jesus compares the birds, who do not work, with disciples, who do not work either. Jesus' disciples or early Christian wandering preachers who did not engage in economically productive labour are assured that God will provide for them just as he does for the birds. In my view it is unlikely that either of these possibilities is the point.

The point is rather that, because the birds do not have to labour to process their food from nature, their dependence on the creator's provision is the more immediate and obvious. (It is not that birds do not have to exert energy in order to find their food, but they do not have to process the food.) Humans, preoccupied with the daily toil of supplying their basic needs, may easily suppose that it is up to them to provide their own food. This is the root of the anxiety about material needs that Jesus is showing to be unnecessary. The way in which people get their food by labour allows them to focus on their own efforts and to neglect the fact that much more fundamentally they are dependent on the divine provision, the resources of creation without which no one could sow, reap or gather into barns. The birds, in their more immediate and obvious dependence on the creator, remind us that ultimately humans too are no less dependent on the creator.

When we recognize the rootedness of Jesus' argument in Old Testament creation theology, three important consequences follow. First, in contrast to the way the passage has very often been understood, the divine provision of material needs of which Jesus speaks cannot be a special providential provision for Jesus' followers or for those who live by faith. It is God the creator's provision for all his creatures. It is the resources of creation that God provides for all to live from. Jesus' point is that when people recognize this provision, when they see that in the end they are dependent not so much on their own efforts to provide for themselves but on what the creator gives them in the form of the resources of the natural world, then they can trust God instead of worrying. People obsessed with their own efforts to provide for themselves, driven by the insecurity of the situation as they see it, never have enough. People who recognize their dependence on the creator can be content with his day-by-day provision for them and are liberated from anxiety in order to seek the kingdom of God.

Second, if the kingdom of God were some kind of alternative to creation, then the command to seek first the kingdom (Matthew 6:33) would come very incongruously after the creation theology of the rest of the passage. Rather, God the creator's fatherly provision for all his creatures is a characteristic precisely of his rule over his creation – his kingdom – which in Jesus he is re-establishing against all opposition and bringing to perfection. For Jesus' disciples to know him as Father is to rediscover him as the fatherly Creator who cares for his creation, and to seek his kingdom is to live as creatures in his creation, to treat the world as his creation, to seek his will for his creation.

Third, Jesus' references to the birds and the lilies are not mere figurative illustrations of his point, as though the point could stand without the illustrations. Rather they belong to the basis of the whole argument: faith in the creator who provides for all his creatures. We cannot have the moral – that we can trust God for basic material needs – without its premise: that we are creatures along with the birds and the lilies. The attitude to God and to material needs that Jesus demands is possible only when people see themselves as participants in the community of living creatures for which the creator provides – eminent participants, certainly ('Are you not of more value than they?'), but participants nonetheless.

Recalling our contemporary situation, we may now be able to see that Jesus' teaching is not a matter of economic naiveté or irresponsibility as has sometimes been alleged. Rather, it invites us to see the world and ourselves as God's creation and the resources on which we depend to live as God's provision for all his creatures. Certainly, Jesus' concern with subsistence contrasts sharply and instructively with the modern talk of wealth creation. At least in Western industrial society, the instinctive human anxiety about having enough to survive to which Jesus refers has long been superseded by the drive to ever-increasing affluence and obsessive anxiety to maintain economic growth (see Chapters 9 and 12). Western people today are obsessively worried not even about maintaining the standard of living we have, but about maintaining its constant improvement. It is this anxiety that is depleting and destroying the resources of nature and depriving not only other species but many humans of the means even of mere subsistence.

Jesus' creation theology assumes that the God-given resources of creation provide abundantly for the needs of all God's creatures. But he speaks of human needs, not of human affluence, and therefore, of course, also of equitable sharing of the creator's provision for our needs. (In his Jewish context, Jesus can presuppose the provisions of the law of Moses, which are intended to supply the basic needs of the poor, who do not have economic resources of their own.) Of course, the birds of the air are no comfort to those starving in Africa unless they are also a challenge to those who are squandering creation's resources elsewhere. It is only when we live within the proper limits of creatures in the givenness of the created world that God's provision is more than enough for all. The ecological necessity of living within limits is a painful one for those so addicted to excess as ourselves. It requires a different way of looking at the world, which Jesus offers when he invites his disciples to consider the birds and the lilies. They represent a natural world of abundance and beauty, which exists by the creator's generous gift, independently of all our efforts to create our own world of plenty and beauty for ourselves. We need to recover our real relationship to that world of God's creatures if we are to be able to seek God's kingdom and further his purposes for his creation.

Thus Jesus' teaching about material possessions – rejecting acquisitiveness, freedom from anxiety, trust in God for basic needs – coincides with the contemporary ecological requirement to moderate our use of resources. The phrase 'living within limits' could describe both Jesus' teaching and the contemporary ecological need. But this is not just a pragmatic convergence of Jesus' teaching with the demands of the contemporary ecological situation. This passage shows how Jesus' teaching is rooted in creation theology. The attitude to material needs that he recommends requires that we see ourselves as participants in God's creation, creatures alongside other creatures, dependent on the creator's provision for all his creatures, and therefore content to live within the limits given us by the created world to which we belong.

It is not, of course, easy to determine the appropriate limits, but our observations on Jesus' teaching would suggest that they are those limits on our own consumption that enable both other human beings and other species also to live and to flourish. (The slogan 'Live simply so that others may simply live' puts it well.) A useful example of the kinds of distinction we need to make is one that theologian Michael Northcott, addressing the key issue of carbon emissions, makes when he adopts a distinction between 'livelihood emissions' and 'luxury emissions'[349] (and see Chapter 14).

Incarnation and resurrection

So far I have restricted this discussion to the Synoptic Gospels. The special value of the Gospel of John for our present concerns lies in its explicit understanding of Jesus as the incarnation of God in human life. The prologue to the Gospel (1:1–18), with its opening allusion to the opening words of Genesis, depicts the pre-incarnate Christ as the divine word of God, who created the whole cosmos. In incarnation this word's relationship to the cosmos goes a remarkable step further. The one who made the world enters the world (1:10). The strongest statement of this is in the words, 'the Word became flesh'. With this phrase John emphasizes the materiality of being human (cf. 3:6, 6:63). Flesh is human nature in its vulnerability and weakness. It is also human nature in its commonality and kinship with the rest of creation, human nature made out of the dust of the earth, utterly dependent on all the physical conditions of life on this planet, interconnected with other life in diverse and complex ways. Jesus in incarnation is not just part of humanity but also part of this worldly creation, a member of the whole community of creation. When the church in the course of its early history sought a way of stating the full truth of the incarnation, it said that Jesus is both fully divine, like God in every respect, and fully human, like us in every respect except sin. To be fully human, Jesus must be as much part of this material world as the rest of us.

A prominent way in which John's Gospel understands the mission of Jesus – in his incarnation, life, death, resurrection and exaltation – is that he brings eternal life to this mortal creation. As can be seen in 3:3–16, 'eternal life' is John's equivalent to the term 'kingdom of God' as the Synoptics use it. God's renewal of his creation is the imparting of his own eternal life to it, so that it may not perish, as merely mortal life must, but live in union with God eternally. In the famous summary at 3:16, the explicit reference, as always in this Gospel, is to the salvation of humans, but we should note that it begins with the words: 'God so loved the world (*kosmos*)'. The renewal of all creation is certainly not excluded.

In this connection it is important to recognize that human salvation in this Gospel is not the salvation of pure spirits from the world of matter, even though it has sometimes been interpreted in this way. It is rather the giving of eternal life to humans in all their materiality. So the human commonality with the rest of creation is not something left aside in eternal life. Here we should notice that John's Gospel, like Luke's (Luke 24:40–42), puts considerable stress on the bodily materiality of the risen Jesus. He shows his disciples the marks of crucifixion on his hands and his side, and even invites the Apostle Thomas to touch them (20:20, 25, 27). For Jesus himself, resurrection was no mere spiritual survival, but the renewal of his full bodily reality. The same will be true of those to whom he gives eternal life (cf. 5:25–29). This perception of both Jesus' own risen life and the salvation of those who believe in him suggests that we cannot regard the rest of the *kosmos* as no more than a temporary backdrop to the drama of salvation. We belong to it as well as to its creator.

14

Sustaining ethical life in the Anthropocene

MICHAEL NORTHCOTT

A people, we may say, is a gathered multitude of rational beings united by agreeing to share the things they love. To discover the character of any people, we have only to observe what they love.
(Augustine, 'City of God', in O. O'Donovan, *Common Objects of Love* (2003), 3)

H. G. Wells is said to have observed that 'when I see an adult on a bicycle, I do not despair for the future of the human race'. And a character in Iris Murdoch's novel *The Red and the Green* suggests that 'the bicycle is the most civilized conveyance known to man. Other forms of transport grow daily more nightmarish. Only the bicycle remains pure in heart.' But in my home city of Edinburgh, despite the on-road cycle lanes, so long as Accident and Emergency units continue to treat a disproportionate number of cyclists after 'accidents' with motor vehicles, a very small number of commuters will use bicycles as a means to get to work. Though there has been a rise in cycling in London since the introduction of the congestion charge, all other areas of Britain have seen a decline in journeys taken by bicycle compared with 20 years ago. This is in large part because of the increased number of cars on the road and consequent rising dangers to cyclists.[350]

Motor vehicles are the single largest source of luxury greenhouse gas (GHG) emissions (see Chapters 2 and 5). Luxury emissions are the avoidable emissions of the rich and such emissions are responsible for a dramatic growth in global GHG emissions since 1999.[351] Most car journeys in intensively settled European cities such as Edinburgh are avoidable in the sense that there are, albeit less individually convenient, other possibilities. Despite increasing evidence of the unsustainability of this mode of transport, more vehicles are made in Britain today than were manufactured in the heyday of Austin, Healey, Jaguar, Morris, Riley and Wolseley. A staggering 1.26 million people die annually from road accidents and over 10 million are injured.[352] Traffic pollution moreover causes ill health for hundreds of millions.[353]

The marketing of consumption

The obstacles to sustainability are nowhere more evident than in the commercial advertising and marketing of motor vehicles and the hidden public absorption of their many dis-benefits. Psychologically manipulative adverts associate car ownership with effective parenting, personal comfort, power, sexual attraction, sport, social status and wilderness. Cars are rarely advertised in traffic jams and car advertisements never refer to the potential of vehicles to kill and maim. Vehicle advertising is just one example of the ubiquity of advertising in modern industrial societies. Adverts are crucial drivers of unsustainable consumption, for without a constant flow of advertising images people would not purchase and consume as many devices and material objects.[354] Advertising and the rituals of consumption it sustains represent a moral and spiritual system that is insidiously powerful in its hold over the imagination of young people and adults alike.[355]

It is widely assumed in the environmental movement that, if modern industrial societies are to achieve a sustainable relationship with the ecosphere, this will require a change of mind and heart in the citizenry. Aldo Leopold, the twentieth century's most influential advocate of a 'land ethic' that sets the health of the land at the heart of human ecology, suggested that conservation could not be achieved without 'creating a new kind of people'.[356] A recent multidisciplinary investigation of the roots of unsustainability from the Yale School of Forestry and Environmental Studies, America's oldest environmental school, suggested that it is the attitudes and values of citizens that stand in the way of effective public and policy responses to climate change and species extinction.[357] But the report nowhere considers the shaping power of advertising and marketing on those values, arguing instead that it is primarily the modern experience of living apart from nature, the extinction of regular sensory encounter with nature, that is crucially implicated in unsustainable ways of living.

The religious traditions of Judaism, Christianity and Islam have a stronger sense of the power of images to shape lives that arises from their shared critique of idolatry. The ban on idols is the first command-ment given to Moses in a tradition of law that has been handed down over thousands of years, and the ambiguous power of images contin-ued to be a source of controversy in Christian and Jewish history, and in Islam until the present day, as witness the controversy over the Danish cartoons of the Prophet Muhammad. In essence, idolatry is the worship of created things, the conferral of worth on objects made by human hands and the correlative diminution of worth given to the creator. God is described in the book of Exodus (20:5) as a jealous God who is angered by the worship of idols. At the root of this anger is the divine knowledge that when humans devote themselves to things they have made from the divine creation, rather than to the creator, they devote themselves to lies. When they devote themselves to lies they bring destruction and violence into their society and they make sacri-fices – even of their own children – to the gods that they make.

Modern industrial humans are sacrificing their children and their children's children to their current devotion to climate-changing machines such as cars and aeroplanes. The destabilization of the climate system threatens not just the distant but the near future of children now being born. But in the presence of the power of the image to capture the hearts and minds of modern citizens, this threat lacks motive force.

Sources of transformation

The Christian tradition, like the other Abrahamic faiths, suggests that a new people can be fashioned through a story of judgement and redemption that evokes repentance and spiritual transformation. However, repentance, a new way of life, can only come about when there is a change of heart and mind, when the temples of the old gods and the lies that their worship sustains are dethroned and judged as unworthy of worship, and when people devote themselves instead to the worship of the true God who is worthy of love and worship. This is why Christ not only preaches repentance but also condemns the existing religious hierarchy, and predicts the destruction of the Jewish temple, which had become the tax-collecting heart of the colonial Roman economy in Palestine.[358] This is why St Paul inveighs against the gods and sacrifices of Corinth, Galatia and Ephesus and ultimately of Rome itself. Change of heart, exposing lies, condemning idols, brings conflict with the existing order and this conflict ensued in the systematic persecution of Christians when the Roman authorities perceived the threat to the imperium.

Analogously, in the present moment of ecological crisis, appeals to the hearts and minds of citizens will not change the unsustainable direction of modern industrial civilization without a more systematic engagement with modern idolatry and the lies that the idols sustain. The wide-scale promotion of the car and the correlative downgrading of the bicycle, pedestrians and public transport indicate that the change that is needed is not just in the sphere of the human heart. Unless government planners, law makers and transport infrastructure providers make it possible for people to get out of their cars and adopt sustainable forms of mobility, many people will remain wedded to fossil-fuelled 'private' cars until, as now seems entirely possible, peak oil prices and the 'credit crunch' make their use prohibitively expensive.

The fossils that daily fuel the vehicles and other climate-changing machines of *Homo industrialis* represent centuries of the stored energy produced by photosynthesis, which is the response of plants and shellfish to sunlight, by means of which they turn carbon dioxide (CO_2) into oxygen, and so created an atmosphere beneficent to life. As these creatures locked sufficient quantities of mobile CO_2 into their bodies in prehistory, the climate of the planet gradually stabilized and *Homo sapiens* eventually responded to this new stable climate by growing crops, building cities, making music and writing laws. But the present fossil-fuelled civilization shows no respect for the primordial ecosystem service that this stored biomass performs. Coal, oil and gas companies take what historian Rolf Peter Sieferle insightfully calls the 'subterranean forest' from under the earth's crust and release its stored carbon back into the atmosphere.[359] This is changing the relationship between the earth and the sun and bringing to an end the 10,000-year Holocene era of climate stability in which human civilizations have developed.

It is because of this era of climate stability that modern humans possess stories and artefacts that link them across a significant proportion of the Holocene to such seminal figures as Abraham, Noah, Moses, the Buddha, Christ and Muhammad. Climate stability has structured human life in such a way as to make possible a set of religious traditions that sustain a species memory across thousands of years far beyond the capacity of intergenerational memory to sustain storytelling in oral form. These great stories are structured by climate stability,[360] and it is that stability that modern human activity is putting at risk. Humanity now stands on the edge of an era in which climate instability will come to dominate the near future. Nobel Laureate Paul Crutzen has called the new era the Anthropocene, since human emissions have become the principal driver of climate variability.[361]

Ecological limits to growth

As human influence over the planet has increased because of techno-logical power and the weight of human numbers, the sense of human connectedness to and dependence upon the natural order is diminish-ing. This diminution is in part a consequence of the move to cities, in which energy, food and water are brought from beyond the city limits by networks and processes on which citizens rely but which distance them from the natural origins of these biological essentials. It is also related to a refusal to recognize limits to the ability of the earth to sustain the exponential economic growth that is ordered from city offices and to absorb the waste products of the economic processes that cities promote and procure. The goal of economic growth under-girds the political aspirations and economic policies of almost every developed and developing country, and of the corporate bodies and command-and-control centres – the World Trade Organization, the World Bank, the stock exchanges – that oversee and sustain their economic interactions. Consequently the word 'sustainability' tends in everyday economic and political parlance to mean 'sustaining eco-nomic growth'. The word is rarely used in the sense in which it was originally used in the Brundtland Commission report: that present humans should adopt forms of development that are consistent with the renewing capacities of ecosystems and the needs of future gener-ations to live on a planet whose ecosystems are still functioning in ways beneficent to human and non-human life (see Chapter 5).

The climate crisis is part of a larger and systemic ecological crisis that has seen degradation of all ecosystems increase in recent decades. The quantities of fish being caught in fossil-fuelled trawlers are so great that some marine biologists believe the oceans could be emptied of most life forms within 50 years.[362] At the same time, deforestation, particularly in tropical regions, grows apace. In Borneo alone an area of forest equivalent to 47 soccer pitches disappears every day. The Amazon is experiencing an even greater rate of forest loss. In Borneo, deforestation is driven primarily by palm oil companies, who are already turning palm oil into transport fuel in the form of biodiesel. In the Amazon most of the burned forest is replaced with soy and corn to meet the growing demand for animal feed as developing countries follow developed countries in their meat consumption. Palm oil and animal feed from tropical forests have a climate footprint far greater than fuels and feeds derived from other terrains because the burning of the forest is a significant source of GHGs. Moreover, as tropical soils dry out after deforestation they continue to release significant quantities of CO_2 and methane into the atmosphere.

Love and the good society

The word 'ethics' derives from the Latin word *ethos*. Its meanings include not just a set of beliefs or values but a way of life, an orientation to the world. For Aristotle, the greatest moral philosopher of the classical world, ethics means the good life, and the goals that humans need to pursue if they are to realize that good life.[363]Aristotle believed that it was the responsibility of the family and the *polis* (the city state in Ancient Greece) to shape the lives of children and citizens so as to enable them to develop those practices and character traits that he called the virtues. For Aristotle, ethics, organic and material life are intricately related, since the gods who ordered human life to realize the virtues and the ultimate end of contemplation of the divine are also the gods who made the biological and material world. The good life for Aristotle therefore concerns a certain way of taking up the physical world and cannot be reduced, as it is by modern philosophers such as Hume, Kant and Mill, to inner emotional states, rational beliefs or 'values', and judgements of consequences. Aristotle also believed that it was only possible to live the good life in a society whose laws and practices shaped the citizenry to realize the virtues. The good society is a society directed by the supreme virtue of justice, which, for Plato as well as Aristotle, is the virtue that orders all the others.

For Christians, love, not justice, is the ordering virtue. This insight is the defining characteristic of Christ's ethical teaching in the Sermon on the Mount (Matthew 5—7). The crucial import of Christ's moral teaching for *Homo industrialis* is that it is not possible to love and serve two masters: if mammon is the master, then God cannot be. A society that sets monetary measures of expanding wealth – such as the rate of increase of Gross Domestic Product – at its heart is a society that has dethroned God and that therefore prevents its citizens from realizing the good life. Such a society is an idolatrous society that will sacrifice people and species and the earth system itself to the gods of mammon. Just as Christ recognized that the ordering power of mammon was in the Temple in Jerusalem, where Rome's financial grip on Palestine was located, so the devotion to modern mammon must be traced back to advertisers and marketers, to the economic ministries, international financial institutions, and corporate headquarters that sustain the lie that economic growth is the definitive source of human well-being (see Chapter 11). To recognize that the ecological crisis is a moral and spiritual crisis does not confine that crisis to the human heart. On the contrary, it roots it in the centres of power in the cities – in Washington and New York, in London and Paris, in Frankfurt, Rome, Stockholm and Tokyo. Modern human beings love created things above the creator, things such as cars and clothes and computers that are not worthy of worship. That is why their societies are committed to policies and programmes that are destroying the planet.

The centrality of love to Christian ethics was further elaborated by Augustine in the fourth century; he argued in *The City of God* that the quality of any society can be discerned from the honour and dignity of the common objects that humans love.[364] If Augustine or St Paul were to revisit the streets of the cities of Rome and Athens that they once knew, the novelty that would assault their senses would be the sight, speed, sound and smell of the motor car. They would soon come to know that the car is the common object of love that more than any other is at the heart of the modern city where so many office blocks are devoted to the quarrying of metal ores, the extraction of oil, the design of engines and bodies, the construction of roads and car parks, and the insurance, financing, advertising and marketing of cars (Figure 14.1).

The extent of devotion to this idol of consumption is represented not just in physical palaces and paved highways but in the way in which the economic measure of welfare deals with the costs and benefits of motoring. That crude contemporary measure of economic well-being, Gross Domestic Product, counts most of the costs, or 'externalities', of motoring including road accidents and deaths, and pollution-related illnesses requiring pharmaceutical or hospital treatment as enhancements of national wealth and well-being. All of these provoke increases

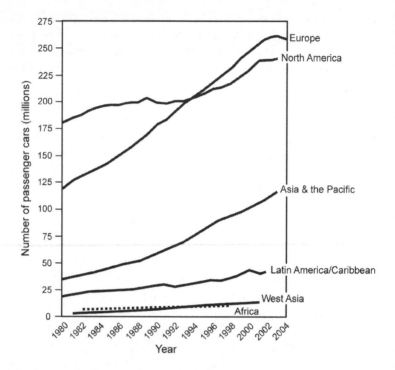

Figure 14.1 Number of passenger cars, by region, 1980–2004. (From GEO Data Portal, compiled with data from Number of passenger cars, by region of the world. (Data source: UN Statistics Division Transport Statistics Database, 'UN Statistical Yearbook', available at <geodata.grid.unep.ch/>).)

in measurable economic activities and hence create employment and grow monetary exchanges. Here again we see the connection between idolatry and lies.

Economism is the name sometimes given to the claim that increased economic activity benefits human welfare. While it is true that growth in the consumption of goods and services has enabled reductions in human mortality and increased well-being in developed and developing countries, research indicates that the relentless pursuit of wealth beyond modest income levels in developed countries has actually diminished human happiness.[365] Ecological economists suggest that it is possible to adapt this foundational assumption of modern economics to the limits of sustainability by attributing monetary values to non-human resources and the ecosystem services that they render to the economy (see Chapter 4).[366] But this adaptation of the presently false materialism of endless growth and consumerism only magnifies its misshaping of modern citizens for it suggests that only when there is a monetary price on everything – including even the air we breathe as is now proposed in the procedures of carbon emissions trading (see Chapter 5) – will it be possible to create a sustainable economy. This revisionist approach completely misses the deep untruth that is at the heart of the money economy, which is the idolatry of the artifactual and monetary form of humanly generated wealth, and the exaltation of mammon above God, of consumption above contemplation.

The origins of consumerism

If we enquire into the historic roots of our consumer revolution we find that it coincides with British colonial expansion.[367] Cheap but high-quality cottons imported from India fuelled demand in an unprecedented way for clothing and cloth in England in the 1690s. Markets in factory-made clothing were advanced by the invention of 'fashion', which necessitated changes in clothing style from year to year, while markets for linen, crockery, cutlery, furniture and other household goods also rapidly expanded. The shift towards fashion was accompanied by a new cultural individualism in which personal expression in clothes and possessions became more central to the sense of self and the orientation of self in the world. Consumption and style rose in cultural significance and a new focus on domestic interiors, personal comfort and luxuries, and designed rather than productive landscapes expressed an emergent shift to everyday life and material possession as the focus of human fulfilment in the seventeenth and eighteenth centuries.

Colonial expropriation of land overseas not only acted as a driver of the new consumer capitalism. It also provided the paradigm for the enclosure of common land at home: the peasant classes were driven from areas whence they had sustainably derived food, fuel and animal fodder, into the polluted slums of early industrial towns and cities, where they provided a pool of labour for the workshops and factories that produced the fashion items. This process continues today in Africa, Asia and the Americas as food surpluses, subsidized to fuel low-waged factory workers, undermine viable rural food economies and force subsistence farmers off the land and into city slums and wage slavery.

According to the growth-oriented theories of economists, these new coerced urban migrants will eventually also make the transition from slavery to volitional consumerism; but, if all 3.5 billion urban dwellers were to consume at levels close to those of the present urban rich, the planet would not only run out of carbon sinks and oil but land for animal feeds, forests, fish, minerals and metal ores, and clean drinking water (see Chapters 6 and 10).

Recognition of the continuing injustice of coercive wage slavery has been taken up in the consumer-driven movement, in the USA and beyond, against sweatshop labour, and in the ecclesiastically originated practice of Fair Trade in Europe. However, the relatively small number of goods that have yet had conferred on them a Fair Trade label indicates how hard it is in practice to trace, in a long supply chain, all the material and social impacts of a commodity such as a tropical banana or a cotton shirt. This indicates another conundrum at the heart of consumer culture. The nineteenth-century thinker and historian Alexis de Tocqueville (1805–59) in *Democracy in America* predicted that materialism would ultimately come to undermine democracy as people pursued private comfort and the enervating distractions of their acquisitive desires at the expense of their own peace of mind and the moral fabric of society itself. He feared that people caught up in covetousness would no longer cultivate those public goods such as charity, honesty and religion without which societies would spiral into a vicious decline.[368] As modern capitalist democracies have pursued the utilitarian philosophy of raising the satisfaction of acquisitive desire to the central goal of social life, the basis for the common good, for collective action, civic virtue, and the very consent to common social goals on which these societies depend, has been undermined.

As if in confirmation of de Tocqueville's prediction, the governments of the developed North that are responsible for 86 per cent of historic GHG emissions have been unable to agree on a legal and regulatory framework for reducing these emissions to a level that will stabilize the earth system (see Chapter 5).[369] In consequence, many turn instead to a focus on the carbon footprint of the individual consumer. This reflects the emergence in the past 30 years of a new political concept known as 'consumer sovereignty'. The efforts of a growing minority of ecologically aware individuals in advanced capitalist societies to reduce their carbon footprints by changing their individual consumption patterns are impressive and demonstrate significant moral leadership. These individuals devote considerable efforts to what is known as 'green consumerism'. They buy smaller cars, low-energy light bulbs, locally grown food. They turn the domestic thermostat down. They take the train when possible instead of the plane, and the most dedicated install solar panels or windmills on their roofs. But while these myriad small and virtuous choices are clearly important both morally and symbolically, they will not on their own address the unsustainable character of the fossil-fuelled economic engine that is driving the climate crisis.

A recent report from the Stockholm Institute at York University shows that GHG emissions within British borders are not declining nearly as much as they need to, even in terms of what the government has promised.[370] If account is taken of the emissions produced in the manufacture of goods abroad that are consumed in the UK the level is 46 per cent higher than government estimates of domestic emissions. This figure still excludes the costs of transporting the imported goods back to the UK because national GHG emission-accounting methods, agreed under the Kyoto Protocol (see Chapter 5), exclude the emissions from international shipping and air transport. To make matters worse, international companies headquartered in the UK facilitate the production of resources such as oil, gas and coal that others burn overseas and in so doing these companies are responsible for 10 per cent of the global total of CO_2 pollution, which is about five times greater than official estimates of British CO_2 emissions.[371]

The UK has a moral responsibility in this area because it is British companies that are fostering this GHG production and use. Focusing on individual actions when they constitute only a tiny part of 20 per cent of the total carbon emissions for which all UK economic actors are actually responsible may even be a dangerous distraction from the real sources of climate pollution. It would be like assuming that persuading individual drivers to drive more slowly would be enough to make sustainable the total energy use of all of the world's car manufacturing, fuelling and maintainance industries, and associated infrastructure.

Environmental law and sustainable business

Multinational corporations have one overarching goal in common, and that is the growth of their share value. Like politicians who commit societies to economic growth regardless of the poor correlation between continued growth and well-being, the corporate commitment to share value above all other values necessitates destruction both of human and other than human values. There is, however, one parameter that can force a company to respect values other than that of the shareholder: the law. While individuals may experience a change of heart and strive to pursue love and justice in their relations with the victims of climate change in Bangladesh or sub-Saharan Africa, the only major way in which companies can be brought to care for such victims is through the medium of law. It does little good asking a company to repent. But if the legally regulated accounts that companies must use to estimate shareholder value were to include ecological or social costs, this would generate a tremendous change in corporate behaviour. Similarly, if governments consistently – and not just in the more affluent parts of the world – outlawed environmental pollution and poverty-level wages, then companies would have to adopt practices and policies that promoted social and environmental justice. If, through the Climate Change Convention process, governments commit to the legal regulation of fossil-fuel emissions – and not trading them in markets that are rife with fraud – then companies will be forced to reduce their carbon emissions.

It is not as if the leaders of some of the world's largest companies do not know that there is a problem in the relationship between their corporations and the planet. This is why 100 chief executive officers of the world's largest companies signed a collective letter in June 2008 asking the leaders of the G8 (the world's eight most industrialized countries) to reliably price carbon and other GHG emissions so as to make it possible for the companies to work together to reduce their pollution of carbon sinks.[372] But how did the G8 leaders respond? They continue to rely on exhortation of their citizens and corporations to more sustainable actions, failing to understand that unless and until they regulate across every legal domain for mandatory reductions in GHG emissions, neither corporate nor citizen actions will be capable of producing a sustainable economy.

What has misled the present generation of politicians to the point at which they are unwilling to regulate the global economy even when it is clearly threatening climate stability is the neoliberal claim that only continued and unfettered growth in the consumption of goods and services in a borderless international 'free' trade regime can advance human well-being. This claim is a reconceptualization of the colonial expansion and expropriation of common resources that began the consumer revolution in the first place. It masks the present power imbalances in a world economy in which 200 large corporations have incomes larger than the poorest 100 countries, and in which Africa and parts of Asia and the Americas continue to be net exporters of wealth to the rich North. It is in these same wealth-exporting poorer regions of the world, not in the cities in the North, that communities are already threatened by drought and flood caused by anthropogenic (human-instigated) climate change brought about by the luxury carbon emissions of the rich.

Sharing the commons

The atmosphere is a 'commons'. The only way to manage it equitably, justly and sustainably is for every national domain, and every trans-national corporation and organization, to agree to a commons management agreement that limits corporate and national use of the commons to a level that is sustainable (see Chapter 5). Such an agree-ment will require that every political unit, from the household to the village to the corporation to the city to the region to the nation state to the transnational corporation to the United Nations, is prepared to acknowledge a moral responsibility no longer to treat the atmosphere as a virtual land-fill, or an 'air-fill', for waste emissions. Such an agree-ment ought at the same time to permit local communities who tend and live off forests and soils – apart from the ocean, the two most sig-nificant carbon sinks (places where carbon emissions are absorbed) – to be involved in the procedures for managing these sinks and not excluded from them by carbon emissions trading regimes that many in Africa and Asia see as an excuse for another neo-colonial land grab.

Some, particularly in the USA, argue that such an agreement is economically and politically unfeasible. However, an agreement that looks very like what I have just proposed was signed into international law by 189 nations in 1987. The Montreal Protocol introduced a gradu-ated ban on the production and use of ozone-depleting chemicals (principally chlorofluorocarbons or CFCs) and inaugurated schemes for technology transfer so that developing countries, for whom the ban on CFCs would be more costly, were both given more time to end their use, and given technical assistance in developing alternatives. So suc-cessful has been the Montreal Protocol that there are no longer CFCs in most households, factories, vehicles and offices in Europe and North America, and their presence is diminishing in the developing world. And as a result the ozone hole over the Antarctic is no longer expanding and may eventually heal.[373] This success with CFCs shows that legal international environmental regulation of invisible gases can work.

There remains the problem of political acceptability in societies shaped for so long by advertising, consumerism and marketing. Here we need again to return to the moral and spiritual teachings of the Christian tradition and their parallels in the other Abrahamic faiths. I have already referred to research which shows that economic growth and growth in human well-being do not correlate beyond modest levels of income. Other studies indicate that economic growth beyond a certain level of economic activity can actually diminish well-being significantly.[374] Furthermore, there is extensive work by the medical epidemiologist Richard Wilkinson charting the link between income inequality and *ill* health.[375] The challenge then in finding ways to promote and shape a more sustainable way of life in the affluent North and then the South is to promote a lower-consumption and low-carbon way of life as one that increases rather than decreases well-being. In this sense, actions taken by Christians and others to pursue lower-carbon lifestyles, while they make only a small impact on global GHG emissions, nonetheless are crucial in that they exemplify that it is possible to live a lower-carbon, lower-consumption lifestyle while experiencing a high quality of life that actually enhances the well-being of those who choose to live this way.

Sustainability and well-being

For all the pollution and danger that I encounter every day as a cyclist, I still enjoy commuting on a bicycle. On the bike there is a sensual quality to life that is not available in a car or a bus. The bike moves more freely in the city than either of these other vehicles and when cycling I am exposed to the elemental forces at work on the planet. I feel the sun and the wind on my face, the rain makes sloshing noises on my wheels and mudguards and makes the grey cobbles shine. And cycling up towards Edinburgh Castle on its volcanic plug of rock from the Firth of Forth every day gets more oxygen to my brain so I can greet my morning classes of undergraduates with more energy and enthusiasm. I also feel that, though I am part of a small minority, on the bicycle I am nonetheless doing something to help the planet on my daily commute. Cycling enables me to acknowledge in a daily ritual that the climate is changing and that it is possible to make a difference. Being part of the change sustains hopefulness in place of the denial and passivity often engendered by the seemingly impossible challenge of anthropogenic climate change. It is not so much that I get a self-righteous glow from cycling instead of driving. On the contrary, the obstacles in terms of traffic jams and roadworks and the hostility and increasing rage and frustration of other road users make the emotional experience of cycle commuting a very up-and-down affair (Figure 14.2). Nonetheless, there is a quality of life that comes from being in the environment, from moving in the midst of natural forces, and feeling the wind on my face, that is not available in a fossil-fuelled metal-and-glass bubble. Ultimately cycling makes me feel good.

Perhaps that is the answer to the political acceptability of the measures that will be necessary to resolve the ecological and climate crises. Hair-shirt environmentalist self-denial is not going to win the argument. Instead, the environmentalist case needs to be linked to the

Figure 14.2 A commuter cyclist in the London morning rush hour, kitted out in specialist cycling gear for protection against accidents and inhalation of exhaust fumes. (Photograph ProfDEH, courtesy of <commonswikimedia.org> under <creativecommons.org/licenses/by-sa/3.0/>.)

true sources of human well-being as revealed by the world's great religious traditions: the love of God and neighbour, the pursuit of justice and mercy, and the quest for beauty, goodness and truth. If more people realized that an ecological lifestyle is more enjoyable, more enriching, more enthralling, as well as more ethical, than the present fossil-fuelled way of life, then it is possible that *Homo industrialis* might find its way out of the climate change conundrum. But in order for this to happen, it will be crucial that the advertising industry, and those who guide and direct the economies of nations, cease their promotion of the lie that economic growth, having and wanting to have, grows human well-being.

15

Creation and new creation: transforming Christian perspectives

DOUGLAS J. MOO

There are no solutions for the systemic causes of ecocrisis, at least in democratic societies, apart from religious narrative.
(M. Oelschlaeger, *Caring for Creation* (1994), 5)

The solution to the ecological crisis we face is a transformation in human values. People must learn to think differently about themselves and the world in which they live. The current unsustainable rate at which we are spoiling and depleting our world's resources, amply documented in other chapters in this book, is rooted in selfishness. For Christians, this should be no surprise. The Bible describes a human history that matches all too closely what we perceive in our world every day: people pursuing their own pleasure and well-being at the expense of others. But the Bible also describes the solution to this pervasive human problem: those who are joined to Christ by faith are liberated from sin's power so that they can love God and one another as they were intended to do. Why, then, do we not see more Christians taking a bold lead in seeking to overturn our present course of ecological destruction? One reason is ignorance: many Christians have simply not taken the time to come to grips with what is really going on. Another reason is a failure to appreciate that the gospel message of liberation has direct and significant consequences for our treatment of the environment in which we live.

In this chapter, I argue that the message of ecological responsibility has a clear basis in the theology of the Apostle Paul (Figure 15.1). I focus on his language of 'new creation' to make this point. The idea of new creation in Paul is built on the foundation of his eschatology. By 'eschatology', I do not mean what many Christians mean when they use the word. I am not referring only to the very end of human history.

Rather, 'eschatology' in the New Testament sense of the word encompasses all the events of God's programme, from the first coming of Christ to his second coming. The 'last things' (Greek *eschata*, from which we get the word 'eschatology') that God promised his people in the Old Testament have been initially fulfilled through Christ's death and resurrection but will be consummated some time in the future. Chapter 16 in this volume addresses the future, or 'not yet', side of eschatology, as it argues that there is far more continuity between this creation and the new creation in the New Testament than has often been realized. My focus here is on the implications of the present, on the 'already' phase of eschatology. What has God already done that has a bearing on Christian attitudes towards the created world?

Figure 15.1 'St Paul' by El Greco (1541–1614). (Courtesy of Casa Museo El Greco, Toledo, Spain.)

'New creation': new creature, new community, new cosmos

The language of 'new creation', as we might expect, occurs frequently in books and articles on the biblical teaching about the created world. Many writers use the phrase 'new creation' to refer to a concept, the idea that new covenant restoration will ultimately include the whole created order in its scope. For instance, in his book *The God of Hope and the End of the World*, physicist and theologian John Polkinghorne devotes a chapter to 'new creation', in which he discusses the degree of continuity and discontinuity between the 'old' creation and the new.[376] It is, of course, quite legitimate to use 'new creation' in this broad conceptual way, but most of the writers who use the phrase appear to want to claim, however implicitly, some biblical warrant for the ideas they are presenting.

The phrase 'new creation' is indeed biblical language, occurring twice in the letters of Paul (Galatians 6:15; 2 Corinthians 5:17). But few of the writers who employ the phrase actually try to explain how their use of 'new creation' language might relate to Paul's use of the same terminology. Of course, writers trying to survey the broad biblical teaching on environmental responsibility rarely have the time to provide such justification, but some such justification is needed if such allusions are to carry any legitimate biblical authority. The need for some justification is indicated at a quite fundamental level by the diversity in English translations. The Authorized Version (King James Version), for instance, does not even contain the phrase 'new creation' (it uses 'new creature'). Other English versions use the phrase but suggest by their renderings that it refers only to human beings and not to the created world more generally (see the translation of 2 Corinthians 5:17 in the RSV, ESV, NASB, NAB, NIV, NET and NLT[377]). As is often the case, translations provide a window into underlying interpretive difficulties. New Testament scholars are quite divided over just what Paul intends by his two allusions to 'new creation'.

I therefore propose to provide brief justification for the following proposals:

- 'New creation' alludes to a concept of universal restoration found in the Old Testament (and especially the latter part of Isaiah) and certain Jewish apocalyptic texts.

- 'New creation' participates in Paul's broad inaugurated eschatology theme, finding its initial fulfilment in the salvation of individual human beings and the creation of a new humanity (the Church) and its ultimate consummation in a renewed universe.
- 'New creation' carries with it wide-ranging ethical implications for those who belong to it, involving especially a shift from a self-focus to an 'other' focus.
- Those who have been transformed as participants in the 'new creation' are accountable to God and responsible to others for the way they use and the way they view the resources of the natural world.

Galatians 6:15

Paul's first reference to 'new creation' occurs in the closing verses of his letter to the Galatians: 'Neither circumcision nor uncircumcision means anything; what counts is the new creation' (6:15, TNIV).[378] The reference to circumcision touches on Paul's central concern in Galatians: to convince the newly converted gentile Christians in Galatia to renounce a false gospel being propagated by people he calls 'agitators' (5:12). These agitators were apparently seeking to supplement the gospel that Paul had proclaimed to the Galatians by insisting that gentiles could truly belong to God's people only if they placed themselves under the law of Moses (2:16, 4:21, 5:4) – a condition marked above all by undergoing the rite of circumcision (5:3, 6:12). Paul counters this false teaching by stressing the far-reaching epochal significance of the death and resurrection of Christ. He sounds this note at the very beginning of the letter, referring to God the Father as the one who 'raised [Jesus Christ] from the dead' (1:2) and to Christ as the one 'who gave himself for our sins to rescue us from the present evil age' (1:4). The cross occupied centre stage in Paul's original preaching in Galatia: 'Before your very eyes Jesus Christ was clearly portrayed as crucified' (3:1). Through Christ's death God 'redeems', 'buys people out of', their condemned status under the curse of the law (3:13; cf. 4:5). And, as Christ's death effects the transfer from old age to new, so, as believers identify with Christ, they find themselves transferred from the old age to the new. Referring to his own experience as representative of other believers, Paul claims that he has 'been crucified with Christ', and so lives a totally new life (2:20). Similarly, he claims that he will boast only about the cross of Christ, because it is through Christ that 'the world has been crucified to me, and I to the world' (6:14).

This last text, which immediately precedes the verse I am interested in, is particularly significant. Paul describes a dramatic and thorough-going shift in his value system.[379] The 'world' is used in the typically biblical sense of the fallen and sinful world, with particular focus on the value system of that world. 'New creation' in 6:15 stands as the counterpart to that world and its values. In a move typical of Paul's polemics in Galatians, he dares to associate God's old covenant requirement of circumcision with this worldly system of values that has now been judged and ended by Christ's death and resurrection. Significantly, it is not only circumcision that has no value in this new 'world', but uncircumcision as well. This pair of terms reminds us forcefully of a similar claim Paul makes earlier in the letter: 'There is neither Jew nor Gentile, neither slave nor free, neither male nor female, for you are all one in Christ' (3:28). People who are 'in Christ' enter a realm in which the distinctions of ethnicity, social class and gender that are determinative for this world no longer matter.[380] All 'simply human' factors become meaningless in the face of God's world-transforming work in his son Jesus Christ.

With this context in view, we can now ask: why, in place of circumcision and uncircumcision, does Paul claim that what truly matters is the 'new creation'? I noted above that the English versions reveal some differences in the way this phrase is translated. These differences arise from the fact that the Greek word *ktisis* that occurs here can refer either to the totality of what God created (the 'creation') or to individual members of that creation ('created thing' or 'creature'). The New Testament uses the word with both meanings, but more often with the broad meaning 'creation'.[381] Most contemporary interpreters therefore agree that the phrase should be translated 'new creation'. But to what does the phrase refer? Is 'new creation' a metaphor that describes the Christian as one who, in passing from death to life, becomes totally new? Or does it describe the new humanity created in Christ? Or does 'new creation' refer to the entire created world, made 'new' in Christ? In fact, we do not need to choose among these options. Three lines of evidence suggest that Paul uses 'new creation' to depict the total new state of affairs that Christ has inaugurated in his first coming and will consummate in his second coming. This new state of affairs includes transformed people, a new community and a renewed universe.

The first line of evidence is the way the language of 'new creation' was being used in Paul's day. This consideration is especially important because the phrase appears nowhere else in the New Testament – and yet Paul does not think he has to explain it to his readers. Clearly, he expects them to know to what he is referring. When we consider the Old Testament and Jewish writings that would have formed Paul's (and his readers') conception of 'new creation', it is clear that the phrase itself, as well as the concept to which it points, was somewhat flexible in meaning.[382] Most interpreters, correctly in my view, point to the latter chapters of Isaiah and apocalyptic Judaism as the texts that formed the dominant idea of 'new creation' in Paul's day. Creation language is pervasive in Isaiah 40—55, used particularly often to portray the return of Israel from exile. Isaiah 43:18, which is linguistically very similar to 2 Corinthians 5:17, is a good example: 'Forget the former things; do not dwell on the past. See, I am doing a new thing!' The 'former things' are God's past acts of deliverance – especially the rescue of his people from Egypt at the time of the exodus. Isaiah's point is that the new deliverance that God will accomplish for Israel is so much greater, so decisive, and so far-reaching that it will be as if they have been created anew. In the latter chapters of Isaiah, these 'new things' are referred to again, but now with a much more explicit cosmic orientation: Israel's restoration will take the form of (or inaugurate) nothing less than a 'new heavens and new earth' (Isaiah 65:17–22; cf. 66:22–24). The cosmic connotations of the phrase continue to be seen in post-biblical Judaism. The actual phrase 'new creation' is used before Paul only in two and possibly three Jewish texts, and these texts also refer broadly to a reconstitution of the entire universe.[383] The probable background from which Paul draws the language of new creation, then, suggests that it would include reference to a total renovation of the universe: a new creation as extensive as the old creation it replaces.

The second line of evidence to pursue in seeking to pinpoint the sense of new creation in Galatians 6:15 is context. Of course, as we noted above, the overriding concern of the letter is to argue that gentiles (apart from the law) now stand on the same footing as Jews before God. This being the case, new creation could denote the Christian community as a place where the usual worldly barriers between people are broken down (see Galatians 3:28 and the argument of Ephesians 2:11–22). This second set of data is certainly important. However, our brief analysis of the letter's theme suggests that both these pictures are too narrowly focused. To convince the Galatians to renounce the agitators and their insistence on coming under the authority of the law, Paul puts great emphasis on the wholly new state of affairs that Christ's cross has inaugurated. Everything comes under the judgement of the cross.

Galatians 3:28, which I quoted earlier, supports this direction of interpretation. It is puzzling at first glance why, granted the letter's argument, Paul does not content himself with referring to how Christ brings together Jew and gentile. Why add the apparently extraneous pairs 'slave and free' and 'male and female'? It is possible that Paul is simply citing tradition (note the parallels in 1 Corinthians 12:13 and Colossians 3:10–11). But we have good reason to believe that Paul does not simply take over tradition unless it suits his purposes. A better explanation is that Paul is deliberately setting the oneness between Jew and gentile in the broader context of God's general reconciling work in Christ. This is probably why Paul has chosen to use the words 'male' and 'female' (instead of 'man' and 'woman'): he is deliberately echoing the language of the original creation, when God made human beings 'male' and 'female'.[384] In effect, Paul suggests, belonging to Christ means belonging to a re-created humanity. Just how fundamental is this transformation is revealed in the way Paul associates the agitators and the law they espouse with 'the world' (6:14; see above) and 'the elements of the world' – the fundamental building blocks of the material universe (4:3; cf. 9).[385] 'New creation' is the letter's climactic summing up of this new state of affairs. It is the opposite of the 'old age' that Paul mentioned in the opening of the letter (1:4).

A third reason for thinking that 'new creation' in Galatians 6:15 includes reference to ultimate cosmic transformation are other passages in Paul that plainly include such transformation in the scope of God's work in Christ. The two most important are Romans 8:19–22 and Colossians 1:20. In Romans 8, Paul is arguing that God will ultimately transform believers, bringing them into God's own state of glory (8:18, 30). Christ's resurrection initiates the transformation in which believers will also share (see v. 11), but Paul also makes clear that this transformation will include more than just believers: the whole created world will be liberated, participating in the glory of God's own children (vv. 19–22). The transformation of the entire universe is part of God's plan for the future, and it is surely the case that 'new creation' must include reference to this liberation.

Colossians 1:20, similarly, climaxes what was probably an early hymn about Christ with the claim that God has 'reconciled to himself all things'. This reconciliation, while applied in the context to Christians (vv. 21–23) cannot be limited to human beings. For Paul elaborates the 'all things' in verse 20 by referring to 'things on earth or things in heaven'. Moreover, the 'hymn' (vv. 15–20) repeatedly uses the language 'all' in a universal sense. Of course, the 'reconciliation' Paul has in view here is not equivalent to 'salvation'; Paul has no notion of a final universal salvation of all things. Paul's language of 'making peace' in verse 20 provides the clue to the meaning of reconciliation. The Old Testament frequently predicts that God would, in the 'last days', establish his *shalom*, his 'peace' or 'well-being' (see especially Isaiah 52:6–10; and also, among others, Isaiah 9:7, 26:3, 12, 27:5, 52:7, 55:12, 66:12; Jeremiah 29:11, 30:10, 33:6, 9, 46:27; Ezekiel 34:29, 37:26; Micah 5:5; Haggai 2:9; Zechariah 9:10). What is meant is that God would bring all things into appropriate relationship to himself: his people would be vindicated, his people's enemies vanquished, his world made new. It is this universal reign of peace that Christ's cross has brought into being. Of course, this peace is not yet fully established. The 'already/not yet' pattern of New Testament eschatology must be applied to Colossians 1:20. While secured in principle by Christ's crucifixion, universal 'peace' is not yet established. But believers do experience this reconciliation now, and are, as a result, to be God's agents of reconciliation in our world today: extending the message of reconciliation to other human beings so that they can also become God's own people, seeking to bring reconciliation among humanity and reconciliation between humanity and the rest of the created world. Thus Colossians 1:20 is an important indication that reclamation of the world of nature must be included in God's new creation work of transformation.

2 Corinthians 5:17

I turn now, much more briefly, to the second (and only other) occurrence of 'new creation' in the New Testament: 2 Corinthians 5:17. My concern is simply to suggest some reasons why the phrase here should be given the same basic sense that it has in Galatians 6:15. This is a case that needs to be made, for many interpreters are convinced that the context in which the phrase occurs in 2 Corinthians suggests that it refers simply to the renewed individual.[386] Many English versions make this clear by translating something like 'if anyone is in Christ, he is a new creation' (RSV; ESV). In fact, however, the 'he is' in this translation has no clear basis in the Greek, which is abrupt and elliptical: 'If anyone is in Christ, new creation!' We could equally validly expand this in English translation to 'if anyone is in Christ, the new creation has come' (TNIV) or 'if anyone is in Christ, that person belongs to the new creation'. I think this general rendering is closest to Paul's intention.

First, since Paul uses the phrase 'new creation' only twice in his letters, we would expect it to have the same meaning in each case – and we have seen good reason to take it in Galatians 6:15 as a general reference to the new redemptive work of God in Christ. Making it further likely that the phrase means the same thing in both texts is the fact that they are focused on similar issues. In Galatians, Paul uses 'new creation' to remind the readers of the new set of values that should guide them in evaluating false teaching. In contrast to the 'agitators', who focus on the flesh (specifically circumcision) and are world oriented, true believers should focus on the new creation. Paul is engaged in a similar attempt to reorient values in 2 Corinthians. The Corinthians, apparently under the influence of some rival teachers (10:10–12, 11:4–5, 12–15, 19–23, 12:11), are questioning Paul's ministry credentials and procedures. Central to this dispute are the criteria by which his work and character are to be evaluated. Paul makes specific reference to these rivals in our context: 'We are not trying to commend ourselves to you again, but are giving you an opportunity to take pride in us, so that you can answer those who take pride in what is seen rather than in what is in the heart' (5:12). What are the criteria of evaluation? In verses 14–15, Paul cites the death of Christ as the great turning point in human history – just as he does in Galatians. Christ's death, in which all people participate, means that people should live by a new standard: no longer 'for themselves' but 'for him who dies for them and was raised again'. Then, in verse 16, Paul draws out the consequences of this new perspective for the way in which he, and other Christians, view others, and especially Christ: 'From now on we regard no one from a worldly [or 'fleshly'; *sarx* in Greek] point of view. Though we once regarded Christ in this way, we do so no longer'. The temporal 'from now on' (emphasized in the contrast in the second part of the verb between 'once' and 'no longer') suggests allusion to Paul's typical contrast between the two ages of salvation history. The old age, ruled by Adam, sin and death, has been replaced by a new age, ruled by Christ, righteousness and life. His point in verse 16, then, is that when people enter into the new age of redemption, their standards of evaluation necessarily change.

The claim about 'new creation' in verse 17 relates to verses 14–15 and verse 16. Christ's death and resurrection, because it is the turning point in history, means that one who is 'in Christ' belongs to the new creation Christ has inaugurated and has therefore left behind the 'worldly' standard of evaluation typical of the old creation. As biblical scholar Victor Paul Furnish puts it, to be in Christ means a 'total re-orienting of one's values and priorities away from the world (self) and toward the cross (Christ, others)'.[387] 'New creation' functions here, as in Galatians, to indicate broadly the new age, the new state of affairs that Christ has inaugurated, as the crucial context for a Christian system of values. Theologian Herman Ridderbos says it well: 'When he [Paul] speaks here of "new creation", this is not meant merely in an individual sense (a "new creature"), but one is to think of the new world of re-creation that God has made to dawn in Christ, and in which everyone who is in Christ is included.'[388]

Finally, and more cautiously, we might ask whether it is possible that the note of universal reconciliation sounded in Colossians 1:20 might also be heard in 2 Corinthians. There are some intriguing parallels between 2 Corinthians 4—5 and the 'Christ hymn' of Colossians 1:15–20. Both texts feature creation language (2 Corinthians 4:4, 6; Colossians 1:15–17), both refer to Christ as 'the image of God' (2 Corinthians 4:4; Colossians 1:15), and both use the language of 'reconciliation'. The clear movement in Colossians 1 from 'universal' reconciliation (v. 20) to the reconciliation of Christians (vv. 21–23) might be found also in 2 Corinthians 5. Verse 18 ('reconciled *us*') and verse 19b ('not counting people's sins against them') clearly have Christians in view. But verse 19a is couched in broader terms: 'God was reconciling the world to himself in Christ'. Might this be a reference, parallel to Colossians 1:20, to universal reconciliation?[389] Most scholars think not, arguing that the pronouns in the second part of verse 19 clearly presuppose that 'world' refers to the world of humanity. Yet it is possible, since the syntactical sequence is awkward and the idea is similar to the probably traditional Colossians 1:20, that verse 19a is a piece of tradition that Paul is quoting and then applying to the Corinthians.[390] We would not even entertain this way of reading the verse were it not for Colossians 1:20. But this possible parallel, along with the all-embracing character of 'new creation' in verse 17, at least opens the door to think Paul might have universal reconciliation in view in verse 19a.

We are now in a position to summarize the results of our consideration of Paul's use of the phrase 'new creation'. In both texts where Paul uses this phrase, he applies the language to the current situation of Christian believers. But, as I have argued, there are good reasons for claiming that the phrase refers to the ultimate state of affairs that God is bringing into being as a result of his redemptive and transformative work through Christ. Paul, as he so often does, appropriates a key theme from Isaiah, who stresses the radical and far-reaching nature of God's promised redemption by referring to it as a 're-creation'. Those who are 'in Christ' (2 Corinthians 5:17; see Galatians 3:28) belong, though they still live in the world, to this newly created world, a world that awaits its full establishment but which is experienced even now by faith.

On the one hand, then, those who use the concept 'new creation' as if it simply designates the new material universe that will ultimately replace this creation, are restricting the scope of the phrase in a way that does not do justice to its biblical usage. Moreover, it is significant in this regard that Paul contrasts 'new creation' not with the existing 'creation', but with the 'world' (Galatians 6:14) and the 'flesh' (2 Corinthians 5:16). On the other hand, it is equally illegitimate to confine 'new creation' only to existing spiritual realities. In Isaiah, as we have seen, 'new creation' includes a 'new heavens and new earth'; and, for Paul also, as Romans 8:19–22 teaches and Colossians 1:20 intimates, a renewal of the material world is part of God's redemptive plan. Interpretation of Scripture in the West has suffered from a dualism, inherited from the Greeks, that tends to remove the material world from the sphere of God's ultimate purposes. But we cannot remove creation from 'new creation'. Those who use the phrase to refer only to the future transformed universe and those who confine it only to present spiritual realities separate what Paul ultimately wants to keep together. 'New creation' participates fully in Paul's framework of inaugurated eschatology. Just as the kingdom of God can be both presently enjoyed (for example, Colossians 1:14) and yet will be inherited in the future (for example, Galatians 5:21), so 'new creation' refers to the totality of God's redemptive and transformative work, experienced now in renewed individuals and renewed relationships (focused especially in the Church) and to be climaxed in the eschaton in a renewal of 'all things' (Acts 3:21; cf. Colossians 1:20).

New creation and stewardship of this creation

Now I will spell out briefly some of the specific implications of this new creation concept for the Christian attitude towards the natural world. 'New creation' is the ultimate reality that Christians are to recognize as governing their attitudes and actions. This being the case, participation in the new creation has fundamental ethical implications. Indeed, Paul makes this explicit in Galatians 6:16. In this verse, after mentioning the 'new creation' in verse 15, he pronounces a blessing on 'all those who keep in line with this standard'.[391] What is this 'standard'? The nearest and most likely referent is the 'new creation'. Christians live by a new set of values, the 'standard' of new creation. As so often in the New Testament, Christian thinking and Christian behaviour are tied to what God has done in Christ. New creation values, which Paul elaborates briefly in Galatians 5:13—6:10, revolve around the central demand of love, the 'fulfilment' of the Old Testament law (5:14) and the heart of new covenant law, 'the law of Christ' (6:2). Living on the basis of the new creation requires a 'total re-orienting of one's values and priorities away from the world (self) and toward the cross (Christ, others)'.[392] The 'others' we are to love are, first of all, our fellow believers, as the 'one anothers' found throughout Galatians 5:13 to 6:10 indicate. But the 'others' we are to love ultimately extend to the whole world. The 'neighbour' in 5:14 must be seen in light of Jesus' extension of the word to refer to anyone we encounter (even, or especially, a 'different' anyone!) in the parable of the Good Samaritan. Note also the concluding verse in the ethical section of Galatians: 'let us do good to all people, especially to those who belong to the family of believers' (6:10).

Application to the theme of this book should be obvious: living in a way that sustains rather than depletes the earth's resources is incumbent on believers because we are to live by new covenant values. We may summarize those values, as Jesus did, in the two great commandments.

The context of Galatians provides plenty of evidence that love for the 'other' is a central new creation value. These 'others' we are to love are people all over the world, and we cannot love these others without caring for the environments in which they live. My decisions about using and conserving resources must be governed by the new creation imperative to love others as myself. We must also include among the 'others' we are to love our children, grandchildren, and people yet unborn. I am not loving them if I use up so many of the earth's resources that they have too little left to get by on.

The other, and first, great commandment is, of course, that we love the Lord our God. While not explicit in Paul's elaboration of new creation, love for God is implicit in all that he says about it, taking the form of specific commandments by which he directs the course that our love for others is to take. This vertical dimension in our new creation value system is critical, preventing love for others from becoming a vague and open-ended principle that we can use to justify almost anything we want. With respect to our topic, love for God, in addition to providing direction and substance to our love for others, contributes in two important ways.

First, to love God is to love and value the things he loves and values. The Old Testament provides abundant testimony to the importance and significance of the created world in God's eyes. Such evidence is much harder to discover in the New Testament, especially in the letters of Paul and the writings attributed to John the Evangelist. Yet, as we have seen, Paul himself includes the created world in God's redemptive programme. By doing so, Paul reveals that he maintains the Old Testament perspective on creation as something to be valued in its own right. Richard Bauckham has noted the limitations of 'love for others' by itself as a directing force in our attitude towards the natural world: it can justify exploitation of nature, as long as some ultimately human benefit might be seen to result (see also Chapter 13).[393] To be sure, humans, created uniquely in God's image, have pride of place in creation: there is a certain kind of anthropocentrism in Scripture. But that anthropocentrism is always subordinated to the theocentrism that is the warp and woof of Scripture. Loving the Lord our God is the practical and ethical expression of this theocentrism. It reminds us of our creaturely status and the humility incumbent on us as creatures and that our attitude towards the natural world must have in view not just the needs of others but also the value that God himself places on the natural world.

A second way in which love for God contributes to our theme relates to our appointment as stewards of God's creation.[394] Genesis 1:26–28 charges human beings specifically with the task of 'ruling' and 'subduing' the earth (see also Psalm 8:5–8) and, in the very language 'image of God', points to the responsibility of human beings to act as the 'sub-regents' of God with respect to the earth. (I am assuming the widely held view that our creation in the 'image of God' has some reference to our responsibility, specified in the context, to 'rule' the creation God has made.) Participation in the new creation rescues our stewardship of creation from the self-serving turn that it took as a result of the Fall. Through the 're-creation' of conversion, Christians are conformed to the image of Christ, himself *the* 'image of God' (Romans 8:29; see 2 Corinthians 4:4; Colossians 1:15). We can become again the faithful, self-sacrificing stewards we were originally created to be. But if we are to steward God's earth well, we require knowledge – knowledge, of course, about God's concerns and purposes for the earth, but knowledge also of that earth itself. Our love for God requires, then, that we acquire wisdom to carry out our tasks as his stewards. The institution at which I teach (Wheaton College, IL, USA) has adopted as its slogan 'All truth is God's truth'. The truth that scientists discover about the nature of the earth and its implications for the future of the earth and its resources is, indeed, God's truth – and Christians, out of love for God, are obligated to learn this truth. Theological ethicist William Schweiker is right: 'Any form of ethics that in principle undercuts the input of the natural and social sciences in our assessment of courses of action and the limits on human desire is dangerous'.[395] Both love – for God and for others – and wisdom are essential to a robust and credible Christian ethic of the natural world. A basic problem confronting Christians in our pursuit of such an ethic is our tendency either to ignore the truth of God revealed in the natural world or to seek interpretations of that truth that will not interfere with a comfortable lifestyle or particular economic system. Such attitudes are manifestations of a failure to love God as we are supposed to.

I end, appropriately, with the note of grace. Participation in the new creation not only imposes a new set of values; equally important, it provides, through the transforming power of the Holy Spirit, the power to live by those values. The ecological crisis is, at bottom, a human crisis – a crisis created by ignorance and selfishness. As those living in the 'already' of eschatological realization, Christians are being renewed in their thinking (Romans 12:2; Ephesians 4:23), progressively being given the ability to look at all the world as God does and to love others. We should therefore be in the vanguard of efforts to create a sustainable world.

16

Environmental unsustainability and a biblical vision of the earth's future

JONATHAN MOO

There are people who regard it as frivolous, and some Christians think it impious for anyone to hope and prepare for a better earthly future. They think that the meaning of present events is chaos, disorder, and catastrophe; and in resignation or pious escapism they surrender all responsibility for reconstruction and for future generations. It may be that the day of judgment will dawn tomorrow; in that case, we shall gladly stop working for a better future. But not before.

(D. Bonhoeffer, *Letters and Papers from Prison*,
ed. E. Bethge (1953), 16–17)

According to the New Testament, the present world is inherently and inescapably unsustainable. It is only the 'scoffers', subject of scathing attack by the author of 2 Peter, who claim that 'everything carries on as it has since the beginning' (3:4) and wish, perhaps, that things keep going that way. The promise of Christ's return means that Christians, by contrast, are meant confidently to expect a future cosmic judgement and look forward to – even hasten – the coming of 'a new heaven and a new earth' (2 Peter 3:13; cf. Revelation 21:1). For 'biblical' Christians, then, working towards environmental sustainability might seem to be beside the point, at best a waste of time and at worst a misdirected desire for things to carry on as they always have.

This scenario is not merely hypothetical; such a reading of the New Testament has demonstrably contributed to the failure of portions of the Christian Church to demonstrate the sort of counter-cultural insight, prophetic critique, and leadership in environmental issues for which one might otherwise have hoped. In a provocative editorial in *Conservation Biology*, David Orr has with some justification blamed

American evangelicals in particular for their active opposition to conservation measures and for their collusion with those who – usually for short-term and self-interested reasons – fight against any sort of environmental regulation. Orr explicitly contrasts the conservationist's goal of 'sustainability' with what he calls the Christian evangelical's goal of 'a redeemed world that fulfills the promise of creation'.[396] If Orr is right – that such a vision of the future is necessarily opposed to environmental sustainability – it is worrying that his surprisingly robust way of characterizing biblical hope could apply to the teaching of a much wider swath of Christianity than just American evangelicalism.

A place for hope?

It is not my intention in this chapter to analyse or critique Orr's thesis, but I want to take seriously the potential that visions of the future can and do play in shaping religious thought and practice. Orr's conclusions – shared by many others – must challenge biblical scholars, theologians and all Christian believers to re-evaluate biblical eschatology (the doctrine of 'last things') and to take seriously its implications for the mission of today's Church. The negative results that have often been observed when millennial passions are stirred up understandably prompt many both within and outside the Church to ignore or despise eschatology generally; but however badly it has sometimes been applied and however uncomfortable it makes many Westerners, I am not convinced that Christianity can merely dispense with biblical hope and still remain recognizably Christian. The outworking of God's faithfulness and righteousness is linked throughout Scripture to the future vindication and full revelation of his divine justice, and the theology of creation that emerges in the New Testament is inescapably directed towards this future. As Christoph Schwöbel points out, Christian eschatology is ultimately rooted in the theological character of the 'christological' story: 'Jesus' story discloses the character of God's relationship to his creation as one by which God maintains his relationship to creation through the discontinuity of death, [and so] this story is a promise for all.'[397]

It is Christ's resurrection that displays God's faithfulness to and purposes for the entire creation, and it is Christ's resurrection that drives Christian hope (Figure 16.1). Chapter 15 in this volume shows how this conviction plays out in the cosmic scope of redemption envisioned by the Apostle Paul, and it emphasizes – against purely anthropocentric readings – the inextricable link between human beings and the rest of creation that is maintained in Paul's conception of 'new creation'. The question addressed in the present chapter is more limited, concerning the precise shape and implications of this envisaged cosmic new creation. For even if the 'eschaton (the 'end')' includes the remaking of both humankind and material creation, the radical discontinuity implied by passages such as 2 Peter 3 can still in practice lead to the sort of anthropocentric or existentialist worldview that leaves little room for caring for creation.

Before such a task is even attempted, however, we need to be reminded that whatever Scripture might say about the world to come, both Old and New Testaments contain plenty of challenges to Christians for living rightly on earth in the present. There are, among other things, the instructions to Adam to care for the earth, the profound

Figure 16.1 'Cross in the mountains' (The Tetschen Altar) by Caspar David Friedrich (1774–1840). (Courtesy of Staatliche Kunstsammlungen Dresden.)

interest in land and justice that emerges in Old Testament law and which is a frequent concern of the prophets (see Chapters 8 and 12), and above all the commands to love God and neighbour and to follow the self-sacrificial example of Christ – with the many radical implications that follow. As Paul reminds the Corinthians, of faith, hope and love, 'the greatest of these is love' (1 Corinthians 13:13).

Nevertheless, Paul also affirms that faith and hope remain indispensable in this in-between time of imperfect knowledge and limited sight, in this age of seeing 'through a glass darkly'. Christian ethics, finding their wellspring in the life-giving power of Christ's resurrection, are necessarily orientated towards the kingdom of God proclaimed by Christ, a kingdom that has broken into the present and yet remains only partially realized. As Jesus taught his disciples to pray, Christians still yearn for the day when God's will is fully done 'on earth as in heaven'.

It is also the case that contemporary environmentalism – whether it is concerned with preventing and mitigating catastrophic climate change, reforming agriculture towards sustainable practices, stemming the frightening tide of species extinction, or conserving wild places – is badly in need of vision and of hope (see Chapters 7 and 11–13). Here, if anywhere, a Christian perspective should have much to offer. A biblical wisdom writer observed long ago that, 'without a vision, people cast off restraint', citing the example of a servant who cannot be corrected with mere words, for 'though he understands, he will not give heed' (Proverbs 29:18–19). The parallel with the situation we face today is prescient; more and more of us understand more and more about the threats facing the earth, yet few of us do much about it. As for restraint, it was cast off long ago. We need a fresh vision that reminds us of the futility of unrestrained consumption and points us towards truer sources of joy and fulfilment, a vision that compels us to find new ways to live and gives us hope to go on working for change even in the face of failure and despair. The question addressed in this chapter is whether the New Testament can provide such a vision. Can New Testament expectations of the future contribute anything towards a constructive, distinctively Christian ethos that addresses the root causes of environmental unsustainability and points us towards solutions?

The vision of 2 Peter 3 seems at first sight to have the least potential to be of much help, and the temptation is undoubtedly to ignore it in preference for more 'earth-friendly' texts. But the difficulties of the passage must finally be faced, not least because, for many 'biblical' Christians, it represents a genuine obstacle to engagement with the sort of issues treated in this volume, while for others it serves as a handy excuse for inaction. Nonetheless, any Christian interpretation of 2 Peter 3 must also acknowledge that the description here represents but one of a variety of ways in which the new creation is pictured in the New Testament, and 2 Peter's distinctive voice – though worth hearing – cannot be allowed to drown out the others.

If we apply the well-established principle of interpreting the less clear in the light of what is more clear in Scripture, it is in fact prudent to begin with the description of Christian hope found in Romans 8:19–23, itself an enigmatic passage but one which provides important canonical constraints on how 2 Peter 3 is read by the Church. It is intriguing that some commentators think that the author of 2 Peter himself may have been familiar with the book of Romans; Richard Bauckham, for example, finds a possible echo of Romans 8:21 in 2 Peter 2:19.[398] The evidence is insufficient to determine it with any certainty, but if the author of 2 Peter did know Romans 8, it is unlikely that someone who commends Paul's letters as highly as he does (see 2 Peter 3:15–16) would undermine or contradict Paul's teaching just a few lines earlier. There is therefore some justification from both a canonical and a historical perspective to consider the contours of Paul's cosmic eschatology in Romans 8 before we turn to an examination of 2 Peter 3.

A future for creation in Romans 8

Romans 8:19–23 is one place where the cosmic scope of Paul's conception of the new creation emerges quite clearly:

(v. 19) For the creation waits with eager longing for the revealing of the children of God; (v. 20) for the creation was subjected to futility, not of its own will but by the will of the one who subjected it, in hope (v. 21) that the creation itself will be set free from its bondage to decay and will obtain the freedom of the glory of the children of God. (v. 22) We know that the whole creation has been groaning in labour pains until now; (v. 23) and not only the creation, but we ourselves, who have the first fruits of the Spirit, groan inwardly while we wait for adoption, the redemption of our bodies.

The interpretation of this passage is not as straightforward as some Christian environmentalists might like, but for our purposes it is necessary only to observe three things that do seem indisputable.

1 Creation has its own voice, which is distinct from that of the 'children of God', even if the expression of this voice is here limited to groaning in anticipation of a longed-for release from bondage.
2 Creation's hope is inextricably bound up with the 'revealing of the children of God', connected in verse 23 with the resurrection, what Paul calls the 'redemption of our bodies'.
3 It is the same creation that is now groaning which finds a future in the new creation and which participates in the 'freedom of the glory of the children of God'. The last point is particularly important; whatever elements of discontinuity there may be in Paul's understanding of the cosmic new creation, the implication of Romans 8:19–22 is that it must be fundamentally the same created world that finds its purposes fulfilled and its hopes realized when it is released from its slavery to ruin and brought into the 'freedom of the glory of the children of God'.

If this freedom pertains entirely to the future resurrection, it may justly be queried whether there is any space here for human action to participate in helping creation realize its freedom in the present age. Chapter 15 sketches something of an answer to this apparent conundrum by emphasizing the 'inaugurated' side of new creation theology. Here, in Romans 8, it can be observed that the 'children of God' may not be fully revealed for who they are until the future redemption, but Paul affirms in the very same passage that they nonetheless already bear the status of God's adopted children – and so are expected to begin to live as such even now.[399]

When Christians begin to live as God's reconciled children, they will necessarily find themselves in a new relationship with God and with the rest of creation, a relationship constituted and determined by their inclusion in Christ. As beachheads of the new creation (cf. 2 Corinthians 5:17; Galatians 6:15), those who are in Christ are expected to bear witness by their lives and their actions to God's in-breaking kingdom, trusting that God's faithfulness to his creatures and to his creation means that their labour will not be in vain (1 Corinthians 15:58). There is, then, according to Paul's teaching on the resurrection and new creation, no more reason for Christians to give up caring appropriately for the earth than there is for them to give up praying, pursuing virtue, proclaiming the gospel, or helping the poor; all such activity finds its ultimate fulfilment in the complete realization of the new creation, but its value and importance in the present is not thereby diminished. In Paul's view, it is in fact the future hope reaching back into the present that lends all work done 'in the Lord' its true weight and significance.

Cosmic catastrophe in 2 Peter

Returning to 2 Peter 3, it may seem that the atmosphere has changed considerably – from the fresh sea breezes of resurrection hope to the scorching heat of fiery judgement:

> (v. 10) But the day of the Lord will come like a thief, and then the heavens will pass away with a loud noise, and the elements will be dissolved with fire, and the earth and everything that is done on it will be disclosed. (v. 11) Since all these things are to be dissolved in this way, what sort of persons ought you to be in leading lives of holiness and godliness, (v. 12) waiting for and hastening the coming of the day of God, because of which the heavens will be set ablaze and dissolved, and the elements will melt with fire? (v. 13) But, in accordance with his promise, we wait for new heavens and a new earth, where righteousness is at home.

It is often assumed that this passage unequivocally portrays the complete dissolution of the present cosmos and its replacement with a new one. After a careful and thorough study, Edward Adams, for example, concludes that 'the writer has expressed the conviction that the existing created order will come to a violent end as emphatically as he could'.[400] We may find reasons to revise or nuance Adams's conclusion, but there can be no doubt that the emphasis of 2 Peter 3 is on the radical discontinuity envisioned between the present age and the age to come.

Throughout our discussion, however, it is worth bearing in mind that the allusive language and imagery used in 2 Peter 3 requires readers to sit rather lightly to the cosmology it portrays. An ancient author's view of the structure of the universe will obviously be quite different from our own, but the purpose of a text like 2 Peter 3 is not in any case to teach something about cosmology per se. The author of 2 Peter no doubt intends to describe a real future event in time and space, an event that he considers to represent the culmination of earth's history, but his way of describing that event is more in the way of a painter or a poet than in the way of a reporter or a physicist. We will miss the point if we merely comb the text for cosmological data and fail to consider its purpose in the context and the overall effect the imagery is intended to have in transforming the way readers think and act in their world.

With that in mind, let us return to the description of the events associated with the 'day of the Lord' in verse 10:

> the heavens will pass away with a loud noise,
> and the elements will be dissolved with fire,
> and the earth and everything that is done on it will be disclosed.

Older translations of the final phrase have the earth and the works on it being 'burned up' rather than 'disclosed' or 'found', a difference due to several textual variants in the ancient manuscripts that contain this verse. But nearly all present-day commentators accept what is the best-supported, though more difficult reading, *heurethēsetai* ('will be found'/'will be disclosed'), not only because of the powerful manuscript evidence for it but precisely because all of the other variants can be explained as attempts to clarify this rather unusual way of describing the final judgement.[401] I will shortly consider the possible significance of this language of 'being found', but first it is necessary to examine the meaning of another difficult term in the verse.

The referent of the 'elements' (*stoicheia*), which are said to be destroyed by 'fire' or 'burning' in verse 10 and to 'melt with fire' in verse 12, has been the subject of much scholarly debate. For most readers of 2 Peter in English translation, 'elements' straightforwardly denotes the basic building blocks of the physical world – and that is indeed how many scholars interpret the Greek term *stoicheia*. Adams is the most recent and perhaps most forceful advocate of this view, suggesting that the 'elements' are essentially equivalent to the 'earth'. The point of verse 10, on Adams' reading, is that the heavens and the earth will be destroyed by fire and, in the process, the earth and the works on it will be 'found' in the sense of being judged.

Such an interpretation cannot be entirely ruled out, especially because the usage of *stoicheia* for 'elements' in this sense is well attested in other Hellenistic sources, including in the context of Stoic portrayals of the world's cyclical destruction and regeneration (which many commentators find paralleled in 2 Peter 3). There is, however, an alternative explanation of *stoicheia* that takes more seriously the Old Testament and Jewish background of 2 Peter and may also better account both for the unique use of 'will be found' in verse 10 and for the progression in this verse from 'heavens' to 'elements' to 'earth'.

By the second century, *stoicheia* is indisputably used in some instances with the meaning 'heavenly bodies', referring to the stars, sun and moon;[402] it is also possible (though this is less certain) that these material elements of the heavens could be associated with spiritual forces, as may be the case in Paul's use of *stoicheia* (Galatians 4:3, 9; cf. Colossians 2:8, 20). 2 Peter would be the first extant example of an author using *stoicheia* for 'heavenly bodies', whether or not associated with spiritual forces, but this meaning for 3:10, 12 has nevertheless managed to garner fairly widespread scholarly support – primarily because it fits the context so well.[403] In this scenario, the picture presented in verse 10 is something like this: the outer heavens are torn away, the intermediary heavenly bodies are dissolved with fire, and then the earth and all the deeds of human beings are laid bare before God, being 'found' before him, with nothing to separate them from the testing fire of his judgement.

Support for such an interpretation can be adduced from the parallel between the way in which the elements are described as 'melting with fire' in 2 Peter 3:12 and the description of God's judgement in Isaiah 34:4, where a Greek translation reads, 'all the powers of the heavens will melt'. There are good reasons to think that 2 Peter 3:12 (like the nearly contemporaneous 2 Clement 16:3) is echoing this biblical text and, if so, *stoicheia* is being used in 2 Peter to refer to the 'powers of heaven' and not to the melting or destruction of the four components of the earth itself.

Translating *stoicheia* in this way yields a somewhat different interpretation of 2 Peter 3:10 from that with which we began. We are left with the cataclysmic fire of God's judgement, but its function in the context is primarily to lay the earth bare before God, to reveal it as it is, and to leave human beings and their works without any place to hide. A similar theme can be discerned in Paul's caution that a

Christian worker 'build' carefully on the 'foundation' of Christ: 'the work of each builder will become visible, for the Day will disclose it, because it will be revealed with fire, and the fire will test what sort of work each has done' (1 Corinthians 3:13). In another application of the same imagery, 1 Peter 1:7 encourages Christians to rejoice in their hope even in the midst of trials so that 'the genuineness of your faith – being more precious than gold that, though perishable, is tested by fire – may be found to result in praise and glory and honour when Jesus Christ is revealed'. And, just a few verses after the claim that the earth and its works 'will be found' in 2 Peter 3:10, readers are encouraged '*to be found at peace*' (v. 14) when the Lord returns. Al Wolters builds on this to suggest that the fire of 2 Peter 3:7, 10 and 12 must be envisioned as a purifying fire that destroys human evil but leaves everything else intact or renewed; he goes so far as to claim that, rather than picturing the end of this creation, 'the text of 2 Pet. 3:10 . . . stresses instead the permanence of the created earth, despite the coming judgement'.[404]

Wolters may press his argument too far, but it is striking that nowhere in 2 Peter 3 is the end of the earth unambiguously described. In 2 Peter 3:7, the author claims that 'the present heavens and earth have been reserved for fire, being kept until the day of judgement and destruction of the godless'; but though both heaven and earth are 'reserved for fire', the purpose of this fire is expressly stated to be for the 'judgement and destruction of the godless' – in other words, to do away with *human* evil. In 2 Peter 3:12, it is again only the heavens and the elements that are said to be burned with fire before the appearance of the new creation. More challenging might be 3:11, where the author's ethical admonitions are rooted in the fact that 'all these things are to be dissolved in this way'. The referent of 'all [these] things' would seem in the context to include the heavens, the elements, and the earth of the previous verse. Nonetheless, Peter Davids points out that if 3:10 is taken 'at face value as expressing the vision of the future that our author wishes to communicate, then "all these things" [in v. 11] are [limited to] the heavens and the elements (heavenly bodies)'; whatever effects such a judgement might also have on the earth, the author's focus remains on 'the positive vision of the future and what it means for the present'.[405]

It is worth asking what the significance might be in any case if the author of 2 Peter 3, in contradiction to Wolters and Davids, does intend to describe the ultimate destruction of the present earth. What would 'destruction' mean in such a context? Adams points out that even when (as in his reading of 2 Peter 3) early Jewish and Christian texts do describe a genuine cosmic catastrophe, the absolute destruction of the world into non-existence (which is sometimes what modern readers assume is meant) is never what is in view. Scripture regularly uses the language of 'destruction' to denote something that has been rendered unfit for its purpose – a land made desolate by drought or flood, a burst vessel that no longer holds liquid, a ship's stern that waves have broken up, even a coin that has been lost.[406] The sense is of something wrecked, ruined, broken apart, or put beyond use, but there is no sense in which the thing destroyed has been obliterated into nothingness, however beyond human repair it may be. The parallel used by the author of 2 Peter himself is instructive; he compares the future judgement by fire with the past destruction of the cosmos by the flood (3:6). Though this sounds like an intensification of the effects of the Noahic flood described in Genesis, the author of 2 Peter surely does not envision the world that emerged after the flood as anything other than one that was in 'material continuity' with what went before.

In fact, it is worth looking briefly at 2 Peter's compact description of the new world that emerges after the final judgement: 'a new heavens and a new earth . . . where righteousness is at home' (3:13). The language of 'a new heavens and a new earth' is borrowed from Isaiah 65 and 66, and there is a much fuller picture of this new creation in Revelation 21—22: a creation wondrously transformed, taken beyond all threat of harm or evil, and suffused with God's glorious presence. But 2 Peter focuses only on the central idea that in this new heaven and new earth, God's will is done, because here 'righteousness dwells'. This remarkable personification of righteousness as 'making its home' in the new creation is taken from Isaiah 32, where, following a description of God's desolating judgement upon human habitation in the land, Isaiah 32:15–16 describes the time when 'a spirit from on high is poured out on us' and the wilderness itself becomes a 'fruitful field', a fruitful place where 'righteousness will dwell'.[407] 'The effect of righteousness', Isaiah 32:17 goes on to say, 'will be peace (*shalom*)'. In the same way, 2 Peter encourages readers, as they await the day of the Lord and the new heaven and new earth, to 'be found by him at *peace*' (3:14). 2 Peter's hope for the future, then, does not sound far from the ecological vision of Isaiah 32, where the wilderness, cleared of human injustice, is renewed by God's spirit as a fruitful field where righteousness dwells and peace is found (Figure 16.2).

Figure 16.2 'The New Jerusalem' by Gustave Doré (1832–83). (Courtesy of <www.creationism.org>.)

In the light of all this, Wolters and Davids are probably right to emphasize greater continuity between the ages than Adams and others have been prepared to recognize. But we should not finally miss 2 Peter's essential insight that God's purposes for his creation and for his people cannot be realized unless and until all things are put to rights, and this putting to rights will require in the end a radical rupture with the past, God's definitive judgement of evil, and his making of all things new (cf. Revelation 21:5). It is perhaps our discomfort with a God who acts in the world and our unwillingness to take seriously our own involvement in sin and injustice and need for grace and mercy that tempts us to reject such 'apocalyptic' visions; but the claim of 2 Peter is that this is where we must begin (and end) if we are to learn to live in a way that is in keeping with a world 'where righteousness is at home'.

Ethics for a new earth

Whatever precise interpretation we adopt for the cosmology of 2 Peter 3, it is important to consider the implications that the text itself draws from its eschatological expectation. Here, as elsewhere in Scripture, eschatology is not taught to satisfy idle curiosity, stoke millennial passions, or even merely to comfort the suffering; it is intended to profoundly reorient readers' perceptions of the world, to challenge them out of complacency, and to motivate radical commitment to the ways of God's kingdom. So it is that 2 Peter moves immediately from the concise depiction of the events attending the future 'day of the Lord' in verse 10 to its significance for the present life of the believer:

> (v. 11) Since all these things are to be dissolved [*or* are being dissolved] in this way, what sort of persons ought you to be in leading lives of holiness and godliness, (v. 12) waiting for and hastening the coming of the day of God? . . . (v. 13) But, in accordance with his promise, we wait for new heavens and a new earth, where righteousness is at home.

It might seem strange that the author of 2 Peter expects his readers not only to await but even to hasten – to 'speed on' – this coming day of God. It is equally surprising, however, that whereas the events pertaining to the day of the Lord are consistently portrayed throughout this chapter as belonging to the future, the author switches to the present tense to describe the 'dissolving' of 'all these things' in verse 11 and the present 'dwelling' of righteousness in the new heavens and new earth in verse 13. There is apparently for 2 Peter a sense in which these climactic events are already beginning to happen in the present time. Perhaps, as in Paul's 'already/not yet' eschatology, there is a hint here that the form of the old creation is even now passing away as those who are in Christ begin to live in the light of God's future and the new creation breaks into the present.

But how can those who are in Christ 'hasten' the coming of that day? It should go without saying that there is no sense in which believers are being told to help things along by contributing to the destruction or ruin of the earth, by using up its resources and trying to provoke God, as it were, or pre-empt his judgement; the author of 2 Peter would no doubt agree with Revelation that those who destroy the earth should expect to be destroyed themselves (Revelation 11:18). For 2 Peter, the day is hastened by 'holy ways of living and godly acts' as the Lord's followers 'strive to be found by him at peace' (v. 14). The plurals in the Greek text ('holy ways of living and godly acts') are not always evident in English translation, but, as Steven Kraftchick points out, they 'underscore that many kinds of godliness characterize the Christian life'.[408] Presumably this will include cultivating the virtues listed in 2 Peter 1:5–8, where readers are called on to 'support your faith with goodness, and goodness with knowledge, and knowledge with self-control, and self-control with endurance, and endurance with godliness, and godliness with mutual affection, and mutual affection with love'. But it will also include the very many practical things that constitute 'godly acts', concrete examples of goodness, self-control, and love that will necessarily find expression in different ways in different times and places. It is precisely here, of course, that our scientific knowledge about the present state of the earth, the plight of its creatures and peoples, and its probable future if things carry on as they have, enters in to supply the context and material with which Christian love and hope must do its work.

When Jesus talked about the coming of the Son of Man 'like a thief' – the saying echoed in 2 Peter 3:10 – he immediately followed this with parables about the responsibilities incumbent upon servants who are awaiting their master's return (Matthew 24:45–51; Luke 12:42–8). According to Luke, Jesus finished by saying, 'From everyone to whom much has been given, much will be required; and from the one to whom much has been entrusted, even more will be demanded' (12:48). Jesus' stern challenge leaves his followers in the Western world today – rich in monetary wealth, technology, and scientific knowledge – with little excuse but to face up to the radical demands being made of them. What does it mean to be responsible servants of the Lord, to lead 'lives of holiness and godliness', to love God and neighbour and care for the earth in a world of staggering inequalities, in countries built upon profligate use and abuse of the planet's resources, in societies addicted to unsustainable practices that endanger the earth's life, alter its atmosphere, and threaten all who live at the margins? It surely will involve something more than 'business as usual', than merely economic calculations of costs and benefits, and more than half-measures that leave our sacrosanct 'standard of living' intact.

There is in fact a more negative way of envisioning the situation in which we find ourselves that can be drawn from Habakkuk, an Old Testament book to which (not incidentally) 2 Peter 3:9 alludes and which, like 2 Peter, presents 'a vision for the appointed time' that 'speaks of the end, and does not lie' (Habakkuk 2:3). Habakkuk is also well aware of the dangers of falling into complacency or despair when God's future seems unrealized in the present: 'If it seems to tarry, wait for it; it will surely come, it will not delay.' Habakkuk's vision of the future is intended to comfort the oppressed and those who long for God's justice; but it serves at the same time as a warning to the 'proud' who 'never have enough', who 'gather all nations for themselves and collect all peoples as their own' (v. 5), who 'heap up what is not [their] own' (vv. 6–7). Habakkuk accuses 'you who get evil gain for your house, setting your nest on high to be safe from the reach of harm' (v. 9) and who 'have devised shame for your house by cutting off many peoples' (v. 10). In the end, even the very materials with which the proud have hoarded and built their houses accuse them before the Lord: 'The very stones will cry out from the wall, and the plaster will respond from the woodwork. "Alas for you who build a town by bloodshed, and found a city on iniquity!"'

The tone is severe and the vision focused on judgement; but it is a judgement in favour of the oppressed, and the warning serves to challenge hearers – then and now – to pursue justice and righteousness, to renounce greed, bloodshed, and what we might today call 'unsustainable development'. There is also a note of hope, the promise of a day when 'the earth will be filled with the knowledge of the glory of the Lord, as the waters cover the sea' (v. 14). Universal 'knowledge of the glory of the Lord' is for Habakkuk the ultimate answer to pride and injustice; in such a world – as in 2 Peter 3:13 and Isaiah 32:16 – righteousness is at home.

The book of 2 Peter and the biblical tradition of which it is a part lend support and motivation for Christians today to be involved in all kinds of work and ways of living that are directed towards God's transcendent future – and this will without question involve the sort of restoration of relationships with other human beings and with the whole of creation that requires, among many other things, 'environmental sustainability'. Not only do these texts make ethical demands on their readers for living in the present, but the future to which they point is not so discontinuous with the present that readers have reason to question God's faithfulness or ability to confirm and carry over into his new creation all the work that is done now 'in the Lord'. There is no sense in these biblical texts of the sort of other-worldly piety that can serve to mask a self-absorbed search for personal fulfilment and to excuse by its silence the greed-fuelled exploitation of fellow creatures and the earth. We are presented instead with an active and a living hope, a hope that, as Jürgen Moltmann has put it, is for 'combatants, not onlookers'.[409] It is a hope that derives not from optimism in the ability of human projects to bring about God's future or from Enlightenment notions that ever-increasing progress is simply what we should expect; it is a hope that begins and ends with the death, resurrection and exaltation of Christ. With such a hope, Christians are enabled to go on working even when failure seems the only prospect and to go on living in a way that is in keeping with a world where righteousness dwells, even when that world seems impossibly distant. With such a hope, neither bland optimism nor despair – both fatal enemies of environmental sustainability – is an option.

The scoffers of 2 Peter and the jaded and disillusioned of today do not like the notion of a final judgement or even of a new heavens and a new earth; we often prefer to embrace a 'freedom' (2:19) that derives from the rejection of any transcendent God who might involve himself in the world. As Jerome Neyrey suggests, the scoffers 'are concerned only with "today," not the future . . . In their concern for "today," they reject God's future time.'[410] The 'scoffers', then – to return to where we began – are precisely those who live as though everything does and should carry on as it always has (getting and spending) and fail to live in the light of a differently envisaged future. In this respect, one of the root causes of environmental unsustainability is a failure of the imagination, an acceptance of the status quo, and – for Christians – a rejection of the new identity we are meant to have in Christ.

Notes

1 Introduction

1 For a sober assessment of what is currently happening to the environment, biodiversity, water and global warming, see United Nations Environment Programme, *Global Environment Outlook GEO4* (Malta: Progress Press Ltd, 2007).

2 J. Lovelock, 'The Earth is about to catch a morbid fever that may last as long as 100,000 years', *The Independent*, Monday, 16 January 2006.

3 J. Lovelock, *The Revenge of Gaia* (London: Penguin, 2006).

4 M. Rees, *Our Final Century* (London: Arrow Books, 2004).

5 M. Rees, *Anniversary Address 2006* (London: The Royal Society, 2006).

2 Sustainable climate and the future of energy

6 For the years 2001 to 2008 there has been little if any increase in global average temperature. Like other example of interannual variability in the record, this is most likely due to variations in El Niño events in the Pacific Ocean that have a substantial influence on surface temperature. See D. M. Smith *et al.* 2007, *Science*, **317**, 796–9.

7 W. T. Pfeffer, J. T. Harper and S. O'Neel, 'Kinematic constraints on glacier contributions to 21st-century sea-level rise', *Science* (2008) **321**: 1340–3. They suggest that if all variables in the melting process are quickly accelerated to extremely high limits, the rise could be up to 2 metres.

8 See 'Technical summary', in *Climate Change 2007 – Impacts, Adaptation and Vulnerability: Working Group II contribution to the Fourth Assessment Report of the IPCC*, ed. M. Parry, O. Canziani, J. Palutikov, P. van der Linden and C. Hansen (Cambridge: Cambridge University Press, 2007), 52, Fig. TS 13.

9 S. N. Jonkman, 'Global perspectives on loss of human life caused by floods', *Natural Hazards* (2005) **34**: 151–75; the losses due to flooding only include those from rainfall and not those from storm surges from the sea, for instance in tropical cyclones.

10 For example, see T. N. Palmer and J. Räisänen, 'Quantifying the risk of extreme seasonal precipitation events in a changing climate', *Nature* (2002) **415**: 512–14.

11 E. J. Burke, S. J. Brown and N. Christidis, 'Modeling the recent evolution of global drought and projections for the twenty-first century with the Hadley Centre climate model', *Journal of Hydrometeorology* (2006) **7**: 1113–25.

12 N. Myers and J. Kent, *Environmental Exodus: An Emergent Crisis in the Global Arena* (Washington, DC: Climate Institute, 1995).

13 See 'Summary for policymakers', in *Climate Change 2007, Impacts, Adaption and Vulnerability, Working Group II Contribution to the Fourth Assessment Report of the IPCC Intergovernmental Panel on Climate Change*, ed. M. Parry, O. Canziani, J. Palutikov, P. van der Linden and C. Hansen (Cambridge: Cambridge University Press, 2007), 7–22.

14 Nicholas Stern, *The Economics of Climate Change: The Stern Review* (Cambridge: Cambridge University Press, 2006).

15 The IPCC was formed in 1988 jointly by two UN bodies, the World Meteorological

Organization and the United Nations Environment Programme. See IPCC, *Climate Change 2007* (Cambridge: Cambridge University Press, 2007), 3 vols; also available on the IPCC website: <www.ipcc.ch> (last accessed 17 December 2008). My book, John Houghton, *Global Warming: The Complete Briefing*, 4th edn (Cambridge: Cambridge University Press, 2009) is strongly based on the IPCC reports.

16 The statements can be found on <www.royalsoc.ac.uk> (last accessed 17 December 2008).

17 UN Framework for Climate Change Convention (UNFCCC), see <unfccc.int> (last accessed 6 February 2009).

18 Global Commons Institute, see <www.gci.org.uk> (last accessed 17 December 2008).

19 Personal communication from Steve Howard of The Climate Group.

20 IPCC, *Carbon Sequestration, IPCC Report 1999*, see <www.ipcc.ch> (last accessed 6 February 2009).

21 S. Pacala and R. Socolow, 'Stabilization wedges: solving the climate problem for the next 50 years with current technologies', *Science* (2004) **305**: 968–72.

22 IEA, *Energy Technology Perspectives* (Paris: IEA, 2008); see also IEA, *World Energy Outlook* (Paris: IEA, 2008).

23 By 2050 the BLUE Map scenario reduces CO_2 emissions by 50 per cent from 2005 levels. For a 50 per cent chance of achieving the 2°C target, the reduction must be at least 50 per cent from 1990 levels – see the curve in Figure 2.8.

24 Stern, *The Stern Review*.

25 IEA, *Energy Technology Perspectives*, chap. 6, 221ff.

26 IEA, *Energy Technology Perspectives*, chap. 6.

27 G. Nelson with S. Campbell and P. Wozniak, *Beyond Earth Day: Fulfilling the Promise* (Madison: University of Wisconsin Press, 2002).

28 G. Brown, Address to the Energy and Environment Ministerial Roundtable, 15 March 2005; see <www.hm-treasury.gov.uk/speech_chex_150305.htm> (last accessed 15 January 2009).

29 J. Tollefson, 'Not your father's biofuels', *Nature* (2008) **451**: 880–3.

30 Royal Society, 'Sustainable biofuels: prospects and challenges', report by Royal Society of London, 2008, see <www.royalsoc.org> (last accessed 9 January 2009).

31 Grameen Communications, see <www.grameen-info.org> (last accessed 16 December 2008).

32 J. Oswald, 'Defence and environmental security', in *Threats Without Enemies*, ed. G. Prins (London: Earthscan, 1993), 113–34.

33 See Environment News Service, <www.ens-newswire.com/ens/dec2007/2007-12-10-01.asp> (last accessed 7 February 2009).

34 Patriarch Bartholomew of Constantinople and Pope John Paul II have both addressed this point; see M. S. Northcott, *A Moral Climate: The Ethics of Global Warming* (London: Darton, Longman and Todd, 2007), 153.

35 E. Burke, '1 December 1783, Speech on Mr Fox's East India Bill', in *The Writing and Speeches of Edmund Burke*, ed. P. J. Marshall and Paul Langford, vol. 5, *India: Madras and Bengal 1774–1785* (Oxford: Oxford University Press).

3 Climate science and its distortion and denial by the misinformation industry

36 J. P. Holdren, 'Convincing the skeptics', in *International Herald Tribune*, 4 August 2008; see <http://belfercenter.ksg.harvard.edu/publication/18467/convincing_the_climatechange_skeptics.html?breadcrumb=> (last accessed 1 May 2009).

37 See S. R. Weart, *The Discovery of Global Warming* (Cambridge, MA: Harvard University Press, 2003).

38 Paleontological Research Institution, see <www.priweb.org/ed/pgws/history/pennsylvania/pennsylvania.html> (last accessed 1 May 2009).

39 See J. R. Fleming, *The Callendar Effect: The Life and Work of Guy Stewart Callendar (1898–1964), the Scientist Who Established the Carbon Dioxide Theory of Climate Change* (Boston, MA: American Meteorological Society, 2007).

40 J. Imbrie and K. P. Imbrie, *Ice Ages: Solving the Mystery* (Cambridge, MA: Harvard University Press, 1979).

41 J. E. Penner, M. Andreae, H. Annegarn *et al.*, 'Aerosols, their direct and indirect effects', in *Climate Change 2001: The Scientific Basis. Contribution of Working Group I to the Third Assessment Report of the Intergovernmental Panel on Climate Change*, ed. J. T. Houghton, Y. Ding, D. J. Griggs *et al.* (Cambridge: Cambridge University Press, 2001), chap. 5.

42 Imbrie and Imbrie, *Ice Ages*.

43 J. Imbrie, 'Editorial: a good year for Milankovitch', *Paleoceanography* (1992) **7**: 687–90. On the dominance of the 100,000-year period in ice age cycles during the past million years of earth history, see for example P. Huybers, 'Glacial variability over the last two million years: an extended depth-derived age model, continuous obliquity pacing, and the Pleistocene progression', *Quaternary Science Reviews* (2007) **26**: 37–55.

44 J. Morgan and N. Morgan, *Roger: A Biography of Roger Revelle* (San Diego, CA: Scripps Institute of Oceanography, University of California, 1996).

45 I. C. Prentice, G. D. Farquhar, M. J. R. Fasham *et al.*, 'The carbon cycle and atmospheric carbon dioxide', in *Climate Change 2001: The Scientific Basis. Contribution of Working Group I to the Third Assessment Report of the Intergovernmental Panel on Climate Change*, ed. J. T. Houghton, Y. Ding, D. J. Griggs, *et al.*(Cambridge: Cambridge University Press, 2001), chap. 3.

46 D. L. Albritton, M. R. Allen, A. P. M. Baede *et al.*, 'Summary for policymakers: a report of Working Group I of the Intergovernmental Panel on Climate Change', in *Climate Change 2001: The Scientific Basis. Contribution of Working Group I to the Third Assessment Report of the Intergovernmental Panel on Climate Change*, ed. J. T. Houghton, Y. Ding, D. J. Griggs, *et al.*(Cambridge: Cambridge University Press, 2001), 11, Fig. 4.

47 P. J. Crutzen and E. F. Stoermer, 'The "Anthropocene"', *IGBP Newsletter* (2000) **41** (May): 17–18.

48 K. A. Emanuel, 'Increasing destructiveness of tropical cyclones over the past 30 years', *Nature* (2005) **436**: 686–8; P. J. Webster, G. J. Hollard, J. A. Curry and H.-R. Chang, 'Changes in tropical cyclone number, duration, and intensity in a warming environment', *Science* (2005) **309**: 1844–6; P. A. Stott, D. A. Stone and M. R. Allen, 'Human contribution to the European heatwave of 2003', *Nature* (2004) **432**: 610–14; S. Rahmstorf, A. Cazenave, J. A. Church *et al.*, 'Recent climate observations compared to projections', *Science* (2007) **316**: 709.

49 IPCC, '16 years of scientific assessment in support of the climate convention', *Tenth Anniversary Brochure* (2004); see <www.ipcc.ch/about/index.htm> (last accessed 1 May 2009).

50 'Policymakers Summary', in *Climate Change. The IPCC Scientific Assessment. Report Prepared for IPCC by Working Group I*, ed. J. T. Houghton, G. J. Jenkins and J. J. Ephraums (Cambridge: Cambridge University Press, 1990).

51 UNFCCC International, see <unfccc.int/essential_background/convention/background/items/1349.php> (last accessed 1 May 2009).

52 'Summary for policymakers', in *Climate Change 1995. The Science of Climate Change. Contribution of Working Group I to the Second Assessment Report of the Intergovernmental Panel on Climate Change*, ed. J. T. Houghton, L. G. Meira Filho, B. A. Callander *et al.* (Cambridge: Cambridge University Press, 1995), 1–7.

53 Albritton *et al.*, 'Summary for policymakers', 10; Q. K. Ahmad, O. Anisimov, N. Arnell *et al.*, 'Summary for policymakers', in *Climate Change 2001: Impacts, Adaptation, and Vulnerability. Contribution of Working Group II to the Third Assessment Report of the Intergovernmental Panel on Climate Change*, ed. J. J. McCarthy, O. F. Canziani, N. A. Leary, D. J. Dokken and K. S. White (Cambridge: Cambridge University Press, 2001), 4–7.

54 National Academies, 'Joint science academies' statement: Global response to climate change' (2005); see <www.nationalacademies.org/onpi/06072005.pdf> (last accessed 1 May 2009).

55 S. Solomon, D. Qin, M. Manning *et al.*, eds, *Climate Change 2007. The Physical Science Basis. Working Group I Contribution to the Fourth Assessment Report of the Intergovernmental Panel on Climate Change* (Cambridge: Cambridge University Press, 2007), 6.

56 N. Oreskes, 'The scientific consensus on climate change', *Science* (2004) **306**: 1686.

57 These and many other myths about climate change are exposed for what they are in publications like The Royal Society, *Climate Change Controversies: A Simple Guide* (London: The Royal Society, 2007); see <royalsociety.org/page.asp?id=6229> (last accessed 1 May 2009). Another good source of responses to questions about what is and is not happening to earth's climate is 'Frequently asked questions', in Solomon *et al.*, *Climate Change 2007. The Physical Science Basis*, 93–127. A good place in which to find a full exchange of expert views on recently published scientific papers is <www.realclimate.org> (last accessed 1 May 2009).

58 T. C. Peterson, W. M. Connolley and J. Fleck, 'The myth of the 1970s global cooling scientific consensus', *Bulletin of the American Meteorological Society* (2008) **89**: 1325–37.

59 United States Senate, Committee on Commerce, Science, and Transportation', *Hearing on Intergovernmental Panel on Climate Change (IPCC) Third Assessment Report. Statement of Hon Chuck Hagel, U.S. Senator from Nebraska*, 107th Congress, First Session, 1 May 2001 (Washington, DC: US Government Printing Office, 2004), 5.

60 C. Wunsch, see <puddle.mit.edu/~cwunsch/> (last accessed 1 May 2009).

61 N. Lawson, *An Appeal to Reason: A Cool Look at Global Warming* (London: Duckworth Overlook, 2008).

62 J. Houghton, 'Full of hot air', *Nature Reports* (2008) **2**: 92–3.

63 McKinsey and Company, 'Reducing U.S. greenhouse gas emissions: how much at what cost' (2007); see <www.mckinsey.com/clientservice/ccsi/greenhousegas.asp> (last accessed 1 May 2009). N. Stern, *The Economics of Climate Change: The Stern Review* (Cambridge: Cambridge University Press, 2007).

64 G. Monbiot, *Heat: How to Stop the Planet Burning* (London: Allen Lane, 2006), 27; see <www.guardian.co.uk/environment/2003/mar/04/usnews.climatechange> (last accessed 1 May 2009) and <www.huffingtonpost.com/david-horton/time-of-the-preacher_b_96847.html> (last accessed 1 May 2009).

65 UCS, *Smoke, Mirrors and Hot Air: How ExxonMobil Uses Big Tobacco Tactics to Manufacture Uncertainty on Climate Science* (Cambridge, MA: Union of Concerned Scientists, 2007).

66 Monbiot, *Heat*, 39.

67 J. Murray, BusinessGreen, see <www.businessgreen.com/business-green/news/2217825/exxon-repels-climate-change> (last accessed 1 May 2009).

68 B. Lomborg, *Cool It: The Skeptical Environmentalist's Guide to Global Warming* (New York: Knopf, 2007).

69 J. P. Holdren, 'Convincing the skeptics', in *International Herald Tribune*, 4 August 2008; see <http://belfercenter.ksg.harvard.edu/publication/18467/convincing_the_climatechange_skeptics.html?breadcrumb=> (last accessed 1 May 2009).

70 Lomborg, *Cool It*; B. Lomborg, 'An inconvenient Peace Prize', in *The Boston Globe*, 13 October 2007.

71 O. Anisimov and B. Fitzharris, 'Polar Regions (Arctic and Antarctic)', in *Climate Change 2001: Impacts, Adaptation and Vulnerability: Working Group II contribution to the Fourth Assessment Report of the IPCC Intergovernmental Panel on Climate Change*, ed. J. McCarthy, O. Canziani, N. Leary, D. Dokken and K. White (Cambridge: Cambridge University Press, 2001), 814.

72 G. Ekström, M. Nettles and V. C. Tsai, 'Seasonality and increasing frequency of Greenland glacial earthquakes', *Science* (2006) **311**: 1756–8.

73 Solomon *et al.*, *Climate Change 2007. The Physical Science Basis*, 13.

74 W. T. Pfeffer, J. T. Harper and S. O'Neel, 'Kinematic constraints on glacier contributions to 21st-century sea-level rise', *Science* (2008) **321**: 1340–3.

75 Solomon *et al.*, *Climate Change 2007. The Physical Science Basis*, Table SPM-2.

76 Q. K. Ahmad, O. Anisimov, N. Arnell *et al.*, 'Summary for policymakers', in *Climate Change 2001: Impacts, Adaptation, and Vulnerability. Contribution of Working Group II to the Third Assessment Report of the Intergovernmental Panel on Climate Change*, ed. J. J. McCarthy, O. F. Canziani, N. A. Leary, D. J. Dokken and K. S. White (Cambridge: Cambridge University Press, 2001), 1–17.

4 Responding to climate change: how much should we discount the future?

77 For a survey of the issues, see D. A. Hay, 'Sustainable economics', in *When Enough is Enough*, ed. R. J. Berry (Leicester: InterVarsity Press, 2007), chap. 6.

78 N. H. Stern, *The Economics of Climate Change: The Stern Review* (Cambridge: Cambridge University Press, 2007).

79 W. D. Nordhaus, 'A review of the *Stern Review on the Economics of Climate Change*', *Journal of Economic Literature* (2007) XLV: 686–702. Nordhaus is the leading economist of climate change in the USA: see also W. D. Nordhaus, *Managing the Global Commons: The Economics of Climate Change* (Cambridge, MA, and London: MIT Press, 1994); W. D. Nordhaus and J. Boyer *Warming the World: Economic Models of Global Warming* (Cambridge, MA, and London: MIT Press, 2000)

80 The *Stern Review* is not explicit on the discount rates it employs. These rates are cited in I. Byatt, I. Castles, I. M. Goklany *et al.*, 'The Stern Review: a dual critique: Part II Economic aspects', *World Economics* (2006) 7(4): 165–232. The authors note that they obtained this information directly from the UK Treasury.

81 R. S. J. Tol, 'The marginal damage costs of carbon dioxide emissions: an assessment of the uncertainties', *Energy Policy* (2005) 33: 2064–74. Tol has recently updated that review in R. S. J. Tol, 'The social cost of carbon: trends, outliers and catastrophes', *Economics: The Open Access, Open-Assessment E-Journal* (2008) 2(25): 12 August; see <www.economics-ejournal.org/economics/journalarticles/2008-25/> (last accessed 19 December 2008).

82 Nordhaus, *J. Econ. Lit.* (2007) XLV: 686–702; P. Dasgupta, 'Commentary. The Stern Review's economics of climate change', *National Institute Economic Review* (2007) 199: 4–7.

83 See Hay, 'Sustainable economics', especially 101–7.

84 F. P. Ramsey, 'A mathematical theory of saving', *Economic Journal* (1928) 38: 543–59.

85 See, for example, Nordhaus, *Managing the Global Commons*; P. Dasgupta, *Human Wellbeing and the Natural Environment* (Oxford: Oxford University Press, 2004).

86 The parameter η is defined as the elasticity of the marginal utility of consumption. Consider two people: person A with initial consumption three times greater than person B. An additional unit of consumption given to B is worth three times as much as giving it to person A if η is set at 1, but nine times as much if η is set at 2. A higher η is more egalitarian.

87 Nordhaus, *J. Econ. Lit.* (2007) XLV: 686–702.

88 Dasgupta, *Nat. Inst. Econ. Rev.* (2007) 199: 4–7.

89 The book version of the *Stern Review* was able to respond to these criticisms to some degree: see the 'Technical annex to the postscript', in Stern, *Economics of Climate Change*, 658–71.

90 But see the discussion in M. L. Weitzman, 'A review of the *Stern Review on the Economics of Climate Change*', *Journal of Economic Literature* (2007) XLV: 703–24. Weitzman points out that there is no single market rate of discount, and that the choice of an appropriate rate is crucial.

91 IPCC, 'Climate Change 2007: the Physical Science Basis. Summary for Policymakers', see <www.ipcc.ch> (last accessed 18 December 2008).

92 Weitzman, *J. Econ. Lit.* (2007) XLV: 703–24.

93 J. Broome, 'Discounting the future', *Philosophy and Public Affairs* (1994) 23: 128–56.

94 Ramsey, *Econ. J.* (1928) 38: 543–9.

95 This description of the practice of economists is not entirely fair. For example, the *Stern Review* seeks to convert consumption into an aggregate measure of 'social welfare' with weights depending on initial income (the parameter η described in the text) – and the *Review* notes that other indicators of human welfare should be included in the analysis such as health, education and quality of the environment.

96 The discussion here is derived directly from S. Caney, 'Cosmopolitan justice, rights and global climate change', *Canadian Journal of Law and Jurisprudence* (2006) XIX: 255–78, and an unpublished paper which he has made available to me.

97 Caney, *Can. J. Law Jurisprud.* (2006) XIX: 255–78.

98 J. Raz, *The Morality of Freedom* (Oxford: Clarendon Press, 1986).

99 D. Bookless, 'Towards a theology of sustainability', in *When Enough is Enough*, ed. R. J. Berry (Leicester: InterVarsity Press, 2007), chap. 2, also identifies a third approach – the ecocentric – which views human beings as just one small element of an interdependent biosphere, with no greater rights than any other element.

100 These points are adapted, with permission, from a presentation by Alister McGrath in November 2007. C. J. H. Wright, *Old Testament Ethics for the People of God* (Leicester: InterVarsity Press, 2004), chap. 4, has an excellent summary of the relevant texts. For a discussion of the Old Testament materials, see also C. B. DeWitt, *Earth-Wise: A Biblical Response to Environmental Issues* (Grand Rapids, MI: CRC Publications, 1994); C. B. DeWitt, *Caring for Creation* (Grand Rapids, MI: Baker Books, 1997).

101 Wright, *Old Testament Ethics*, 122–3, argues that it is better to think of the human race as 'shepherds' rather than 'stewards' of the creation. The former concept ties in with Old Testament concepts of kingship, and should characterize our delegated authority over the natural world – we are vicegerents. Stewardship implies management: shepherding implies care.

102 For details, see the discussion in D. A. Hay, *Economics Today: A Christian Critique* (Leicester: Apollos, InterVarsity Press, 1989), chap. 3.

103 Wright, *Old Testament Ethics*, chap. 5.

5 International governance and root causes of unsustainability

104 Brundtland Commission, *Our Common Future,* Report of the World Commission on Environment and Development (Oxford: Oxford University Press, 1987).

105 J. Diamond, *Collapse: How Societies Choose to Fall or Succeed* (New York: Viking, 2005).

106 P. Wilkinson, *International Relations* (Oxford: Oxford University Press, 2007).

107 Article 2, The United Nations Framework Convention on Climate Change, see <unfccc.int/resource/docs/convkp/conveng.pdf> (last accessed 27 January 2009).

108 D. M. Liverman, 'Survival into the future in the face of climate change', in *Survival: The Survival of the Human Race*, ed. E. Shuckburgh (Cambridge: Cambridge University Press, 2006), 187–205.

109 S. Pacala and R. Socolow, 'Stabilization wedges: solving the climate problem for the next 50 years with current technologies', *Science* (2004) **305**: 968–72.

110 Pacala and Socolow, 'Stabilization wedges'.

111 G. Monbiot, see <www.monbiot.com/archives/2006/10/19/selling-indulgences/> (last accessed 16 July 2008).

112 UK government, see <www.hm-treasury.gov.uk/media/9/9/CLOSED_SHORT_executive_summary.pdf>; *Guardian* newspaper, see <www.guardian.co.uk/environment/2008/jun/26/climatechange.scienceofclimatechange> (both last accessed 16 July 2008).

113 N. H. Stern, *The Economics of Climate Change: The Stern Review* (Cambridge: Cambridge University Press, 2006).

114 M. Parry, J. Palutikof, C. Hanson and J. Lowe, 'Squaring up to reality', *Nature Reports Climate Change* (2008) **2**: 1–3.

115 S. Boehmer-Christiansen, 'Science, equity, and the war against carbon', *Science, Technology & Human Values* (2003) **28**: 69–92.

116 B. Lomborg, *Cool It: The Skeptical Environmentalist's Guide to Global Warming* (New York: Knopf Publishing Group, 2007).

117 M. Paterson, 'Global warming', in *Encyclopedia of International Relations and Global Politics*, ed. M. Griffiths (London: Routledge, 2008), 338–47.

118 J. C. Waterlow, D. G. Armstrong, L. Fowden and R. Riley, *Feeding a World Population of more than Eight Billion People* (Oxford and New York: Oxford University Press and Rank Prize Funds, 2008); K. M. Leisinger, K. M. Schmitt and R. Pandya-Lorch, *Six Billion and Counting: Population Growth and Food Security in the 21st Century* (Washington, DC: International Food Policy Research Institute, 2002), and see website <www.wfp.org/operations/introduction/index.asp?section=5&sub_section=1> (last accessed 19 October 2008).

119 F. Comim, 'Climate injustice and development: a capability perspective', *Development* (2008) **51**: 344–9.

120 All Party Parliamentary Group on Population, Development and Reproductive Health, 'Return of the population growth factor: its impact upon the Millennium Development Goals', Report of Hearings, January 2007; see <www.appg-popdevrh.org.uk> (last accessed 16 July 2008).

121 United Nations, see <www.un.org/millenniumgoals/pdf/The%20Millennium%20Development%20Goals%20Report%202008.pdf> (last accessed 19 October 2008).

122 R. B. Heap and F. Comim, 'Consumption and happiness: Christian values and an approach towards sustainability', in *When Enough is Enough,* ed. R. J. Berry (Nottingham: APOLLOS, 2007), 79–98.

123 N. Myers and J. Kent, *The New Consumers* (Washington, DC: Island Press, 2004).

124 Heap and Comim, 'Consumption and happiness'; see <www.defra.gov.uk/Environment/business/scp/> (last accessed 16 July 2008).

125 IAASTD, see <www.agassessment.org/docs/SR_Exec_Sum_280508_English.pdf> (last accessed 18 October 2008); C. Pollock, J. Pretty, I. Crute, C. Leaver and H. Dalto, eds, Sustainable agriculture: Parts 1 and 2. *Philosophical Transactions of the Royal Society Biological Sciences* **363** (London: The Royal Society, 2008); C. Pollock, J. Pretty, I. Crute, C. Leaver and H. Dalton, eds, Sustainable agriculture 2. *Philosophical Transactions of the Royal Society Biological Sciences* **363** (London: The Royal Society, 2008); see <www.agrioutlook.org/dataoecd/54/15/40715381.pdf> (last accessed 16 July 2008).

126 IAASTD, see <www.agassessment.org/docs/SR_Exec_Sum_280508_English.pdf> and <www.agassessment.org/docs/Global_Press_Release_final.doc> (last accessed 19 October 2008).

127 J. Pretty, 'Agricultural sustainability: concepts, principles and evidence', in 'Sustainable agriculture 1', *Philosophical Transactions of the Royal Society B: Biological Sciences* (2008) **363**: 447–66.

128 Pollock *et al.*, 'Sustainable agriculture 1'; Pollock *et al.*, 'Sustainable agriculture 2'; Pretty, *Phil. Trans. Roy. Soc. B: Biol. Sci.* (2008) **363**: 447–66.

129 IAASTD, see <www.agassessment.org/docs/SR_Exec_Sum_280508_English.pdf> and <www.agassessment.org/docs/> (last accessed 16 July 2008).

130 *China Daily* newspaper, see <www.chinadaily.com.cn/china/2008-07/11/content_6836524.htm> (last accessed 16 July 2008).

131 IAASTD, see <www.agassessment.org/docs/SR_Exec_Sum_280508_English.pdf> and <www.agassessment.org/docs/Global_Press_Release_final.doc> (last accessed 19 October 2008).

132 IAASTD, see <www.agassessment.org/docs/SR_Exec_Sum_280508_English.pdf> (last accessed 18 October 2008); <www.agassessment.org/docs/SR_Exec_Sum_280508_English.pdf> and <www.agassessment.org/docs/Global_Press_Release_final.doc> (last accessed 19 October 2008).

133 S. Barrett, *Why Cooperate? The Incentive to Supply Global Public Goods* (Oxford: Oxford University Press, 2007).

134 P. Dasgupta, 'Nature in economics', *Environmental Resource Economics* (2008) **39**: 1–7.

135 H. Daly and J. B. Cobb, *For the Common Good: Redirecting the Economy toward Community, the Environment, and a Sustainable Future* (Boston, MA: Beacon Press, 1989).

136 Professor Jose Eli da Veiga addressed this argument at a seminar at St Edmund's College, Cambridge, UK, on 10 July 2008. See University of São Paulo, <www.econ.fea.usp.br/zeeli/papers/TIME%20TO%20DITCH%20GDP%20-%20Cambridge%2010jun08.pdf>.

137 J. R. Vincent and T. Panayotou, 'Consumption: challenge to sustainable development or distraction?' *Science* (1997) **276**: 55–57.

138 Heap and Comim, 'Consumption and happiness'; Myers and Kent, *New Consumers*.

139 Diamond, *Collapse*.

140 Pew Research Center, see <people-press.org/report/417/a-deeper-partisan-divide-over-

global-warming> (last accessed 4 August 2008).

141 European Commission, see <ec.europa.eu/public_opinion/archives/ebs/ebs_295_en.pdf (last accessed 17 October 2008).

142 Heap and Comim, 'Consumption and happiness'.

143 M. C. Nussbaum, *Frontiers of Justice: Disability, Nationality, Species Membership* (Cambridge, MA: Belknap Press, 2006).

144 L. T. White, Jr, 'The historical roots of our ecologic crisis', *Science* (1967) **155**: 1203–7.

145 R. J. Berry, *Environmental Stewardship* (New York and London: T. & T. Clark, 2006).

146 The American Muslim, see <www.islamfrominside.com/Pages/Articles/Ecology%20 Environment%20and%20Islam.html> (last accessed 16 July 2008).

147 All Party Parliamentary Group, 'Return of the population gowth factor'.

148 P. Dasgupta, 'Nature and the economy', *Journal of Applied Ecology* (2007) **44**: 475–87.

149 L. Levidow and C. Marris, 'Science and governance in Europe: lessons from the case of agricultural biotechnology', *Science and Public Policy* (2001) **28**: 345–60.

150 Paterson, 'Global warming'.

151 Churches Together in Britain and Ireland, *Prosperity with a Purpose: Christians and the ethics of affluence* (London: Churches Together in Britain and Ireland, 2005).

152 Wilkinson, *International Relations*.

153 N. Spencer and R. White, *Christianity, Climate Change and Sustainable Living* (London: SPCK, 2007).

154 Churches Together, *Prosperity with a Purpose*.

155 Diamond, *Collapse*.

156 G. Vogel, 'The evolution of the Golden Rule', *Science* (2004) **303**: 1128–31.

157 J. G. Speth and P. M. Hass, *Global Environmental Governance* (Washington, DC: Island Press, 2006).

6 Population matters: voluntary contraception for environmental sustainability

158 J. Guillebaud and P. Hayes, 'Editorial: Population growth and climate change', *British Medical Journal* (2008) **337**: 247–8; see <www.bmj.com/cgi/content/full/337/jul24_2/a576> (last accessed 29 January 2009); WWF, GFN and ZSL, *Living Planet Report* (London: Worldwide Fund for Nature, with Global Footprint Network and Zoological Society of London, 2008), 1–40; see <www.panda.org/news_facts/publications/living_planet_report/index.cfm> (last accessed 5 January 2009).

159 J. Cohen, *How Many People can the Earth Support?* (New York: W. W. Norton & Company, 1995).

160 WWF, GFN and ZSL, *Living Planet Report*.

161 J. van den Bergh and P. Rietveld, 'Reconsidering the limits to world population: meta-analysis and meta-prediction', *BioScience* (2004) **54**: 195–204.

162 WWF, GFN and ZSL, *Living Planet Report*.

163 *World Population Data Sheet* (Washington, DC: Population Reference Bureau, 2008); see <www.prb.org> (last accessed 5 January 2009).

164 WWF, GFN and ZSL, *Living Planet Report*.

165 Guillebaud and Hayes, *Br. Med. J.* (2008) **337**: 247–8.

166 H. Haberl, M. Wackernagel and T. Wrbka, 'Land use and sustainability indicators', *Land Use Policy* (2004) **21**: 193–8.

167 UNEP, *Global Environment Outlook: Environment for Development (GEO-4) Report* (United Nations Environment Programme, 2007); see <www.unep.org/geo/geo4> (last accessed 5 January 2009).

168 P. Ehrlich and A. Ehrlich, *The Population Explosion* (London: Arrow Books, 1990), 58–9.

169 N. Spencer and R. White, *Christianity, Climate Change and Sustainable Living* (London: SPCK, 2007), 165–77.

170 R. Sider, *Rich Christians in the Age of Hunger* (Nashville, TN: Thomas Nelson, 1973).

171 FAO, see <www.fao.org/newsroom/en/news/2006/1000448/index.html (Food and Agricul-

ture Organization, 2006)> (last accessed 5 January 2009).

172 L. Grant, *The Collapsing Bubble- Growth and Fossil Energy* (Santa Ana, CA: Seven Locks Press, 2005), 45–64.

173 L. Grant, *Valedictory: The Age of Overshoot* (Alexandria, VA: Negative Population Growth Inc., 2007), 5–38; see <www.npg.org> (last accessed 5 January 2009).

174 M. Potts, 'The population policy pendulum', *British Medical Journal* (1999) 319: 933–4.

175 T. Hesketh, L. Lu and Z. W. Xing, 'The effect of China's one-child family policy after 25 years', *New England Journal of Medicine* (2005) 353: 1171–6; see <content.nejm.org/cgi/content/full/353/11/1171> (last accessed 29 January 2009).

176 J. Guillebaud. '*Youthquake*': *Population, Fertility and Environment in the 21st Century* (London: Optimum Population Trust, 2007), 1–24; see <www.optimumpopulation.org/Youthquake.pdf> (last accessed 5 January 2009).

177 House of Commons, *Return of the Population Growth Factor. Report of Hearings by the All Party Parliamentary Group on Population, Development and Reproductive Health* (London: House of Commons, 2007); see <www.appg-popdevrh.org.uk> (last accessed 5 January 2009).

178 House of Commons, *Return*.

179 Guillebaud, '*Youthquake*'.

180 Guillebaud, '*Youthquake*'.

181 C. Berry, *Beginnings – Christian Views of the Early Embryo* (London: Christian Medical Fellowship, 1993), 17–36.

182 House of Commons, *Return*.

183 J. Porritt, *Letter of Support on Occasion of 10th Anniversary for the Environment Time Capsule* (2004); see <www.ecotimecapsule.com> (last accessed 5 January 2009).

184 House of Commons, *Return*.

185 House of Commons, *Return*.

186 Guillebaud, '*Youthquake*'.

187 Population Reference Bureau, *World Population Data Sheet*.

188 J. Cleland, 'Different pathways to demographic transition', in *Population – the Complex Reality*, ed. F. Graham-Smith (London: The Royal Society, 1994), chaps 3/5, 229–47.

189 Cleland, 'Different pathways'; J. Cleland, S. Bernstein, A. Ezeh, A. Faundes, A. Glasier and J. Innis, 'Family planning: the unfinished agenda', *Lancet* (2006) 368: 1810–27.

190 Guillebaud and Hayes, *Br. Med. J.* (2008) 337: 247–8.

191 Cleland, 'Different pathways'.

192 Guillebaud and Hayes, *Br. Med. J.* (2008) 337: 247–8.

193 M. Campbell, N. Sahin-Hodoglugil and M. Potts, 'Barriers to fertility regulation: a review of the literature', *Studies in Family Planning* (2006) 37: 87–98.

194 Cleland, 'Different pathways'.

195 M. Campbell, 'Consumer behaviour and contraceptive decisions: resolving a decades-long puzzle', *Journal of Family Planning & Reproductive Health Care* (2006) 32: 241–4.

196 Guillebaud, '*Youthquake*'.

197 Guillebaud, '*Youthquake*'.

198 Population Media Center, see <www.populationmedia.org (Population Media Center, 2008)> (last accessed 5 January 2009).

199 M. J. Hodson and M. R. Hodson, *Cherishing the Earth* (Oxford: Monarch, 2008), 28–30.

200 Hodson and Hodson, *Cherishing the Earth*; R. Berry, ed., *The Care of Creation* (Leicester: InterVarsity Press, 2000), 7–194; Spencer and White, *Christianity*, chaps 3–4, 75–119.

201 J. Guillebaud, 'Two sides of the same coin', *Green Christian* (2008) 65: 8-11; see <www.christian-ecology.org.uk/population-guillebaud.htm> (last accessed 5 January 2009).

202 For more on environmental ethics, see M. Northcott, *The Environment and Christian Ethics* (Cambridge: Cambridge University Press, 2008); R. Attfield, *The Ethics of the Global Environment* (Edinburgh: Edinburgh University Press, 1999).

203 Guillebaud and Hayes, *Br. Med. J.* (2008) 337: 247–8.

204 Guillebaud, *'Youthquake'*.

205 Guillebaud, *Green Christian* (2008) **65**: 8–11.

206 Pope Paul VI, 'Humanae Vitae', *Papal Encyclical* (Vatican, 1968); see <www.vatican.va/holy_father/paul_vi/encyclicals/documents/hf_p-vi_enc_25071968_humanae-vitae_en.html> (last accessed 5 January 2009).

207 L. Cahill, *Sex, Gender & Christian Ethics* (New York: Cambridge University Press, 1996), 187.

208 Berry, *Beginnings*.

209 O. Hotonu, *Contraception: a Pro-Life Guide* (Newcastle: The Christian Institute, 2005), 5–72.

210 Berry, *Beginnings*.

211 J. Guillebaud. *The Pill – the Facts*, 6th edn (Oxford: Oxford University Press, 2005), 207–10.

212 J. Grant, *The State of the World's Children* (Oxford: Oxford University Press for UNICEF, 1992), 58–60.

213 WWF, GFN and ZSL, *Living Planet Report*.

214 UN Population Division, <www.un.org/esa/population/publications/worldfertility2007/worldfertility2007.htm> (UN Population Division, 2008) (last accessed 5 January 2009).

215 Brundtland Commission, *Report of the World Commission on Environment and Development* (New York: United Nations, 1987), General Assembly Resolution 42/187; see <www.un.org/documents/ga/res/42/ares42-187.htm> (last accessed 5 January 2009).

216 Guillebaud, *Green Christian* (2008) **65**: 8–11.

7 Natural disasters: acts of God or results of human folly?

217 S. Bondevik, 'The sands of tsunami time', *Nature* (2008) **455**: 1183–4.

218 UN, *Disaster Risk Reduction: Global Review 2007* (Geneva: United Nations, 2007).

219 IPCC, *Climate Change 2007 – Synthesis Report* (Fourth Assessment Report of Intergovernmental Panel on Climate Change, 2007); see <www.ipcc.ch> (last accessed 26 May 2009).

220 For further details, see *Climate Change 2007 – Impacts, Adaptation and Vulnerability, Working Group II contribution to the Fourth Assessment Report of the IPCC Intergovernmental Panel on Climate Change*, ed. M. Parry, O. Canziani, J. Palutikof *et al.* (Cambridge: Cambridge University Press, 2008).

221 UN, *Disaster Risk Reduction*.

222 C. J. Humphreys and R. S. White, 'The eruption of Santorini and the date and historicity of Joseph', *Science and Christian Belief* (1995) **7**: 151–62.

223 R. S. White, 'Volcanic eruptions and deaths', *Geology Today* (1995) **11**: 27–8.

224 C. J. Humphreys, 'Famines and cataclysmic volcanism', *Geology Today* (1994) **10**: 181–5.

225 B. Franklin, 'Meteorological imaginations and conjectures', *Memoirs of the Literary and Philosophical Society, Manchester* (1784) **2**: 373–7.

226 R. Bilham, 'Urban earthquake fatalities: a safer world, or worse to come?', *Seismology Research Letters* (2004) **75**: 706–12.

227 T. Waltham, 'The flooding of New Orleans', *Geology Today* (2005) **21**: 225–31.

228 P. A. Stott, D. A. Stone and M. R. Allen, 'Human contribution to the European heat wave of 2003', *Nature* (2004) **423**: 610–14.

229 A. Sen, *Poverty and Famines: An Essay on Entitlement and Deprivation* (Oxford: Oxford University Press, 1981).

230 R. Conquest, *The Harvest of Sorrow: Soviet Collectivization and the Terror-Famine* (Edmonton: The University of Alberta Press in Association with the Canadian Institute of Ukrainian Studies, 1986).

231 FAO, *The State of Food Insecurity in the World* (Geneva: Food and Agriculture Organization of the United Nations, 2006); see <www.fao.org> (last accessed 26 May 2009).

232 From a letter by Timothy Richard quoted by P. R. Bohr in *Famine in China and the Missionary: Timothy Richard as relief administrator and advocate of national reform, 1876–1874* (Cambridge, MA: Harvard University Press, 1972).

233 C. E. Trevelyan, 'The Irish crisis', *Edinburgh Review* (1848) **175**: 201.

234 A helpful book on this is C. Ash, *Out of the Storm: Grappling with God in the Book of Job* (Leicester: InterVarsity Press, 2006).

235 D. K. Chester, 'The theodicy of natural disasters', *Scottish Journal of Theology* (1998) 51: 485–505.

236 C. S. Lewis, *Mere Christianity* (London: Fontana, 1971) 116.

8 Just food: a biblical perspective on culture and agriculture

237 Millennium Ecosystem Assessment, *Ecosystems and Human Well-Being*, vol. 1, *Current State and Trends* (Washington, DC: Island, 2005), 777.

238 See T. Hirsch, 'The incredible shrinking Amazon Rainforest', *World Watch* (May/June 2008) 21(3): 14.

239 K. Bradsher and A. Martin, 'Shortages threaten farmers' key tool: fertilizer', *The New York Times*, 30 April 2008.

240 CNN morning broadcast, 18 February 2008.

241 All translations are my own.

242 On wide hybridization and marker-assisted selection as modes of technologically 'assisted evolution', see J. D. Glover, C. M. Cox and J. P. Reganold, 'Future farming: a return to roots?' *Scientific American* 297: 82–9.

243 Among numerous publications of Jackson and others at the Land Institute, see most recently W. Jackson and B. Vitek, eds, *The Virtues of Ignorance: Complexity, Sustainability, and the Limits of Knowledge* (Lexington: The University Press of Kentucky, 2008).

244 See C. Tudge, *So Shall We Reap* (London: Allen Lane, 2003).

245 W. Berry, 'Faustian economics: hell hath no limits', *Harper's Magazine* (May 2008), 36–8.

246 See C. J. H. Wright, *God's People in God's Land: Family, Land, and Property in the Old Testament* (Exeter: Paternoster Press, 1990).

247 For examples, see N. Wirzba, *The Paradise of God: Renewing Religion in an Ecological Age* (New York: Oxford University Press, 2003); W. Berry, 'The gift of good land', in *The Gift of Good Land: Further Essays Cultural and Agricultural* (San Francisco: North Point Press, 1981), 267–81.

248 On the ecology of the land the Israelites settled, see C. Meyers, *Discovering Eve: Ancient Israelite Women in Context* (Oxford: Oxford University Press, 1988), 47–71; D. Hillel, *The Natural History of the Bible: An Environmental Exploration of the Hebrew Scriptures* (New York: Columbia University Press, 2006), especially 26–39.

249 The term 'catastrophic agriculture' is used in R. Manning, *Against the Grain: How Agriculture Has Hijacked Civilization* (New York: North Point, 2004).

250 W. C. Lowdermilk, *Conquest of the Land through 7,000 Years*, Soil Conservation Agricultural Bulletin (Washington, DC: United States Department of Agriculture, 1948) see <www.journeytoforever.org/farm_library/Lowd/Lowd3.html> (last accessed 6 January 2009).

251 The phrase 'the end of food' echoes the titles of two recent analyses of the food system: P. Roberts, *The End of Food* (Boston, MA: Houghton Mifflin, 2008); T. F. Pawlick, *The End of Food: How the Food Industry is Destroying our Food Supply – And What You Can Do about It* (Vancouver: Greystone Books, 2006).

252 For extended studies of 1 Kings 21, Psalm 37, and other agrarian texts, see E. F. Davis, *Scripture, Culture, and Agriculture: An Agrarian Reading of the Bible* (Cambridge: Cambridge University Press, 2009).

253 See Davis, *Scripture, Culture, and Agriculture*, chap. 6.

254 On these and other examples of community-based agriculture, see D. H. Boucher, ed., *The Paradox of Plenty: Hunger in a Bountiful World* (Oakland, CA: Food First Books, 1999), 274–329.

9 Unsustainable agriculture and land use: restoring stewardship for biospheric sustainability

255 D. Hillel and C. Rosenzweig, 'Biodiversity and food production', in *Sustaining Life: How Human Health Depends on Biodiversity*, ed. E. Chivian and A. Bernstein (Oxford: Oxford

University Press, 2008), 325–81.

256 M. Polanyi, 'Life's irreducible structure', *Science* (1968) **160**: 1309–12.

257 V. W. Rattan, 'The transition to agricultural sustainability', *Proceedings of the National Academy of Sciences, USA* (1999) **96**: 5960–7 (5960).

258 P. Bardhan, ed., *The Economic Theory of Agrarian Institutions* (Oxford: Clarendon, 1991).

259 D. C. North, *Understanding the Process of Economic Change* (Princeton, NJ: Princeton University Press, 2005), 49.

260 North, *Understanding the Process*, 49.

261 M. Schwaninger, *Intelligent Organizations: Powerful Models for Systemic Management* (Heidelberg: Springer, 2009).

262 R. T. Watson and A. H. Zakri, 'Foreword', in *Ecosystems and Human Well-Being: Policy Responses*, vol. 3, *Millennium Ecosystem Assessment* (Washington, DC: Island Press, 2005), xiii.

263 Details are available at <www.millenniumassessment.org> (last accessed 19 January 2009).

264 D. Pimentel, E. C. Terhune, R. Dyson-Hudson *et al.*, 'Land degradation: effects on food and energy resources', *Science* (1976) **194**: 149–55 (150).

265 D. Pimentel, C. Harvey, P. Resosudarmo *et al.*, 'Environmental and economic costs of soil erosion and conservation benefits', *Science* (1995) **267**: 1117–23.

266 C. B. DeWitt, 'Biogeographic and trophic restructuring of the biosphere: the state of the earth under human domination', *Christian Scholar's Review* (2003) **32**: 347–64.

267 E. N. Broadbent, G. P. Gregory, M. Keller, D. E. Knapp, P. Oliveira and J. N. Silva, 'Forest fragmentation and edge effects from deforestation and selective logging in the Brazilian Amazon', *Biological Conservation* (2008) **141**: 1745–57.

268 D. Skole and C. Tucker, 'Tropical deforestation and habitat fragmentation in the Amazon: satellite data from 1978 to 1988', *Science* (1993) **260**: 1905–10.

269 DeWitt, *Christ. Schol. Rev.* (2003) **32**: 347–64.

270 D.W. Bromley, 'Resource degradation in the African commons: accounting for institutional decay', *Environment and Development Economics* (2008), **13**: 539–63.

271 D. B. Henriques, 'Food is gold, so milllions invested in farming', *New York Times*, 5 June 2008, see <www.nytimes.com/2008/06/05/business/05farm> (last accessed 22 January 2009).

272 D. W. Bromley, 'Environmental regulations and the problem of sustainability: moving beyond "market failure"', *Ecological Economics* (2007) **63**: 676–83 (676).

273 W. P. George, 'Grotius, theology, and international law: overcoming textbook bias', *Journal of Law and Religion* (1999–2000) **14**: 605–31 (605).

274 H. Grotius, *Mare liberum* [The free sea], 1609; C. Darwin, *On the Origin of Species by Means of Natural Selection* (London, John Murray, 1859).

275 George, *J. Law Religion* (1999–2000) **14**: 606.

276 J. Cauvin, *Commentary on Genesis* (1554).

277 J. N. Pretty, A. S. Ball, T. Lang and J. I. L. Morison, 'Farm costs and food miles: an assessment of the full cost of the UK weekly food basket', *Food Policy* (2005) **30**: 1–20.

278 J. N. Pretty, A. D. Noble, D. Bossio *et al.*, 'Resource-conserving agriculture increases yields in developing countries', *Environmental Science and Technology* (2006) **40**: 1114–19.

10 Water, water . . .

279 United Nations, 'Millennium Development Goals', see <www.un.org/millenniumgoals> (last accessed 5 February 2009).

280 Joint Monitoring Programme, *Progress in Drinking-water and Sanitation: Special Focus on Sanitation* (Geneva: WHO/UNICEF, 2008).

281 United Nations, 'Millennium Development Goals', see <www.un.org/millenniumgoals> (last accessed 5 February 2009).

282 UNDP, *Human Development Report 2007/08* (Basingstoke: United Nations Development Programme, Palgrave Macmillan, 2007); UNFPA, *State of World Population 2008* (New York: United Nations Population Fund, 2008).

283 UN-Habitat, *The State of African Cities 2008: A Framework for Addressing Urban Challenges in Africa* (Nairobi: United Nations Human Settlements Programme, 2008); see <www.unhabitat.org> (last accessed 5 February 2009).

284 JMP, *Progress in Drinking-water*; data for 2006.

285 D. D. Mara and R. G. A. Feachem, 'Water- and excreta-related diseases: unitary environmental classification', *Journal of Environmental Engineering* (1999) 125: 334–9.

286 JMP, *Progress in Drinking-water*.

287 UN-Water, *The Second UN World Water Development Report: Water, A Shared Responsibility* (Paris: World Water Assessment Programme, 2006).

288 R. C. Carter and A. Parker, 'Climate change, population trends and groundwater in Africa', *Hydrological Sciences Journal* (2009), in press.

289 IPCC, *Climate Change 2007: The Physical Science Basis. Contribution of Working Group I to the Fourth Assessment Report of the Intergovernmental Panel on Climate Change*, ed. S. Solomon, D. Qin, M. Manning *et al.* (Cambridge: Cambridge University Press, 2007).

290 Cranfield/Aguaconsult/IRC (2006) 'Landscaping and review of approaches and technologies for water, sanitation and hygiene, opportunities for action'; see <www.irc.nl/page/35950> (last accessed 14 January 2009).

291 Comprehensive Assessment of Water Management in Agriculture, *Water for Food, Water for Life: A Comprehensive Assessment of Water Management in Agriculture* (London: Earthscan, and Colombo: International Water Management Institute, 2007); see <www.iwmi.cgiar.org/assessment/Publications/books.htm> (last accessed 23 February 2009).

292 For example, see R. C. Carter, R. Rwamwanja and G. Bagamuhunda (2005) 'Achieving a lasting impact in rural water services: a case study from south-west Uganda', paper presented at the 31st WEDC International Conference, Kampala, Uganda, 2005, and see <wedc.lboro.ac.uk/conferences/pdfs/31/Carter.pdf> (last accessed 14 January 2009); R. C. Carter and R. Rwamwanja, 'Functional sustainability in community water and sanitation: a case study from south west Uganda' (Diocese of Kigezi/Cranfield University/Tearfund, 2006), and see <www.tearfund.org/webdocs/website/Campaigning/Policy%20and%20research/Uganda%20Watsan%20final.pdf> (last accessed 14 January 2009).

293 See WaterAid, <www.wateraid.org/uk/what_we_do/policy_and_research/citizens_action/default.asp> (last accessed 14 January 2009).

294 United Nations, 'Millennium Development Goals', see <www.un.org/millenniumgoals> (last accessed 5 February 2009).

11 Globalization, ecology and poverty

295 For a detailed list of the detrimental effects of climate change in Asia, Africa and Latin America, see Swiss Agency for Development and Cooperation, <www.deza.admin.ch/media> (last accessed 6 January 2009).

296 L. Sklair, *Globalisation: Capitalism and its Alternatives*, 3rd edn (Oxford: Oxford University Press, 2002), 8–9.

297 Joseph Stiglitz, *Making Globalization Work: The Next Steps to Global Justice* (London: Allen Lane, 2006), 30–2.

298 For the meaning of this term, see J. Williamson, 'What Washington means by policy reform', in J. Williamson, ed., *Latin American Readjustment: How Much has Happened* (Washington, DC: Institute for International Economics, 1989).

299 C. Van Dam, *Ocupación, Degradación Ambiental, Cambio Tecnológico y Desarrollo Sostenible* [Occupation, environmental degradation, technological change and sustainable development] (Salta: FLACSO, 2002).

300 Van Dam, *Ocupación*, 39.

301 Van Dam, *Ocupación*, 85.

302 A. Leake and M. de Ecónomo, *La deforestación del Chaco salteño entre 2004–2007* [The deforestation of Salta's Chaco between 2004 and 2007] (Salta: Fundación ASOCIANA, 2008).

303 See D. Aranda, 'Atrapados entre la minería y los desmontes' [Trapped between the mining industry and the waste products], *La Nación Revista*, 12 October 2007. According to Romina Picoletti, Argentina's Secretary of Environment and Sustainable Development, the number of deforested acres is over 300,000 (121,500 hectares) per year (*La Nación*, 23 March 2008).

304 L. Coutinho and J. Edward, 'Amazonía: cinco preguntas urgentes' [Amazonia: five urgent questions], *La Nación*, 27 April 2008.

305 FAO, see <www.fao.org/foofclimate> (last accessed 7 January 2009).

306 FAO, <www.fao.org/newsroom/en/news/2008/1000877/index.html> (last accessed 7 January 2009).

307 BBC, <www.news.bbc.co.uk/2/hi/in_depth/7432583.stm> (last accessed 7 January 2009).

308 BBC, <www.news.bbc.co.uk/1/hi/world/europe/7435439.stm> (last accessed 7 January 2009).

309 A. Oppenheimer, *Ojos vendados: Estados Unidos y el negocio de la corrupción en América Latina* [Blindfolded eyes: The United States and the business of corruption in Latin America] (Buenos Aires: Editorial Sudamericana, 2203), 7 (my translation).

310 Oppenheimer, *Ojos vendados*, 7 (my translation).

311 Oppenheimer, *Ojos vendados*, 9 (my translation).

312 Oppenheimer, *Ojos vendados*, 18 (my translation).

313 M. S. Northcott, *A Moral Climate: The Ethics of Global Warming* (Maryknoll, NY: Orbis Books, 2007), 37.

314 E. F. Schumacher, *Small is Beautiful: A Study of Economics as if People Mattered* (London: Abacus, 1974), 20.

315 B. L. Myers, *Walking With the Poor: Principles and Practices of Transformational Development* (Maryknoll, NY: Orbis Books, 1999), 86.

316 T. D. Hanks, *God So Loved the Third World* (Maryknoll, NY: Orbis Books, 1983), 38.

317 A. J. Heschel, *Los profetas: Concepciones históricas y teológicas* [The prophets: historical and theologial concepts] (Buenos Aires: Ediciones Piados), 77 (my translation).

318 W. Brueggemann, *Theology of the Old Testament: Testimony, Dispute, Advocacy* (Minneapolis, MN: Fortress Press, 1997), 612.

319 S. Hiatt, ed., *A Game as Old as Empire: The Secret World of Economic Hit Men and the Web of Global Corruption*, with Introduction by John Perkins (LaVergne, TN: Ingram Publisher Services, 2007).

320 W. Brueggemann, *Biblical Perspectives on Evangelism: Living in a Three-Storied Universe* (Nashville, TN: Abingdon Press, 1993), 40.

321 Stiglitz, *Making Globalisation Work.*

12 Justice for all the earth: society, ecology and the biblical prophets

322 Friends of the Earth, <www.foe.co.uk/resource/faqs/questions/environmental_justice.html> (last accessed 11 May 2008).

323 'Rights and Means to a Healthy Environment', Friends of the Earth, 2000, see <www.foe.co.uk/resource/index.shtml> (last accessed 11 May 2009).

324 Environmental Justice Foundation, see <www.ejfoundation.org/> (last accessed 11 May 2009).

325 Environmental Health Coalition, see <www.environmentalhealth.org> (last accessed 11 May 2009).

326 *Encyclopedia of the Atmospheric Environment*, see <www.ace.mmu.ac.uk/eae> (last accessed 11 May 2009).

327 KAIROS, see <www.kairoscanada.org/en/ecojustice/> (last accessed 11 May 2009).

328 For a philosophical perspective, see S. Hailwood, *How to Be a Green Liberal: Nature, Value and Liberal Philosophy* (Chesham: Acumen, 2004).

329 C. J. H. Wright, *Living as the People of God: The Relevance of Old Testament Ethics* (Leicester: InterVarsity Press, 1983); C. J. H. Wright, *The Mission of God: Unlocking the Bible's Grand Narrative* (Leicester: InterVarsity Press, 2006); C. J. H. Wright, *Old Testament Ethics for the*

People of God (Leicester: InterVarsity Press, 2004).

330 W. Houston, *Contending for Justice: Ideologies and Theologies of Social Justice in the Old Testament* (London and New York: T. & T. Clark, 2006).

331 K. Whitelam, *The Just King: Monarchical Judicial Authority in Ancient Israel*, Journal for the Study of the Old Testment Supplement Series no. 12 (Sheffield: JSOT Press, 1979).

332 All translations from the Hebrew in this chapter are my own.

333 For a wide-ranging discussion of divine world order, see R. Murray, *The Cosmic Covenant: Biblical Themes of Justice, Peace and the Integrity of Creation* (London: Sheed & Ward, 1992).

334 E. Hammershaimb, *The Book of Amos: A Commentary*, trans. J. Sturdy (Oxford: Basil Blackwell, 1970), 65.

335 J. A. Loader, *A Tale of Two Cities: Sodom and Gomorrah in the Old Testament, Early Jewish and Early Christian Traditions* (Kampen: J. H. Kok Publishing House, 1990), 37.

336 H. Gossai, *Justice, Righteousness and the Social Critique of the Eighth Century Prophets* (New York: Peter D. Lang, 1993), 249.

337 K. Koch, *The Prophets*, vol. I, *The Assyrian Period*, 2 vols (London: SCM Press, 1982).

338 P. S. White, 'Disturbance, the flux of nature, and environmental ethics at the multipatch scale', in *Religion and the New Ecology: Environmental Responsibility in a World in Flux*, ed. D. Lodge and C. Hamlin (Notre Dame, IN: University of Notre Dame Press, 2006).

339 D. Bentley-Hart, *The Doors of the Sea: Where Was God in the Tsunami?* (Grand Rapids, MI: Eerdmans, 2005).

340 D. Lodge and C. Hamlin, eds, *Religion and the New Ecology: Environmental Responsibility in a World in Flux* (Notre Dame, IN: University of Notre Dame Press, 2006), 7.

341 Vinoth Ramachandra, 'Tsunami Tragedy: Where was God?'; see <www.arocha.org/int-en/460-DSY.html> (last accessed 25 July 2008).

13 Jesus, God and nature in the Gospels

342 This passage is my own translation.

343 I have argued at length for this interpretation of Mark 1:13 in R. Bauckham, 'Jesus and the wild animals (Mark 1:13): A christological image for an ecological age', in *Jesus of Nazareth: Lord and Christ: Essays on the Historical Jesus and New Testament Christology*, ed. J. B. Green and M. Turner (Festschrift for I. Howard Marshall; Grand Rapids, MI: Eerdmans, 1994), 3–21.

344 I have discussed this passage and its ecological relevance more fully in R. Bauckham, 'Reading the Sermon on the Mount in an age of ecological catastrophe', *Studies in Christian Ethics* (2009) **22**: 76–88.

345 Jesus also uses, in parallel to this, the example of the wild flowers or 'lilies of the field,' as they are traditionally called (Matthew 6:28–30). For more on this example, see Bauckham, *Studies Christ. Ethics* (2009) **22**: 76–88.

346 I have altered the NRSV translation here.

347 The theme is also continued, within early Jewish literature, in Psalms of Solomon 5:8–11:

> For if I am hungry, I will cry out to you, O God,
> and you will give me (something).
> You *feed the birds* and the fish
> as you send rain in the wilderness that grass may sprout
> To provide pasture in the wilderness for every living thing,
> and if they are hungry, they will lift their eyes up to you.
> You feed kings and rulers and peoples, O God,
> and who is the hope of the poor and needy, if not you, Lord?

348 See R. Bauckham, 'Jesus and animals. I: What did he teach?', in *Animals on the Agenda: Questions about Animals for Theology and Ethics*, ed. A. Linzey and D. Yamamoto (London: SCM Press, 1998), 33–48 (44–7).

349   M. S. Northcott, *A Moral Climate: The Ethics of Global Warming* (London: Darton, Longman and Todd, 2007), 56–7, following Henry Shue.

14   **Sustaining ethical life in the Anthropocene**

350   D. Milmo, 'Investment in cycling could save £520 million, government told', *Guardian*, 17 September 2007.

351   M. Korbetis, D. S. Reay and J. Grace, 'New directions: rich in CO₂', *Atmospheric Environment* (2006) **40**: 3219–20.

352   C. Kapp, 'WHO acts on road safety to reverse accident trends', *Lancet* (2003) **362**: 1125.

353   B. K. Watson and V. Shepherd, 'Managing respiratory effects of air pollution', *Australian Family Physician* (2005) **34**: 1033–6.

354   T. Gorringe, *The Education of Desire: Towards a Theology of the Senses* (London: SCM Press, 2001), 22–7.

355   R. Williams, 'Formation: Who's bringing up our children?', Citizen Organisation Foundation Lecture, Queen Mary College, University of London, 11 April 2005; see <www.archbish-opofcanterbury.org/> (last accessed 8 February 2009).

356   A. Leopold, *A Sound County Almanac* (London: Oxford University Press, 1982).

357   A. O. Lieserowitz and L. O. Fernandez, *Towards a New Consciousness: Values to Sustain Human and Natural Communities* (New Haven, CT: Yale School of Forestry and Environmental Studies, 2007).

358   W. R. Herzog, *Jesus, Justice, and the Reign of God: A Ministry of Liberation* (Louisville, KY: Westminster John Knox Press, 2000), 122.

359   R. Sieferle, *The Subterranean Forest: Energy Systems and the Industrial Revolution*, English trans. M. Osmann (Whitstable: White Horse Press, 2001).

360   M. Northcott, *A Moral Climate: The Ethics of Global Warming* (London: Darton, Longman and Todd, 2007), 11–12.

361   P. J. Crutzen and E. F. Stoermer, 'The Anthropocene', *IGBP Newsletter* (2000) **36**; see <www.mpch-mainz.mpg.de/~air/anthropocene/> (last accessed 7 August 2008).

362   *New Scientist*, see <www.newscientist.com/article/dn13818-growing-ocean-dead-zones-leave-fish-gasping.html> (last accessed 2 February 2009).

363   Aristotle, *The Nicomachean Ethics*, trans. R. Crisp (Cambridge: Cambridge University Press, 2000).

364   Augustine, 'The City of Love', trans. O. O'Donovan, in O. O'Donovan, *Common Objects of Love* (Grand Rapids, MI: Eerdmans, 2003), 1–29.

365   R. E. Lane, *The Loss of Happiness in Market Democracies* (New Haven, CT: Yale University Press, 2001).

366   R. Constanza, R. D'Arge, R. de Groot *et al.*, 'The value of the world's ecosystem services and natural capital', *Ecological Economics* (1998) **25**: 3–15.

367   N. McKendrick, 'The consumer revolution in eighteenth-century England', in *The Birth of a Consumer Society: The Commercialization of Eighteenth Century England*, ed. N. McKendrick, J. Brewer and J. H. Plumb (London: Hutchinson, 1983), 19.

368   A. de Tocqueville, *Democracy in America*, trans. J. P. Mayer (New York: Perennial, 2000).

369   A. Grubler and Y. Fujii, 'Inter-generational and spatial equity issues of carbon accounts', *Energy* (1991) **16**: 1397–16.

370   SEI and University of Sydney, *Development of an Embedded Carbon Emissions Indicator: A research report to the Department for Environment, Food and Rural Affairs by the Stockholm Environment Institute and the University of Sydney* (London: HMSO, 2008).

371   Henderson Global Investors and Trucost, *The Carbon 100: Quantifying the Carbon Emissions Intensities and Exposures of the FTSE 100* (London: Henderson Global Investors and Trucost PLC, 2005).

372   WBCSD and WEF, *CEO Climate Policy Recommendations to World Leaders* (Geneva: World Business Council for Sustainable Development and World Economic Forum, 2008); see <www.weforum.org/documents/initiatives/CEOStatement.pdf> (last accessed 7 August 2008).

373 NASA, 'The incredible shrinking ozone hole', Nasa Science, 12 December 2000; see <http://science.nasa.gov/headlines/y2000/ast12dec_1.htm> (last accessed 9 January 2008).

374 O. D. Evans, 'Does money buy satisfaction?' *Social Indicators Research* (1975) **2**: 267–74.

375 R. G. Wilkinson, *Unhealthy Societies: The Afflictions of Inequality* (London: Routledge, 1996).

15 Creation and new creation: transforming Christian perspectives

376 John Polkinghorne, *The God of Hope and the End of the World* (New Haven, CT: Yale University Press, 2002). In another context, Polkinghorne ties 'new creation' to Scripture, appealing to 2 Corinthians 5:17 and arguing that the phrase has broad, cosmic connotations because of parallels such as Romans 8:19–22. To cite another example, 'An Evangelical Declaration on the Care of Creation' introduces the phrase 'new creation', citing 2 Corinthians 5:17, and then goes on to implicitly identify new creation with kingdom of God, in which there is the renewal of fellowship with God, with other humans, and with the rest of created world; see <www.creationcare.org/resources/declaration.php> (last accessed 9 January 2009).

377 RSV, Revised Standard Version; ESV, English Standard Version; NASB, New American Standard Bible; NAB, New American Bible; NIV, New International Version; NET, New English Translation; and NLT, New Living Translation.

378 I am assuming that Galatians was written before 2 Corinthians, probably in AD 47–48, but the dating has no bearing on my argument. All references to the English Bible are to the Today's New International Version (TNIV), unless otherwise noted.

379 See especially P. Minear, 'The crucified world: the enigma of Galatians 6:14', in *Theologica Crucis – Signum Crucis* (Tübingen: Mohr Siebeck, 1979), 395–407.

380 J. L. Martyn has drawn particular attention to the strong dualities in Galatians, labelling them 'apocalyptic antinomies' ('Apocalyptic Antinomies in Paul's Letter to the Galatians', *New Testament Studies* (1983) **31**: 410–24); he works these out in detail in his commentary on Galatians (*Galatians: An Introduction with Translation and Commentary*, Anchor Bible Series no. 33A (New York: Doubleday, 1997)).

381 In Romans 1:25, 8:39, and Hebrews 4:13, *ktisis* means 'created thing(s)' in general, in opposition to the creator. Col. 1:23 may refer to 'every creature under heaven' (NRSV, TNIV, NAB) but more likely refers to 'the whole creation under heaven' (ESV, NASB, NET). In 1 Peter 2:13, the word refers to an '[established] authority'. All the other New Testament occurrences of *ktisis* mean 'creation' in a general sense (see Mark 10:6; 13:19; Hebrews 9:11; 2 Peter 3:4; Revelation 3:14).

382 See especially the survey of usage in M. Hubbard, *New Creation in Paul's Letters and Thought*, Society of New Testament Studies Monograph Series no. 119 (Cambridge: Cambridge University Press, 2002), 11–77.

383 *Jubilees* 4:26; *1 Enoch* 72:1; 1QH 13:11. There are, of course, many other texts that, while not using the language 'new creation', probably refer to a similar concept.

384 The Greek terms, *arsēn* ('male') and *thēlys* ('female'), are used in the creation account in Genesis 1 and tend to be confined to 'creation' texts in the New Testament (Matthew 19:4; Mark 10:6; Romans 1:26–27).

385 The phrase 'the elements of the world' (*ta stoicheia tou kosmou*), used in Galatians 4:3 (see v. 9) and Colossians 2:8, 20 (see also *stoicheia* in Hebrews 5:12; 2 Peter 3:10, 12) is one of the most debated in Paul's letters. Many interpreters think it refers to astral spirits (TNIV), while others take it is a reference to 'elementary principles' (see ESV). The view I espouse here is admittedly a minority one but reflects the overwhelming usage of Paul's day. See especially Martyn, *Galatians*, 393–406.

386 See, e.g., Hubbard, *New Creation*, 133–87.

387 V. P. Furnish, *II Corinthians*, The Anchor Bible, vol. 32A (Garden City, NY: Doubleday, 1984) 322.

388 Herman Ridderbos, *Paul: An Outline of His Theology* (Grand Rapids, MI: Eerdmans, 1974), 45.

389 For example, see J. Fitzmyer, 'Reconciliation in Pauline theology', in *No Famine in the Land: Studies in Honor of John L. McKenzie*, ed. J. W. Flanagan and A. W. Robinson (Missoula, MT: Scholars, 1975), 161–2; Furnish, *II Corinthians*, 319.

390 See Ernst Käsemann, 'Some thoughts on the theme "The doctrine of reconciliation" in the New Testament', in *The Future of our Religious Past*, ed. J. M. Robinson (New York: Harper & Row, 1971), 52–7. A good response is M. Thrall, *A Critical and Exegetical Commentary on the Second Epistle to the Corinthians*, 2 vols, International Critical Commentary Series (Edinburgh: T. & T. Clark, 1994), vol. 1, 445–9.

391 This is my own translation.

392 Furnish, *II Corinthians*, 332.

393 R. Bauckham, *God and the Crisis of Freedom: Biblical and Contemporary Perspectives* (Louisville, KY: Westminster John Knox, 2002), 161.

394 The 'steward' analogy, despite its problems, is still, in my view, the best single way to depict human beings' role with respect to the created world. For the spectrum of opinion on the stewardship imagery, see especially the collection of essays in R. J. Berry, ed., *Environmental Stewardship: Critical Perspectives – Past and Present* (London: T. & T. Clark, 2006).

395 W. Schweiker, 'Time as moral space: cosmologies, creation, and last judgment', in *The End of the World and the Ends of God: Science and Theology on Eschatology*, ed. J. Polkinghorne and M. Welker (Harrisburg, PA: Trinity Press International, 2000), 135.

16 Environmental unsustainability and a biblical vision of the earth's future

396 D. W. Orr, 'Armageddon versus extinction', *Conservation Biology* (2005) **19**: 290–2 (291).

397 C. Schwöbel, 'The church as a cultural space: eschatology and ecclesiology', in *The End of the World and the Ends of God: Science and Theology on Eschatology*, ed. J. Polkinghorne and M. Welker (Harrisburgh, PA: Trinity Press International, 2000), 117. Cf. O. O'Donovan, *Resurrection and the Moral Order: An Outline for Evangelical Ethics* (Grand Rapids, MI: Eerdmans, 1986).

398 R. Bauckham, *Jude, 2 Peter*, Word Bible Commentary no. 50 (Waco, TX: Word Books, 1983), 276.

399 See J. Moo, 'Romans 8:19–22 and Isaiah's cosmic covenant', *New Testament Studies* (2008) **54**: 74–89.

400 E. Adams, *The Stars Will Fall From Heaven: Cosmic Catastrophe in the New Testament and its World* (London: T. & T. Clark, 2007), 234.

401 For example, see Bauckham, *Jude, 2 Peter*, 316–21; J. H. Neyrey, *2 Peter, Jude*, Anchor Bible no. 37c (New York: Doubleday, 1993), 243–4; D. J. Harrington, *Jude and 2 Peter*, Sacra Pagina no. 15 (Collegeville, MN: Liturgical Press, 2003), 289; P. H. Davids, *The Letters of 2 Peter and Jude*, Pillar New Testament Commentary (Grand Rapids, MI, and Cambridge: Eerdmans, 2006), 286–7. (Note that I confine myself in this chapter to citing only accessible English language works.)

402 Cf. Theophilus of Antioch, *Autol.* 1.4; Justin, *2 Apol.* 5.2; *Dial.* 23.2.

403 For example, see Bauckham, *Jude, 2 Peter*, 315–16; S. J. Kraftchick, *Jude/2 Peter*, Abingdon New Testament Commentaries (Nashville, TN: Abingdon, 2002), 163; Davids, *2 Peter and Jude*, 284–7.

404 A. Wolters, 'Worldview and textual criticism in 2 Peter 3:10', *Westminster Theological Journal* (1987) **49**: 405–13 (413).

405 Davids, *2 Peter and Jude*, 288.

406 Cf. D. Moo, 'Nature in the new creation: New Testament eschatology and the environment', *Journal of the Evangelical Theological Society* (2006) **49**: 449–88 (466–9).

407 Cf. Bauckham, *Jude, 2 Peter*, 326.

408 Kraftchick, *Jude/2 Peter*, 166.

409 J. Moltmann, *The Coming of God: Christian Eschatology*, trans. M. Kohl (Minneapolis, MN: Fortress, 2004), 146.

410 Neyrey, *2 Peter, Jude*, 237.

Index of biblical and other ancient references

NRSV (New Revised Standard Version) is the default translation. Other translations used are mentioned in the text.

Index of subjects

Page numbers for figures are indicated by **bold** print.